OPEN SKIES,
CLOSED MINDS

OPEN SKIES, CLOSED MINDS

For The First Time
A Government UFO Expert Speaks Out

NICK POPE

With a Foreword by Timothy Good

Best Wishes,

Nick Pope

SIMON & SCHUSTER

LONDON · SYDNEY · NEW YORK · TOKYO · SINGAPORE · TORONTO

First published in Great Britain by Simon & Schuster Ltd, 1996
A Viacom Company

Simon & Schuster Ltd
West Garden Place
Kendal Street
London W2 2AQ

Simon & Schuster of Australia Pty Ltd
Sydney

A CIP catalogue record for this book is available
from the British Library

ISBN 0-684-81664-4

With thanks to Headline for permission to quote from
UFO Encyclopedia by John Spencer

Typeset in Janson by
Palimpsest Book Production Limited, Polmont, Stirlingshire
Printed and bound in Great Britain by
Butler & Tanner, Frome & London

To Mum.
In loving memory.

Author's Note

Unless stated otherwise, the views expressed in this book are my own, and should not be construed as representing the official position of the Ministry of Defence or any other agency.

'Yet, across the gulf of space . . . intellects vast and cool and unsympathetic . . . regarded this earth with envious eyes, and slowly and surely drew their plans against us.'

H.G. Wells
The War of the Worlds
(William Heinemann)

CONTENTS

ACKNOWLEDGEMENTS

As with all books, this one was a team effort, with many people playing a part in producing the finished product. I would like to mention the following key players:

I would like to thank my agent, Andrew Lownie, for all his patient help and encouragement, and for coaching me through the complexities of authorship; without Andrew, this project would never have got off the ground.

I would also like to thank Mei Trow, who collaborated with me in writing this book, shaping it into something that we could both feel proud of. Mei brought common sense and humour into the text, and his sound research and illuminating insights considerably enhanced the whole project.

I am grateful to everyone at Simon & Schuster, who coached me through the various processes associated with turning a manuscript into a book, and provided me with all the help and advice I needed. I am especially grateful to Martin Fletcher, Jacquie Clare, Gillian Holmes, Lisa Shakespeare, Cathy Schofield, Aruna Mathur, Glen Saville, Aniz Damani and Caroline North.

Thanks to Timothy Good for writing an excellent foreword, and for casting an expert eye over the text.

I owe a huge debt of gratitude to a number of ufologists and other researchers of the paranormal, whose enthusiasm first helped convince me that their subjects were deserving of serious investigation, and whose wit and wisdom have continued to shape my own beliefs. We do not necessarily agree on everything, and they do not all believe that UFOs are extraterrestrial in origin, but they have all done ground-breaking work, and are a wonderful group of people. I cannot possibly mention them all, but I would particularly like to thank John Spencer, Timothy Good (again), Budd Hopkins, Graham Birdsall, Philip Mantle, Tony Dodd, Colin Andrews, Jenny Randles, Ralph Noyes and Lucien Morgan.

I am eternally grateful to Mark and Vivienne Birdsall, and everyone at the Quest Picture Library, who tracked down and made available most of the wonderful photographs in the book.

I would like to thank my many friends and colleagues at the Ministry of Defence who have, almost without exception, supported me throughout this venture, offering me encouragement and support through some rather difficult times.

I am grateful to my father for his words of wisdom, expert advice, and all round support. Thanks also to my stepmother, Helen, and my brother, Seb, for their support, and to Michèle Kaczynski for being my chief confidant during the writing of this book.

I would also like to thank Nick Forbes at the Public Record Office, Charles Halt, Ed Walters, Ray Santilli, Ian Macpherson, Lizzie Wickham, Laura Newell, Yetunde Koledoye, Richard Horsley, Jane Goldman and all the other people I've forgotten to mention, but to whom I'm no less grateful.

Finally, I owe a huge debt of gratitude to the various witnesses, named and unnamed, whose stories helped shape my understanding of the UFO phenomenon. I did my best to get to the bottom of the mysteries that intruded upon your lives, and I hope that when I couldn't solve them, I at least helped you come to terms with them. Despite all the traumas and unanswered questions, you are in a sense, the lucky ones. You have actively participated in something that the rest of us are still only beginning to acknowledge, let alone understand.

FOREWORD

by Timothy Good

My first encounter with the Ministry of Defence department which handles UFO reports from members of the public took place in 1963, when I reported by telephone the sighting of an apparently unknown object which hovered over my south-east London suburb as well as the home counties for several hours one August evening. The ministry promised to investigate, and within a few days of the sighting provided me with a valid explanation. In numerous communications with the ministry since that time, my enquiries have always been treated courteously and seriously, and in company with most leading researchers, I share the ministry's official position that the majority (perhaps as high as 90 per cent – though I believe this to be an arbitrary figure) of sightings can be explained in terms of conventional aircraft, airships, balloons, stars, planets, laser displays, and so on. My only disagreement with the ministry is on its insistence that the remaining 10 per cent of sightings represent nothing beyond our present knowledge and do not constitute a threat to national security. Then came Nick Pope.

I had a great deal of correspondence with Nick during his tenure as UFO desk officer at Secretariat (Air Staff) 2a from 1991–1994, and his comments always reflected official policy. Thus, when Nick initiated meetings at his own behest with leading UFO researchers in the UK, I began to wonder if the official policy had changed. As it transpired, I was mistaken, but when first I met Nick in 1993, in company with the well-known author and investigator John Spencer, who arranged the meeting, I was astonished to discover not only that Nick was well informed, but also that he was completely objective about the UFO phenomenon. As he explained to me over a pizza in Whitehall, he was getting paid to do the job so, unlike most of his predecessors, he felt it incumbent upon him to study the subject. 'I made it my business to go out and seek expert opinion,' Nick told me in 1995. 'I needed to know what was going on, and I was keen to meet the key players and to hear their disparate opinions.'

Although Nick's initiative was frowned on by some of his fellow civil servants in Sec(AS)2a – and mocked by others – an unprecedented era of co-operation with UFO researchers ensued. Nick's belief that this co-operation would facilitate the handling of public enquiries was fully justified. For instance, I well recall one case, involving the sighting of an illuminated 'spaceship' reported around the London area in November 1993, when Nick and I shared the task of contacting various civilian authorities to try to identify the object. The 'spaceship' turned out to be an illuminated airship, flown by Virgin Lightships.

Of particular interest in this book are those reports received by Nick during the course of his official duties which appear to defy a conventional explanation. Back in the 1950s, Air Minister George Ward, in his statements to Members of the House of Commons, often explained away UFO sightings as 'balloons' – particularly those reported by Royal Air Force pilots. But in 1954, when he was challenged about this by his friend Desmond Leslie, a second cousin to Sir Winston Churchill and a former Second World War fighter pilot, Ward revealed several reasons why he felt obliged to publically 'explain' these reports. One of these was fear of ridicule. 'What am I to say?' said Ward. '*I* know it wasn't a balloon. *You* know it wasn't a balloon. But until I've got a saucer on the ground in Hyde Park and can charge the public sixpence a go to enter, it *must* be balloons, otherwise the government would fall and I'd lose my job.'

Ward went on to explain the difficult position he found himself in, along with other members of Her Majesty's Government, and said that if he admitted the existence of flying saucers without evidence that the general public could actually touch, they would consider that the government had gone barmy and would lose their faith in it. Evidently, there is a fine line between fear of public embarrassment and concerns relating to national security!

Although British television chiefs have finally caught up with many other countries in recognising that the subject is of great public interest, leading to a number of serious documentaries, the attitude of the national press still leaves much to be desired. It is as mandatory for the tabloids to sensationalise as it is for the broadsheets to ridicule the subject, and doubtless these reactions will typify media response to this book. Neither reaction helps establish a serious appraisal of the phenomenon. As Hungary's minister of defence, György Keleti, responded in 1994, when asked by an apparently sceptical but sensation-seeking Hungarian national newspaper reporter if he feared a UFO 'invasion':

> ... I was a columnist [in Budapest's *Ufomagazin*] and I published UFO cases that were observed and registered within the Hungarian armed forces. I never stated that we were preparing any kind of action against UFO forces; I only pointed out to the public that, as a civilization, we would be unable to defend ourselves here on the Earth ... Around Szolnok many UFO reports have been received by the Ministry of Defence, which obviously and logically means that [the UFOs] know very well where they have to land and what they have to do. It is remarkable indeed that

> ... in general, newspapers everywhere reject the reports
> of the authorities.

I must also touch on the subject of UFOs and national security. Thousands of pages of documents released in many countries – particularly in the United States under provisions of the Freedom of Information Act – reveal quite unequivocally that UFOs have been the subject of intensive investigations by the military and scientific intelligence communities since the 1940s. It is also revealing that in the USA (with the exception of the air force), many agencies long denied any serious involvement, until a flood of released documents proved to the contrary. Furthermore, agencies such as the CIA, the Defense Intelligence Agency, the National Security Agency, and the intelligence branches of the air force, army and navy, admit that many Top Secret documents are still being withheld in the interests of national security. And, as early as 1950, a hitherto Top Secret Canadian government memorandum stated that the results of American investigations into 'flying saucers' were classified higher than the hydrogen bomb. Even a former Director of the CIA, Rear Admiral Roscoe Hillenkoetter, in a statement to the US Congress in 1960, admitted that, 'through official secrecy and ridicule, many citizens are led to believe the unknown flying objects are nonsense'. If there is no cover-up, why all the secrecy?

Nick Pope has found no evidence of a cover-up in the United Kingdom. While I know Nick to be totally truthful, I doubt however that civil servants in Sec(AS)2a are kept fully informed. I am certain, for instance, that the majority of military reports are forwarded to other departments, as confirmed for me by well-informed sources. And, if a former chief of the defence staff, admiral of the fleet Lord Hill-Norton – who is firmly convinced that there is indeed a cover-up – has been frustrated in his attempts to find out more, it is hardly surprising that Nick has been unable to uncover any such evidence.

It is known that Top Secret investigations into the UFO phenomenon were conducted in the 1950s by the Ministry of Defence's scientific and technical intelligence personnel, so why is it that reports relating to well-known encounters by Royal Air Force pilots during that period have not been released to the Public Record Office under the thirty-year rule, and may not be available for public inspection for many years to come? The official explanations that no such records exist, or that they were destroyed routinely, I find difficult to accept, in view of the fact that a few of the more innocuous reports have survived.

Yet Nick *is* unequivocal in his conviction that UFOs pose a potential threat to national security. 'The role of the UK government in UFO research is to evaluate whether there is or is not a threat to the defence of the UK,' he told me in 1995. 'If, as the evidence suggests, structured craft of unknown origin routinely penetrate the UK Air Defence Region, then it seems to me that, at the very least, this must constitute a potential threat. How can we say there's no threat when we do not know what these objects are, where they come from, or what they want?'

In its official policy on the release of UFO reports made by military observers, Britain lags behind other countries. The defence ministries of Belgium, Hungary, Italy, Russia, and particularly Spain, for example, have now released many reports of encounters by air force pilots and other military personnel. Moreover, some European defence chiefs have confirmed the reality of the UFO phenomenon. Following the extraordinary incursions into Belgian airspace in 1989/1990 of large, usually triangular-shaped flying craft, observed by over 2,500 witnesses – including several air force F-16 pilots and numerous police officers – Major General Wilfried De Brouwer, Deputy Chief of the Royal Belgian Air Force, commented: 'The day will come undoubtedly when the phenomenon will be observed with technological means of detection and collection that won't leave a single doubt about its origin. This should lift a part of the veil that has covered the [UFO] mystery for a long time; a mystery that continues to the present. But it exists, it is real, and that in itself is an important conclusion.'

A true pioneer, Nick Pope is to be applauded for his courage in writing this ground-breaking and aptly titled book, at considerable risk to his career in the Ministry of Defence. *Open Skies, Closed Minds* is a fascinating, intelligent and objective overview of this complex and many-faceted subject, which I am sure will do much to dispel the myth that UFOs are a ridiculous nonsense.

Timothy Good is one of the most respected authorities on the UFO phenomenon. He is the author and editor of a number of bestselling books on the subject, including *Above Top Secret: The Worldwide UFO Cover-up*, *Alien Liaison: The Ultimate Secret*, and *Alien Update*. His latest book is *Beyond Top Secret: The Worldwide UFO Security Threat* from which much of the information cited in this foreword has been taken.

INTRODUCTION

Until 1991, I was generally sceptical about the paranormal, although, I liked to think, open-minded. As a career civil servant with the Ministry of Defence, I was certainly not the sort of person who subscribed to any sort of bizarre theory without first seeing some proof. I didn't believe in UFOs; I wasn't aware that there were groups dedicated to UFO research, and I hadn't even heard of the concept of alien abduction. And anyway, paranormal experiences only happened to weirdos, didn't they? But I was about to be given the most bizarre job I had ever done: investigating UFO sightings to ensure that there was no evidence of a threat to the United Kingdom. I was to become, as people would tell me, 'the real Fox Mulder' – hero of the cult TV series *The X-Files*; Nick 'Spooky' Pope, sought after by witnesses and abductees as confidant, seen by ufologists as an ally on the 'inside', and thought of by one or two of my bosses as a maverick.

On this tour of duty I inherited a situation where any UFO report, however bizarre, seemed to be attributed to aircraft lights; case closed. But I was never happy to leave an investigation until I felt I could go no further; I was not prepared to say that UFOs posed no threat until I knew what they were: in short, I was going to call it how I saw it, and pay no attention to the personal prejudices of those who, quite frankly, wouldn't admit there might be things they couldn't explain even if a flying saucer landed in their back garden. Like Fox Mulder, I was the rebel, the man from the corridors of power who wouldn't play by the same 'establishment' rules as everyone else.

One of the first things I did on taking up the UFO post was to read into the subject. Most UFO sightings were of lights in the sky. Obviously, these objects could have been anything, and indeed a great many of them probably were no more than the aircraft lights that most of my predecessors seemed to have been so obsessed with. But there were also things called 'close encounters'. I'd seen Steven Spielberg's film *Close Encounters of the Third Kind*, and thought I knew all about these. Apparently not; it turned out that there were in fact experiences described as 'close encounters of the fourth kind', whereby people were actually abducted by aliens, or so they claimed. There were, it seemed, two common scenarios: some people were taken from their beds; others were the victims of a more proactive abduction, from their cars, usually while driving down a deserted road very late at night. Further research revealed a concept known as 'missing time', where people arrived home much later than they expected, and were unable to account for a lost period of their evening; something had happened, but the mind had no conscious recollection of it. That something, according to many ufologists, was an abduction by alien beings, who took the occupant of the vehicle into a spacecraft, subjecting them to a medical procedure of some sort, and then returned him or her to the car with a hypnotically reinforced instruction not to remember.

The imaginative inventions of attention-seekers? The hallucinations of troubled minds? Perhaps. But I had responsibilities both to the Ministry of Defence and to the public as a whole. I had to investigate all the sightings and experiences in a totally impartial way, irrespective of my own views about a witness or his or her experience. There was no way I could afford to let personal opinions influence me. To start with, many within the world of ufology probably regarded me as just 'the man from the ministry', as likely as not up to my eyeballs in crashed UFOs, dead aliens and cosmic cover-ups. But as I began to deal on a daily basis with people who had experienced events which appeared to go beyond human understanding, I formed working relationships with UFO researchers and a mutual trust developed. I counselled abductees, trying either to explain their experiences, or, more often than not, simply to help them come to terms with them.

Over the next three years I was to build up a huge breadth and depth of understanding of the UFO and alien abduction phenomena. The hundreds of cases I investigated each year were just the tip of the iceberg – 95 per cent of sightings were probably never reported to us at all, either because people weren't aware that there was any official interest, or because they were afraid of ridicule.

My three years were literally a voyage of discovery and one in which my official status gave me an edge over other researchers. Many excellent books have been written on the UFO phenomenon, but the authors are usually enthusiastic amateurs, whose interest stems from a personal experience or a childhood fascination with space and science fiction. The general perception of UFOs as flying saucers carrying little green men has often been shaped by a vociferous handful of cranks whose knowledge is slight, but who manage to shout the loudest. Nowhere is this misunderstanding more apparent than in the perceived role of governments, where the juicy prospect of an official cover-up is a welcoming beacon on a dark and lonely night.

As an official with the Ministry of Defence, I have been able to talk directly to those who have themselves witnessed such phenomena. I have met many key figures in the UFO lobby and had unprecedented access to the raw data on the subject – the files which some lobbyists will tell you the government is anxious to suppress – and other resources not available to civilians. I have also talked to radar experts, astronomers, military pilots and a whole army of civil and military specialists, people to whom civilian UFO researchers are not necessarily denied access, but of whom they are not always aware.

When, finally, I moved on to another posting, having won an important promotion, my mind had been opened to the possibility that the universe is a very much stranger place than conventional science might suggest. Perhaps paranormal phenomena are nothing more than real events that we simply can't yet grasp. A few hundred years ago most people probably thought about lightning in the same way. Perhaps the experiences – frightening though they can be – should be seen in positive terms.

1

'AND OUT OF THE FIRE WENT FORTH LIGHTNING.'

And I looked and behold a whirlwind came out of the north, a great cloud and a fire infolding itself, and a brightness about it, and out of the midst thereof as the colour of amber, out of the midst of the fire. Also out of the midst thereof came the likeness of four living creatures. And this was their appearance; they had the likeness of a man. And every one had four faces, and every one had four wings. And their feet were straight feet; and the sole of their feet was like the sole of a calf's foot; and they sparkled like the colour of burnished brass . . . As for the likeness of the living creatures, this appearance was like burning coals of fire and like the appearance of lamps: it went up and down among the living creatures; and the fire was bright, and out of the fire went forth lightning . . . Now as I beheld the living creatures, behold one wheel upon the earth by the living creature, with his four faces. The appearance of the wheels and their work was like unto the colour of a beryl; and they four had one likeness; and their appearance and their work was

as it were a wheel in the middle of a wheel. When they
went, they went upon their four sides, and they turned not
when they went. As for their rings, they were so high that
they were dreadful; and their rings were full of eyes round
about them four. And when the living creatures went, the
wheels went by them; and when the living creatures were
lifted up from the earth, the wheels were lifted up.

So runs Chapter One of the Book of the Prophet Ezekiel,
according to the *King James Bible* of 1611. Ezekiel the priest,
the son of Buzi in the land of the Chaldeans saw visions of God
'and the heavens were opened.'

Old Testament stories are notoriously open to interpretation.
Ezekiel goes on to describe the throne of God with its rainbow
light in a conventional way, the sort of thing that Michelangelo
would paint centuries later. Yet, even after we weight the balance
of allegories, dreams, fantasies and hallucinations induced by
religious ecstasy, and even after we remember that the *Bible*
has undergone various translations from Hebrew to Greek to
Latin to English, there is something oddly mechanical about
this description. The flame, the lightning, the wheels, even the
curious movement of the vision – 'they went every one straight
forward. . . and they turned not as they went' – corresponds to
many recent eyewitness accounts of unidentified craft landing.
'As for their rings, they were so high that they were dreadful;
and their rings were full of eyes' – could this be the glittering
circles of light emitted from the fuselage of 'flying saucers'?

For centuries, humanity has been fascinated by the skies. The
kingdom of the clouds, the arc of the rainbow, the myriad points
of light in the night; all this has been woven by timid, poetic
humans into an image of their own making. The thunder is
God's barrels rolling around the empty sky. The rainbow is the
symbol of God's promise never to send another flood. And in the

darkness, starlight is the radiance of Heaven shining through the peppered curtain of the night.

What early humans did not understand, they were afraid of, and worshipped as a god. The rain, the sun, the moon, the stars, the thunder and the winds – all these perfectly natural phenomena were attributed to some sort of divinity. And, as our confidence and knowledge grew, we personalised the Heavens, finding animal and human likenesses in the constellations – the Great Bear, Orion the Hunter, the Seven Sisters.

And the Heavens controlled our destinies, so that momentous events on Earth were foretold by bizarre activity in the skies. The Anglo-Saxon Chronicle for the year 793 describes 'fiery dragons' over Northumbria. This was a decade when the Northern Saxon kingdoms were hit time and time again by Viking raids along their coasts. On 8 June of that year, lightning and whirlwinds ravaged the North. A torrent of blood fell on York Minster. The island of Lindisfarne was stormed and its monastery levelled by the marauding Northmen. In Ireland, two years later, dysentery, rabies and smallpox epidemics were heralded by an eclipse of the moon.

Over the Bavarian city of Nuremberg in 1561, eyewitnesses described a battle in the skies, echoing Milton's phrase of nearly a century later – 'There was war in Heaven.' Weird objects – circular and cylindrical – darted above the city's roofs. Perhaps this was an omen too, for Nuremberg was badly hit during the Thirty Years War, when Catholic fought Protestant for control of central Europe.

Shakespeare's plays are full of such incidents. In *Julius Caesar*, the playwright drew on the chronicles of Plutarch. Cassius, one of the conspirators soon to stab the wannabe Emperor, describes sights which echo Ezekiel: 'and there were drawn upon a heap a hundred ghastly women, transformed with their fear; who swore they saw men, all in fire, walk up and down the streets. . . When these prodigies do so conjointly meet, let not men say, these are their reasons – they are natural; for I believe they are portentous things.'

It is impossible now to interpret these experiences accurately. The bewildered Irish in the eighth century had to find a way to explain the inexplicable with very little scientific knowledge to help them. The people of Northumbria in the same period were terrified of the Vikings and their fear caused every little natural phenomenon to become distorted and exaggerated; it may even have given rise to the phenomenon in the first place. And Shakespeare, as a storyteller, needed to seize the imagination of his groundlings, who were hungry for supernatural coincidences. However, it is highly likely that the roots of these phenomena lie in the perfectly natural movements of meteorites or atmospheric conditions: comets, ball lightning, mirages or noctilucent clouds. What is certain is that the notion of inexplicable things from the sky is as old as recorded history itself.

The archaeologist Erich von Däniken, in *Chariots of the Gods?* and *According to the Evidence* has taken these unexplained sightings by the scruff of the neck and has created an intriguing theory – that of the 'ancient astronauts'. The gods – and the particular creed or denomination is irrelevant – were actually extraterrestrial hominids – 'men from outer space' – and their visits to this planet in pre-history have been passed down through the generations in the form of religions, mythologies and folklore. Von Däniken cites the physical evidence for these visits too; from the perfect pyramids of Egypt and Peru; through the ancient Druidic circles of Stonehenge and Avebury; to the secret caves of Equador and the giant stone heads of the Turkish mountains. The evidence is circumstantial, but the question – 'Was God an Astronaut?' – undeniably fascinating.

Dr Jacques Vallée, in *Dimensions*, links unidentified flying phenomena with psychic phenomena. He once made the interesting observation that in one edition of the *Encyclopaedia Britannica*, the entry for 'unidentified flying object' appears between 'unicorn' and 'unified field theory'. Singularly apt, because it places the UFO phenomenon between the realms of magic and science.

The first fully documented sightings of literal unidentified flying objects came to us from the United States at the end of the last century. The country that has given us such fascinating imponderables as Spiritualism (which effectively began in Hydesville, New York State in 1848) and Bigfoot (a reputed hairy hominid living somewhere in the Northern Rockies) might be expected to be first in the modern field of unidentified flying phenomena too. In November 1896, a light was clearly visible in the sky over Sacramento, California, and sightings later in the month were also reported further north, in Washington State and Canada. Above the light appeared to be a dark shape, described as a cigar, an egg or a barrel. By the end of the year, sightings were occurring all over America, accompanied by what may be described as the lunatic fringe of ufology which has never quite gone away. Three Methodist ministers saw a 'flying object' take off at their arrival. Two men walking a lonely country road were attacked by three strange beings, tall with bald heads, who fled in a craft shaped like a cigar. In Michigan, a man claimed that he heard an order for a pot of coffee and four dozen egg sandwiches by a disembodied voice somewhere above the clouds. Not only did he rustle up the order, but an invisible scoop whisked it up to the equally invisible craft!

What made these sightings different is that modern technology had not only created the sightings themselves, but various journalists of the 1890s attributed them – probably correctly – to the maiden flights of airships. The first of these was the steam-driven dirigible of the Frenchman Henri Giffard which flew for the first time in 1852. The French and the Germans in particular were experimenting with lighter-than-air craft in this period, and although the name of Count Ferdinand von Zeppelin is forever linked with this sort of technology, the Americans were not all that far behind. The Massachusetts Institute of Technology had built a wind tunnel and ran courses for the public on propulsion and the behaviour of fluids.

The accounts of those who saw the strange craft on the ground make it fairly obvious that we are talking about flying objects that decidedly originated here on earth. In Beaumont, Texas, on 19 April 1897 and again on the following day at Uvalde in the same state, farmers talked to the craft's crew. They had landed for water, told them the craft ran on electricity, had been made in Iowa and that there were four others just like it. The apparent captain of the craft was a Mr Wilson who lived in Goshen, New York, and he even knew a local sheriff in Texas! There is some evidence to suggest that Wilson had designed these airships himself and urged secrecy on all he met because the designs were still unpatented. The descriptions given by various eyewitnesses, with talk of propellors and cabins, fit exactly the rigid-type craft developed by Thomas Baldwin in Oakland, California, in 1904, and by Santos-Dumont and Zeppelin a few years later.

There is another story of a sighting of what is described as a 'ship' floating in the sky over Ireland. Like some American cases there was talk of an anchor which became snagged on a roof and which was cut free by a crew member climbing down a rope. What is special about this particular sighting? It occurred in 1211, nearly eight hundred years before airships were invented.

Nowadays, for reasons of cost and military importance, no individual is likely to be designing, building and flying aircraft, but in the amateur world of the late nineteenth century, anything was possible. This was also the era in which science fiction had come of age. Jules Verne had produced his *From the Earth to the*

Moon in 1875, and the early books of H.G. Wells, especially *The War of the Worlds* (1898), not only posed the idea of extraterrestrial life, but warned that life could be hostile.

The 1930s saw the arrival of 'ghost aircraft', particularly over Norway and Sweden. Conventional aircraft design had moved rapidly since the turn of the century, partially as a result of the catalyst of the First World War. Orville and Wilbur Wright's 'The Flyer' which had kept to the air for only seconds above Kitty Hawk Beach, North Carolina, on 17 December 1903, had now been superseded by a whole range of military and civil aircraft, bombers and fighters, and the way forward was towards the monoplane, with a single wingspan, rather than the biplanes and triplanes that had flown over the trenches of the Western Front. The Scandinavian sightings were of monoplanes and biplanes usually grey in colour, sometimes lit by searchlights from the ground. But searches over the area by the Swedish Air Force revealed nothing. Twenty-four aircraft flew the fjords, two of them crashing as a result and no trace of a secret base from which the ghost planes could have flown was found.

'It is impossible,' a senior Swedish airman told reporters, 'to explain away the whole thing as imagination. The question is; who are they? And why have they been invading our territory?'

The most plausible explanation, though not without its problems, is that the ghost aircraft, the engines of which seemed to cut out during flight, were experimental prototype missiles which developed into the V1 and V2 rockets by 1944 and 1945. Adolf Hitler, bent on avenging the loss of the First World War and promising to tear up the humiliating Treaty of Versailles, had come to power the previous year (1933). In the year of most sightings (1934) Hitler left the vacillators of the League of Nations and reintroduced conscription on his way to the attempted conquest of Europe. Was he also developing secret aircraft? It would only be three years later that the terrifying

Stuka dive-bomber first appeared in the skies over Guernica, as the German Condor legion flexed its young muscles on behalf of Franco's Phalange in the Spanish Civil War. Such aircraft usually take between ten and fifteen years to take to the air from the designs on the drawing board.

The Second World War was the first truly aerial war. During the Great War, aircraft had been used initially for reconnaissance and officers had to be drafted in to fly them from the existing services, notably the cavalry and infantry. Dog fights developed, at first with pistols and even stones, as reconnoitring aircraft met each other in disputed skies. The year 1939, however, saw the unleashing of Blitzkrieg – Napoleon's 'Lightning War' translated into the air. The phenomenal success of the German armed forces is largely explained by their speed and manoeuvrability in the air and on the ground; and the fact that the Allies, over-keen to appease and pray, were not as ready for war as Hitler.

The increased aerial activity – saturation bombing, aerial photography, fighter interception, nightly missions – created a mythology of its own. Airmen on both sides reported what came to be known by the Americans as 'foo fighters', named after a phrase – 'Where there's foo there's fire' – in the Smokey Stover comic strip, popular in the 1940s. Both sides assumed it was some new weapon developed by the other. Reports were numerous. Lieutenant Schlater of the United States Air Force was flying over the Rhine on a clear night in November 1944 when he was aware of 'ten small balls of reddish fire' bouncing near his fuselage. Two months earlier, two American pilots had been flying over Speyer when 'an enormous burning light' hovered over them. It seemed to be travelling at speeds of about 250 miles an hour. Most airmen who saw foo fighters complained that they damaged their aircrafts' ignition system. There was talk of crashes as a result, but there was no official finding. Nothing in German, Japanese or Allied technology could account for the lights of the foo fighters. Natural explanations included ball lightning, itself a disputed phenomenon. Both the Royal Air Force and the British Eighth Army rather lamely posed the theory that it was a result of mass hallucination, a Second World War version of the Angel of Mons. After 1945, no more was seen of the foo fighters.

Ufology officially came of age perhaps on 24 June 1947. Kenneth Arnold was an experienced pilot, flying on that day over the Cascade Mountains in Washington State, in the direction of the Canadian border. He was looking for the wreckage of a military transport aircraft that had crashed in the area when he saw nine separate objects flying in formation. They were travelling, he estimated, at speeds in excess of 1000 miles an hour, much faster than any known aircraft at the time. Later, when asked by reporters to describe the craft, he said: 'They flew like a saucer would if you skipped it across the water.' This single sentence at once caught the imagination of the public and spelt out an immediate death knell for the UFO as far as the scientific establishment was concerned. Arnold had in fact reported that the craft themselves were crescent-shaped, but it was the saucer image that stayed. Even the cover of the book that Arnold wrote with Ray Palmer, in 1952, showed the now traditional disc-shaped spaceship. It was even called *The Coming of the Saucers*. In the years ahead, there would be hundreds of sightings of saucer-shaped craft. How many of them are as a direct result of the media's misinterpretation of what Kenneth Arnold saw?

Arnold's experience could not be verified. By 1947, radar tracking was sufficiently sophisticated to pick up nine objects racing through the Washington skies, no matter what their speed. There were no radar traces. And no one else saw the craft either.

What had Arnold seen? Was it any one of a dozen possible natural phenomena? Or was it another example of human technology released ahead of its time? On 5 March of the previous year, Winston Churchill had said to the townsfolk of Fulton, Missouri, 'From Stetin in the Baltic to Trieste in the Adriatic an Iron Curtain has descended across the Continent . . .'

Behind the curtain lay the avaricious might of the 'Evil Empire' of the USSR. The former Allies who had shaken hands ceremoniously over the ashes of Hitler's Berlin now drifted apart, into hatred and mistrust. America in particular became obsessed with Communism – Senator Joe McCarthy warned against 'Reds under the Bed'. And in this Cold War which was to prevail for nearly fifty years, both sides stockpiled their conventional weapons and experimented with new ones. Is it possible that, in this context, what Kenneth Arnold saw were prototypes of Jack Northrop's 'flying wing' aircraft, the design of which would eventually be incorporated into the B-2 Stealth Bomber?

Roswell is a typical small town in the arid state of New Mexico. Roswell Air Field (formerly Roswell Army Air Field) lies some one hundred miles east of the White Sands Missile Range. On the night of 2 July 1947, only eight days after Kenneth Arnold's experience, a local Roswell couple, Mr and Mrs Dan Wilmot saw 'a big glowing object' in the night sky over their front porch. It was nearly ten o'clock and the visibility was good. Whatever the object was – and it appeared to be shaped like 'two inverted saucers faced mouth to mouth' – it was moving very fast in the direction of Corona to the north-west.

The next day, rancher 'Mac' Brazel, living near Corona and about 75 miles from Roswell, made an astonishing discovery. There had been an electrical storm the previous night, not unusual in the desert regions of the American south-west, but Brazel had heard a loud explosion that was clearly something other than thunder. In the morning he found an area strewn with wreckage he couldn't recognise, lying in a narrow belt in the direction of Socorro to the west. The fragments he found were thin, foil-like metal, but impossible to crease or bend with his bare hands. The metal's surface seemed to be covered in hieroglyphics or something that resembled writing and had dangling from it a tape-like material which was covered in a floral design.

In Roswell the next day, Brazel visited George Wilcox, the town sheriff, who contacted the Army Air Force Base. It was now that events took a rather sinister turn. Brazel talked to a local radio reporter, Johnny McBoyle, whose transmission was stopped by the authorities who threatened to remove his licence if he continued. His attempt to relay the information to the larger radio station, KOAT, at Albuquerque, was likewise intercepted. Meanwhile Brazel himself was virtually interrogated at the Air Base and the army not only visited his ranch to collect the mysterious debris, but cordoned off the area to keep away fascinated snoopers.

Although radio silence had effectively been achieved, the papers were less easy to control. The *Roswell Daily Record* of 8 July carried the screaming headline – 'RAAF Captures Flying Saucer On Ranch In Roswell Region.' In view of what was rapidly becoming hysterical publicity, Lieutenant Walter Haut, Public Information Officer at the base, issued what is probably a unique press release in terms of official honesty:

The many rumours regarding the Flying Disc became a reality yesterday when the Intelligence Office of the 509*th* Bomb Camp of the Eighth Air Force, Roswell Army Air Field, was fortunate enough to gain possession of a disc through the co-operation of one of the local ranchers and the Sheriff's office of Chaves County.

The flying object landed on a ranch near Roswell some-time last week. Not having phone facilities, the rancher stored the disc until such time as he was able to contact the Sheriff's Office, who in turn notified Major Jesse A. Marcel of the 509*th* Bomb Group Intelligence Office.

Action was immediately taken and the disc was picked up at the rancher's home. It was inspected at the Roswell Army Air Field and subsequently loaned by Major Marcel to higher headquarters.

Haut subsequently claimed that he had cleared this press release (concerning an object he had not personally seen) with his commanding officer, Colonel William Blanchard. Whatever the truth of the situation, Blanchard went on to become a general; Haut resigned his commission the following year.

Most of the wreckage which Major Marcel had collected was now flown to Fort Worth in Texas, where a press conference was called and newsmen were allowed to photograph the debris from a distance. A second photo-opportunity allowed them even closer, but by this time a swap had taken place, and the real debris had been transferred to Wright Field (now the Wright-Patterson Air Force Base). And the authorities now announced that the debris was that of a weather balloon. This was certainly not the recollection of Major Marcel, nor of Bill Brazel, 'Mac's' son, who had kept bits of the wreckage out of curiosity. When the younger Brazel happened to mention in a local bar that he still had three pieces, he was visited by the military who promptly confiscated his collection. This was two years after the crash. Why should the military be so concerned about what they had already said was a weather balloon?

The evidence of Major Marcel is even more important, in

that he was a trained observer and could be expected to know a weather balloon when he saw one. In fact, the base sent up as many as two of these every day. He could not recognise the hieroglyphics on the metal's surface and discovered that, though weighing virtually nothing, the metal could not be dented or burned.

More bizarre than the compelling evidence of the crashed UFO and the subsequent official cover-up is the alleged discovery of a dead crew.

Barney Barnett was a civil engineer, working in the desert area known as the Plains of San Augustin, west of Route 25 that meanders with the Rio Grande. On the morning of 3 July he found 'some sort of metallic, disc-shaped object' lying in the sand. It was about 30 feet in diameter and seemed to have cracked open as a result of its impact with the ground. Inside the craft and scattered around it were dead creatures, humanoid, but the size of children. Their eyes were small in their outsized heads and they had no hair. Their clothing was grey one-piece suits without belts, zips or buttons. Had this sight been witnessed by Barnett alone it would have been wide open to the usual accusations, but he was allegedly joined by a group of student archaeologists from the University of Pennsylvania, carrying out a dig in connection with Native American settlements in the area.

The local undertaker in Roswell, Glenn Dennis, received a number of telephone calls from the Air Base asking about the complexities of preserving bodies in ice. He subsequently received an order for four child-size coffins. A military nurse at the base claimed to have seen autopsy reports on alien bodies.

There, with hearsay, contradiction, denial and unspecified levels of individual and corporate paranoia, the Roswell story lay for several years. But the assassination of John F. Kennedy, the

Watergate scandal and the events in Cambodia led an increasing number of Americans to the realisation that its government could be highly devious and secretive. The Freedom of Information Act, which became law in 1976, forced the release of many (but not all) government papers on UFOs. Papers known as the Majestic-12 documents surfaced in 1984, and they make clear the fact that a group had been set up by the government to study both the Roswell saucer and its alien crew. The government at once denounced these documents as fakes.

Was the Roswell 'saucer' an experimental craft, along the lines of dirigible airships and V1/V2 rockets earlier in the century? Certainly, the White Sands Missile Range near Roswell has fired an estimated 30,000 pieces of military hardware into the sky in the half century since 1945. Until 1964, most of these launches took place at night (which would fit the Wilmot and Brazel evidence) and White Sands admits that 7 per cent of its tests are aborted, allowing for quite a high incidence of crashes. The unusual metal (still, fifty years later, not in general usage) and the unexplained hieroglyphics would seem to rule this theory out, as would, of course, the alien bodies.

Roswell, it seems, will not go away. Recently, New Mexico's Congressman, Steven Schiff, entered the fray as a result of pressure from the public. When he got no satisfactory response, merely the usual stonewalling, he took the matter up with the General Accounting Office which has wide powers of investigation. When pressured by this body, the USAF followed an ever-hopeful policy of retrenchment; the Roswell debris was probably part of a high altitude balloon used in Project Mogul to detect Soviet nuclear tests. Interestingly, Major Marcel worked on this project too, but not until his next tour of duty after Roswell.

Whatever happened in the sun-baked New Mexico desert in the summer of 1947, it marked the coming of age of ufology in two ways. It produced tangible evidence of a craft and crew that were at least likely not to be of earthly origin. And it produced a wall of silence from the authorities that has blocked serious investigation by civilians for years.

George Adamski made history in 1952 by claiming to have met and communicated with an alien from the planet Venus. Now usually discredited as a hoaxer, Adamski sparked a whole series of cases, mostly American, in which such contact had taken place. The craft he described appears in most UFO magazines as one of the 'Adamski' type. The common denominator in these incidents was usually that the aliens, being far more advanced than we are, had a message to convey to humanity, warnings about a nuclear Armageddon or the impending destruction of our eco-system. They were often described as being tall and blond, and these benevolent aliens are always commonly known as Nordics. All this sounds a little pat, and cynics have rejected it as being, perhaps, responses to the paranoia of the Cold War or a precursor of 'hippy' philosophy. Certainly the late 1960s saw a concerted move by the world's youth, centred on West Coast America, to ignore the prejudices and follies of their parents and live together in one vast hippy commune where flowers, beads, love and drugs would provide the answer to every problem. The notion of a paternal, beneficent and wandering band of aliens, concerned for our well-being, seemed to fit that image quite comfortably.

Supporters of Adamski and other 'close-encounter' claimants counter the accusation of fraud with ingenuity. Space research since 1952 has shown that the planets which Adamski claimed to have been inhabited are barren and inhospitable, utterly at odds with his description of them. His supporters claim that this is because the particular aliens whom he met were lying.

This bizarre argument and counter-argument are typical of the warring factions that pervade modern ufology.

F rom the 'four living creatures' who appeared to the priest Ezekiel to the four child-size coffins ordered from Roswell's undertaker, we have travelled through twenty-five centuries of development and progress. But we have also brought with us a fascination and a fear of the unknown.

> From ghoulies and ghosties and long-leggity beasties
> And things that go bump in the night, Good Lord
> deliver us!

Thus runs the traditional Cornish prayer. Yet, in our own time of science and empiricism and rationalism, things still go bump in the night over the sky at Roswell and the desert is a grave for beasties still unknown.

'W e are not alone' – the message was clear. The weird geological formation, thc lure of people into the desert, the bright white light and the 'feelgood factor' all lent a magical glow to Steven Spielberg's *Close Encounters of the Third Kind* which was released in 1977 and which captured the mood of a generation. Interestingly, the largest set in film history was actually the interior of an old dirigible hangar. *Time Out* wrote: 'It somehow combines Disney and 1950s SF and junk food into the most progressive (if arrested) version of the American dream yet.'

The *New Yorker* said: 'It has visionary magic and a childlike comic spirit, along with a love of surprises and a skeptical let's-try-it-on spirit.'

It cost $20,000,000 and much of the dialogue was inaudible.

It also introduced to a largely gullible public what until then had been a technical term used only by ufologists in an attempt to classify UFO sightings. A close encounter of the first kind (CEI) involves the sighting of something unidentified at close range. A close encounter of the second kind (CE2) is one in which the UFO interacts in some way with the environment, leaving tangible evidence such as a depression in the ground. A close encounter of the third kind (CE3) involves the appearance of aliens (like those frail beings whose hands reach out to Richard Dreyfuss and others in the film). The fourth kind (CE4) is one which involves human abduction by aliens. Thousands of reports relate to this last experience, but the first of them to be widely reported dates from 1961:

About midnight on September 20th we were driving in a National Forest Area in the White Mountains in New Hampshire. This is a desolate, uninhabited area. At first we noticed a bright object in the sky, which seemed to be moving rapidly. We stopped our car and got out to observe it more closely with our binoculars. Suddenly it reversed its flight path from the north to the south-west and appeared to be flying in a very erratic pattern. As we continued driving and then stopping to watch it, we observed the following flight pattern: the object was spinning and appeared to be lighted only on one side, which gave it a twinkling effect.

As it approached our car, we stopped again. As it hovered in the air in front of us, it appeared to be pancake in shape, ringed with windows in the front through which we could see bright blue-white lights. Suddenly, two red lights appeared on each side. By this time, my husband was standing in the road, watching closely. He saw wings protrude on each side and the red lights were on the wing-tips.

As it glided closer he was able to see inside this object, but not too closely. He did see several figures scurrying about as though they were making some hurried type of preparation. One figure was observing us from the windows. From the distance this was seen, the figures appeared to be about the size of a pencil and seemed to be dressed in some type of shiny black uniform . . .

So wrote Betty Hill in September 1961 to Major Donald Keyhoe of the National Investigations Committee on Aerial Phenomena (NICAP). It was the beginning of an experience so bizarre that she and her husband were utterly traumatised by it and were plagued by nightmares for years. Betty was a forty-one-year-old child welfare worker. Her husband, Barney, thirty-nine, was a mail sorter in Boston and both were active campaigners in the civil rights movement, then gathering support across the United States. The couple had gone on a spur of the moment holiday to Niagara and Montreal and were driving south along Route 3 from Bolebrook. They had stopped to eat at a diner and were near the town of Lancaster when the flying object appeared.

It was not until late November, two months after their close encounter, that Barney came to realise, in discussion with UFO investigators, that a journey along 190 miles of deserted roads and moving generally between 65–70 miles an hour had taken seven hours. This came to be known as 'missing time'. And neither Betty nor Barney Hill could account for it.

Betty's dreams seemed to continue where her conscious memories of the White Mountain night left off. She and Barney were stopped on the road by eleven men, the crew of the craft whose lights they had seen. They were taken on board the ship and placed in separate rooms. Each was subjected to a physical examination. In Betty's case, samples were taken of her hair, her earwax, scrapings from her skin. A long needle was inserted into her navel as a sort of pregnancy test and she found herself discussing the Universe (of which she knew very little) and the human concept of time with the leader of the crew. Artists' impressions made to Barney's and Betty's specifications show bald-headed beings with mere indentations for ears, large, lidless eyes and vestigial noses. The couple agreed to undergo hypnosis.

Regression hypnosis is now known to have its defects. It was carried out over a seven month period from December 1963 by Dr Benjamin Simon. Simon never committed himself in public to a statement on the case, but it at least seems likely that the couple's anxiety at the time had a bearing on their experience. No one has seriously suggested that the Hills were consciously inventing the visitation, but Barney was working nights, making a round trip of 120 miles a night, and suffered from a worsening ulcer. Betty, at the same time, was separated from the children of her first marriage and came from a family to whom poltergeist activity was a commonplace. Betty was white, Barney was black – a situation which, in 1963, must have carried its own strains.

Hypnosis can indeed aid memory. The police have used hypnotherapy to enable witnesses to remember what they cannot consciously remember. But under hypnosis we now know that the subject can lie and make mistakes. Since the will is suppressed, even manipulated, a subject can become extremely receptive to suggestion. Some subjects become highly chatty, producing a number of details simply conjured up from the imagination.

Whereas the sudden appearance of alien and powerful forces may disturb many people and terrify some, would not most of us, deep down, *like* to believe? Rather as we would like to see, one day, a pleisiosaur or something similar, swimming down Loch Ness?

Whatever the reality of the Hill case – and Betty, now a widow, continues to witness strange lights over New Hampshire

– other, similar claims have been put forward over the last thirty years, and by people who are utterly unaware of the existence of each other.

There is a commonality of experience in these cases and even if not all of them are as dramatic as that which novelist Whitley Strieber describes in *Communion*, the discernible pattern is obvious. The typical alien – known as the 'Grey' – stands about three-and-a-half-feet high, with a hugely distorted head and cadaverous arms and legs. The nose and mouth are vestigial, but the eyes burn deep into the collective memories of abductees. They are large and black, with no discernible pupils, rather like those of an insect. Many describe the hypnotic qualities or calming effect of those eyes. They feel themselves immobilised by a blinding white or blue/white light and a sense of floating from a terrestrial bed or car into a round, white room resembling an operating theatre. The physical examination can be painful and often includes the removal of ova or sperm: the implanting of a small metallic object in a nostril and the carrying out of what we can now describe as keyhole surgery using thin, delicate probes. Actual communication is rare. In fact, Betty Hill's casual chat to her abductors, apparently in colloquial English, poses all sorts of questions about reality. The general memory is that the aliens have no feelings of any kind towards their human captives and regard them rather as we regard laboratory rats.

There is a tendency among ufologists to accept that much of this abduction is related to some kind of breeding programme. Two out of three abductees are female and some claim to have carried alien babies which have been removed before birth during a subsequent abduction. Others claim that they were 're-abducted' and introduced to listless hybrid children, presumably their own, with whom they were encouraged to bond. One of the most lucid examples of this extra-terrestrial stud farming comes however from a man and it predates the

Hill case by four years. It did not reach the English-speaking world until 1965.

Antônio Villas-Boas was a twenty-three-year-old farm labourer living near the town of São Francisco de Sales in Brazil. He and his brother had witnessed bright lights in the sky twice before but on this occasion he was alone ploughing his field when he was grabbed by aliens and carried struggling into their pear-shaped craft. According to Villas-Boas the only sounds the aliens made were, 'low barks and yelps, neither very clear nor very hoarse, some longer, some shorter, at times containing several different sounds all at once and at other times ending in a quaver . . . I can't reproduce them . . . my voice isn't made for that.'

He was smeared with a thick liquid, some of his blood was taken and he was then urged to have sex with a female humanoid about four-and-a-half-feet tall. Her eyes were blue and elongated, her hair almost white, curling inwards towards her face. Her mouth was slit-like and her ears small. She had a very slim body with heavy thighs and bright red hair in her armpits and groin. She smelt feminine and they had sex twice. She grunted and bit him gently on the chin once or twice. When the others called her away, she pointed to her belly and then to the sky.

When Villas-Boas was examined by Dr Fontes of Rio de Janeiro in February 1958, there were still scars on his chin and other parts of his body. The symptoms seemed similar to those of radiation poisoning. Unlike the Hills, Villas-Boas was interrogated quite roughly by the Brazilian military authorities and yet he never wavered from the details of his story.

What is the likely truth behind so many stories of alien abduction? It is inconceivable that everyone is lying. Surely, most people seeking to paint themselves into a fantasy would concoct some benevolent contact, rather than what is almost always an unpleasant and frightening experience. The obvious attractions of fame and fortune may well have induced a few, but the majority of abductees are not seeking to sell their stories; neither do they crave publicity. In fact, a high proportion of them insist that there be no publicity surrounding their case.

Some of those who claim close encounters may of course be mentally ill. Temporal lobe disorders can result in delusions which might explain some abduction stories. A commonly suggested explanation now is that many of the female abductees especially are reliving an incident of childhood sexual abuse. There are no published statistics on this, so that any comparisons between them and the public as a whole is impossible. Since many abductions involve unpleasant gynaecological probings, it does not seem likely that a victim will replace this fantasy for the reality of a situation that is so similar. If the abuse by an adult relative or friend is too traumatic for the mind to accept, why should the mind create something 'even worse'?

It is of course possible to stand this argument on its head. John Mack, Professor of Psychiatry at Harvard Medical School, has created a storm among ufologists and therapists alike with his theories. At first highly sceptical and dismissive of abductees and their supporters, Mack is unusual among the scientific establishment in that he gave them the chance, as it were, to prove their case. Not only does he now believe that some cases are totally genuine, he has postulated the theory that some cases of apparent sexual abuse are actually examples of alien abduction! The authorities at Harvard, upset by his controversial views, launched an inquiry into his conduct. In August 1995 he was publicly censured, but his job, which was rumoured to have been under threat, was safe.

Whitley Strieber is the most famous example of an abductee who has undergone a polygraph or lie-detector test to prove the veracity of his experience to a disbelieving world. These machines are widely used in the United States, but are still inadmissable in a British court of law. Rather like genetic fingerprinting, the lie detector is not 100 per cent foolproof. The theory is that the machine detects physical changes, such as the quickening of the pulse, that occur as a result of telling a lie. A number of control questions are asked where the information is not in dispute, for example the name of the subject undergoing the experiment. This becomes the norm or baseline and any meandering from that will indicate a lie. The greater the area of sensitivity, the further from the baseline the meanderings will be. There are two weaknesses in this system. First, pathological liars exhibit no physical changes as a result of their lying. Secondly, it is possible to give a false baseline during the initial control questions, perhaps by creating physical or mental anguish – biting the lip or recalling a traumatic event. Against this a lie would appear insignificant.

Researchers such as Budd Hopkins have done a great deal in recent years to bring the controversial subject of the Extraterrestrial Hypothesis (ETH) into the public domain. Budd Hopkins is a successful New York artist, who has been investigating alien abductions since 1976. He has investigated some 1500 cases, and is regarded as the world's leading authority in this controversial subject. His primary aim however, is to help those who have had such experiences to come to terms with them.

Whatever the truth behind abduction stories, America has become obsessed by them. From Christopher Walken's cranky, confused Whitley Strieber in the film *Communion*, to a plot-line in the long-running television soap, *The Colbys*, little grey men with huge heads and huge black eyes have become familiar to an entire nation. And bizarre as it may seem, it is now possible to take out insurance cover against alien abductions! The premium is around £45 and the payout is £6 million – twice that if the insured of the first party is killed as a result of a close encounter of the fourth kind. Well over 35,000 people have actually taken out such insurance. Naturally enough, insurance companies demand tangible proof of abduction, such as photographs and medical evidence. The risk taken by insurance companies is actually getting higher. There are now many highly convincing UFO photographs and the injuries sustained by someone like Antônio Villas-Boas are difficult to explain away naturally – how could a Brazilian farmer in the fifties have come into contact conventionally with radioactive material? Photographic laboratories, where there is a high level of expertise, have stated that they do not believe some of the photographs to be fakes. Add to this a corroborative statement from someone with the impeccable credentials of Professor John Mack, and it may well be in the near future that a court of law will decide that the insurance company's conditions have been met. The very existence of such insurance policies however, concedes that the concept of alien abduction is as natural in the States as flood damage or acute appendicitis.

Just as the appearance of inexplicable lights in the sky was known to the ancient world, so there may be historical parallels with alien abduction. In what John Napier has called *The Goblin Universe* are dozens of stories from folklore of humans being taken away by dwarfs, elves, fairies and trolls. What is common to these creatures is their size. They are universally referred to as 'the little people'. Is one person's fairy another's alien? Have we simply come a little nearer than, say, our medieval ancestors to the true origin of these creatures? Let one example suffice. In Welsh mythology, the story is told of Shon ap Shenkin who heard a fairy melody playing in a meadow one morning and rested against a tree trunk to listen to it and to watch the fairies dancing in their ring. When the music stopped, Shenkin stood up to find that the tree against which he had rested had died. When Shenkin returned to his cottage, the place was overgrown with ivy and looked somehow different. The door was opened by an old man who asked the visitor his name. 'I am Shon ap Shenkin,' the visitor replied. The old man in the doorway turned deathly pale and said, 'I often heard my grandfather, your father, speak of your disappearance.' And Shon ap Shenkin crumbled to dust. Washington Irving embroidered this tale in his Rip van Winkle, but it is typical of humans caught up in the parallel world of faerie, where time is utterly different from our own. The missing time concept runs through the goblin universe like an elusive tune, only partly heard, only partly understood.

And if there is a link of some kind between ufology and the goblin universe, might there not also be one between ufology and ghosts? The spirit world is highly complicated and sightings of ghosts (there have been more reported in Britain than anywhere else in the world) are myriad in their form. There is less consistency here than in UFO sightings, but certainly many ghosts appear grey (there are dozens of Grey Ladies who still walk the staircases of ancestral homes) are often seen at night, and some share with aliens the ability to do the 'impossible'; for instance to walk through walls. Again, it is the United States that produces a phenomenon that may bridge the two worlds, of the spirit and space – Spook lights. In the Brown Mountain region of North Carolina some eyewitnesses described these lights hovering in the night sky in 1913 as disappearing 'like a busting skyrocket'. In Silver Cliff, Colorado, in 1965 the assistant editor of *National Geographic* magazine witnessed 'dim round spots of blue white light'. True, they were hovering eerily over a graveyard, but it is the colour, so familiar to ufologists, that is interesting.

Recently in the United States there has been a spate of animal killings. Cattle are the usual target and bodies have been found badly mutilated, often with the genitals cut out. It is of course possible that this is the work of deranged sadists or even some sort of Satanic cult, but several of the bodies have been found in the vicinity of apparent UFO activity. Television producer Linda Moulton Howe, a haematologist and pathologist, as well as Dr John Alshuer, claim that autopsies carried out on some of these animals show that the cuts to the abdomens could have been made with advanced laser technology. What characterises these attacks is the lack of blood and the total absence of tracks of the perpetrator.

Alien abductions and animal mutilations take us away from the friendly cosmonaut mood that dominated the 1950s and 1960s. The cold, harshly-lit interiors of alien craft, the callous kidnaps and probes take us into a nightmarish world where we are the helpless targets of a detached extraterrestrial presence bent on carrying out some sort of genetic programme with little regard for anything other than their own, unknown motives.

Bob Lazar goes further. A controversial figure and the target of much muckraking, Lazar claims to have worked for the American government on a project involving a craft of extraterrestrial origin. He was recruited into a small team based at site S-4, near the mysterious Area 51 at Groom Lake, Nevada. The team was working on the reverse engineering of recovered alien technology. In other words, the government had extraterrestrial vehicles – in fact, nine of them – and the team's job was to take them apart to see how they worked. The vehicles were saucer-shaped, and one, according to Lazar, hovered a few feet off the ground. The seats inside one of the craft were large enough only for children – or aliens. In most cases, there was no sign of damage to these saucers. They had not crashed or been shot down. One theory is that in a United States/extraterrestrial pact, the aliens have *carte blanche* to carry out abductions in exchange for a slice of their technological knowhow. Some even allege that the whole area of technology behind aircraft such as the Stealth fighter has emerged from this.

Lazar's is by no means the only voice. Robotics expert and former NASA mission specialist Bob Oechsler has produced extraordinary information which goes some way to supporting Lazar. During his researches, Oechsler telephoned Admiral

Bobby Ray Inman, a former Director of the US National Security Agency and former Deputy Director of the CIA (an organisation that has always officially debunked UFOs). Oechsler taped the conversation:

> **Oechsler**: Do you anticipate that any of the recovered vehicles would ever become available for technological research? Outside of the military circles?
>
> **Inman**: Again, I honestly don't know. Ten years ago the answer would have been no. Whether as time has evolved they are beginning to become more open on it, there's a possibility.

The obvious implication of this exchange is that we do indeed possess recovered alien technology. The Freedom of Information Act has secured the release of various papers (although many files are – like the time of the abductees – curiously missing).

One paper that has surfaced is signed by Edward Tauss, Acting Chief of the Weapons and Equipment Division of the Office of Scientific Intelligence, dated August 1952: 'It is strongly urged, however, that no indication of CIA interest or concern reach the press or public, in view of their probably alarmist tendencies to accept such interest as "confirmatory".'

A cover-up of some sort appears to have been going on for some time.

Two years ago, Bobby Ray Inman was being tipped as a possible US Secretary of Defense. He was an unexpected choice for the job and some elements of the UFO lobby wondered whether his name on the shortlist might not herald an official change of policy by the government in relation to the existence of UFOs. In the event, the text of the above conversation with Bob Oechsler surfaced in the media, and, at the last moment, Inman turned down the job in very mysterious circumstances. Hints of corruption did not ring true. Was it simply that Bobby Inman had a disarming degree of honesty with which the establishment could not live comfortably? This is what many in the UFO lobby believe. To them it is just one more dimension which suggests that the whole UFO issue is a critically important one at the highest levels in America and one in which disagreements over official policy can claim some very senior victims.

The fifty years since Kenneth Arnold saw crescent-shaped objects flying at incredible speed over the Cascade Mountains have seen the genesis of a new creed. And a realisation that science fiction may well be becoming science fact, whatever the apparent paranoia of various governments to keep information under wraps.

I was aware of the mythology. I had read up on the famous cases and pondered the imponderables. I was ready to throw myself into the new job.

But nothing could have prepared me for those three years. Nothing.

2

THE MOST INTERESTING
JOB IN THE COUNTRY

The Ministry of Defence was created by Act of Parliament in December 1946, seven months before Kenneth Arnold saw saucers in the skies over the Cascade Mountains. It grew out of the wartime need to co-ordinate the three branches of the services – army, navy and air force – as never before and its advisers were the three chiefs of staff of those services. The primary function of the ministry, obviously, is to defend. Quoting from the Statement on the Defence Estimates 1995 (SDE 95), Defence Role 1 is defined as: 'To ensure the protection and security of the United Kingdom and our Dependent Territories even when there is no major external threat.'

The structure of the ministry is vast and complex. When I joined in 1985, approximately 170,000 civilians were employed by the department. The Cold War had not yet warmed – the Gorbachev thaw, though visible, was not yet a torrent. The combine-harvester operator from the North Caucasus who had graduated with a law degree from Moscow University became general secretary of the Communist party and effective leader of the Soviet Union on 11 March. *Glasnost* and *perestroika* still lay ahead, and if Gorbachev's praise of détente and his call for a reduction in arms stockpiles promised much, he was still a communist; there were still grim, grey faces on that Kremlin balcony with him. And there was still a wall dividing Berlin. No one was taking any chances.

In my first weeks, as the new boy, I learned routines, mastered basics, familiarised myself with the department's structure. There were systems to learn, files to grapple with, 'old hands' to talk to for advice. The best place to start was to pore over the Ministry of Defence telephone directory. This huge publication, itself a classified document, spells out chains of command in diagrammatic form and lists the names and job descriptions from the level of executive officer upwards. The executive officer is the junior managerial grade, the rough equivalent of an army captain. Alongside one of these names was written 'UFOs'. I think I chuckled when I read this. It hadn't dawned on me that the department would deal with unidentified flying objects at all and I found myself wondering what the job entailed.

In the Ministry of Defence, tours of duty last between two and three years. After that, in order to provide a breadth of knowledge and experience, personnel are moved on. In the course of my ten-year career to date, I have been involved in the debate over women flying combat aircraft (we won that debate, and now they do); operational duties in the Gulf War and helping to organise the commemorations marking the Fiftieth Anniversary of the end of the Second World War.

On 17 September 1990, I joined the division known as Secretariat (Air Staff) in the grim MOD headquarters buildings along Whitehall, opposite Downing Street. The division's basic role is to provide advice to defence ministers and senior air force officers on policy, political and parliamentary aspects of a host of matters relating to RAF operations. Many of these are outside the NATO area, and involve co-operation with foreign embassies, exercises and deployments, as well as aircraft accidents. It was this division, which focuses particularly on Parliament and the public, that was responsible for UFOs, whatever that term specifically meant in civil service-speak, and an internal shuffle in July 1991 brought me straight to that office and straight into the most interesting job in the country.

My diary entry for Wednesday 17 July reads: 'An interesting day today – was sounded out about taking Owen Hartop's job.' Owen Hartop worked for the section known as Sec(AS)2a – sometimes wrongly called AS2 by the UFO lobby. In what is possibly the most comprehensive catalogue of the UFO phenomenon, *The UFO Encyclopedia*, John Spencer of the British UFO Research Association (BUFORA) includes this entry about it:

> A department of the Ministry of Defence, the full title of which is Air Staff 2, which succeeded Defence Secretariat 8(DS8). These departments are alleged to deal with UFO reports made to the government; in fact a spokesman for that department described AS2 as 'the focal point within the United Kingdom for UFO reports'.

I took the job. Thinking back, I had heard nothing about it in the six years since I had seen it listed in the directory. It was an odd post, because line management has no involvement in the subject, aside from a purely supervisory role. In other words the desk officer was left to get on with it. During the course of my tour of duty in Sec(AS)2a there were three different people in charge of the office where I worked. Their opinions on UFOs ranged from complete scepticism to a more open-minded position. Perhaps because of his other responsibilities, my Head of Division took little interest in the subject. On a daily basis, I was a department of one.

For the first few days, I sat with Owen Hartop as he briefed me on the main duties. As far as UFOs were concerned there were primarily two: to act as a focal point for all UFO sightings in the United Kingdom and to handle general policy questions that arose.

Owen moved to his new post after a lengthy and traditional celebration in the Clarence pub on the Friday. It was generally agreed in the years of the Cold War and the Troubles that if a bomb went off in the Clarence on a Friday lunchtime, half the Ministry of Defence would be wiped out.

But on Monday 29 July, I was on my own.

The term UFO is a misleading one. The initials have become an integral part of the language, and that in itself causes confusion. Dr J. Allen Hynek, one of the most eminent scientists to nail his colours to the mast, pointed out that because we are unaware of any actual UFO in existence, what we actually study – and what I worked on for three years – are UFO *reports*. In 1966, the United States Air Force defined a UFO as 'an aerial object which the observer is unable to identify'. Three years later, the University of Colorado produced a specification which began by describing it as 'the stimulus for a report made by one or more individuals of something seen in the sky . . .' – but the unwieldy definition rumbled on for another seven lines. In 1972, Carl Sagan, the American astrophysicist and television personality, called the UFO 'a moving aerial or celestial phenomenon, detected visually or by radar, but whose nature is not immediately understood'. In the same year Dr J. Allen Hynek offered 'the reported perception of an object or light seen in the sky or upon the land . . . which does not suggest a logical, conventional explanation . . .' The *Oxford Dictionary of Current English* simply gives 'unidentified flying object'. Interestingly, the *Dictionary of Science for Everyone* has no entry for UFO at all!

The question is often asked – and of course I was always being asked it, at courses, parties and in the canteen – 'Do you believe in UFOs?' The answer can only be yes. If I stand a hundred metres from a friend and throw a small object into the air, my friend is unlikely to be able to tell what it is. While in the air, the object is, literally, a UFO. Debasement of the language, even over a few years, has meant that the term UFO has come to be synonymous with alien spacecraft. Most unidentified flying objects can in fact be identified readily, as ordinary, everyday objects. Experts may need to be called in to pronounce on the more difficult cases. It is the small percentage that defy all rational explanation that grab the mind and work on the imagination.

So what was the Ministry of Defence's involvement in something for which even a basic definition is so difficult? It is all a matter of national security. Military Task 1.10, as set out in SDE 95, is concerned that 'The integrity of British airspace in peacetime is maintained through a continuous Recognised Air Picture and air policing of the United Kingdom Air Defence Region'. During the Cold War, Soviet aircraft routinely attempted to penetrate our air defences. There was in one sense nothing overtly aggressive about this. It was rather like the children in *To Kill a Mockingbird* scuttling around the house scaring themselves by calling the mad and terrifying Boo Radley. They would have run a mile if he had come out to play with them, and similarly the Soviet fighters and bombers were testing our defences and trying to evaluate the effectiveness of our radar systems and air defence fighter aircraft, as well as testing the calibre of the crews who operated them. If such an aircraft was detected by the telltale blip on the radar screen, our fighters would be scrambled and the Soviet jet intercepted and politely escorted out of our airspace. It was a friendly, yet deadly serious game of cat-and-mouse, providing essential training for our aircrews and radar teams.

At any time, the report of a UFO in our skies might turn out to be a foreign fighter, missile, reconnaissance device or remotely piloted vehicle. If this 'UFO' is not picked up on radar, then our defences have failed and the ramifications of that are grave indeed. Our air defence system, with its highly sophisticated network of ground-based radar stations and early-warning aircraft, makes few mistakes. But what if such an object escaped detection? Something seen by a harvesting farmer in Sussex; a butcher in Yorkshire; a police officer in the Scottish lowlands? What if this 'something' were the creation of a technology we cannot understand, still less match?

At the beginning of Operation Desert Storm, American F-117 Stealth fighters penetrated the area around Baghdad with total impunity and were able to take out key facilities in the heart of the capital. The general consensus was that such was the accuracy of Allied bombing that it would have been possible to target Saddam Hussein himself, had that been the wish of the United Nations, and had we known where he was. The area around Baghdad was probably one of the most heavily defended in the world at that time, with all sorts of radar systems in operation, yet the radar-absorptive paint and the 'facetin' of the Stealth aircraft beat them all.

This is not the science fiction of H.G. Wells, with the red weed of Mars choking and suffocating our planet. It is science fact. And the Ministry of Defence cannot afford to dismiss it. If alien technology landed in Britain, it would be vital to study it in detail, to duplicate it if possible and to find a defence against it. Does the UFO constitute a threat? If so, then the Ministry of Defence is, very assuredly, interested.

At first, I must admit, my new job was rather disappointing. There were no flying saucers, no aliens, and there was no dark and mysterious government involvement. Try as I might,

I couldn't see a Man in Black anywhere – those sinister, black clad, half-alien, half-human characters who have been known to pay calls on witnesses to UFO sightings, suggesting that they keep quiet about their experiences, and backing up these suggestions with threats. A cursory reading of the files that were now at my disposal revealed nothing more than a handful of reports of vague lights or shapes in the sky which were likely to have been terrestrial aircraft. But I was determined to keep an open mind. It was easy to ridicule; easy to dismiss. I became, I suppose, caught up in it all as I thoroughly immersed myself in the background. I was, after all, in a unique and oddly lonely position: the only official in the country specifically tasked with studying the UFO phenomenon. It was quite a responsibility.

I went to libraries and bookshops. I read voraciously, familiarising myself with cases both celebrated and obscure. At the back of my mind was a sense of professional integrity, honour, call it what you will. It would do me and the department little credit if a UFO researcher, journalist or member of the public asked me a question and I didn't have the answer. In this spirit of detailed study I went back to the files for a closer look, and my initial findings – that the files contained no more than sightings of weather balloons, lenticular clouds, bird formations and aircraft seen from odd angles – were now revised. There were a number of sightings that defied all rational explanation. Something very strange was going on. And clearly, I wasn't the first in the Ministry of Defence to think so.

Lord Hill-Norton, Admiral of the Fleet and Chief of the Defence Staff between 1971 and 1973, remains a steadfast believer in the potential threat of the UFO. A member of the House of Lords All-Party UFO Study Group set up in 1979, Hill-Norton continues to pressurise officialdom on the need for vigilance. Another stalwart was Ralph Noyes, who had been private secretary to Sir Ralph Cochrane, Vice-Chief of the Air Staff from 1950 to 1952 and head of the old DS8. He retired in 1977 as an under-secretary of state and is currently a leading authority on UFOs – he is also a consultant to BUFORA – crop circles and other psychic phenomena. Such distinguished company was light years away from my preconceptions of the UFO lobby. I had fondly imagined them as eccentrics in anoraks, train-spotter types standing on ley-lines at night, staring expectantly up at the heavens, binoculars at the ready. Yet here were senior civil servants and military officers convinced that UFOs were very real. My view of the subject began to change.

Appendix 1 of this book carries the officially reported figures for UFO sightings between 1959 and 1995. It is not clear whether any reports were received before 1959: if they were, they would probably have been handled by the RAF. It is likely that the worldwide media interest in Kenneth Arnold's 'saucers' in 1947 would have generated sightings, however spurious, in Britain. Unfortunately, before 1967, most ministry UFO files were routinely destroyed after a five-year period, so whatever was in them is lost to posterity.

What can we learn from these figures? Practically speaking, not a lot. There are years when great bursts of UFO activity seem to have taken place, notably 1966–7, 1977–8 and 1980–1, but again, there are rational explanations for this. The increase in sightings in 1978 – 550 up on the figure of two years earlier – can probably be attributed to the fascination with Steven Spielberg's hugely successful film *Close Encounters of the Third Kind*. It was the first 'feelgood' movie about extraterrestrials and people wanted to share in that experience. The 1967 peak is more difficult to explain away, however. The only significant space news was grim – in January, 'Gus' Grissom, Ed White and Roger Chaffee died in the capsule of their Apollo spacecraft when a fire roared through the pure oxygen atmosphere on the launchpad, and in April, Soviet cosmonaut Vladimir Komarov was killed when his Soyuz spacecraft plummeted out of orbit and he was unable to release his parachute. Perhaps the sightings had more to do with the fact that the world trembled on the brink of a potential Armageddon as Israel trounced the Arabs in the Six-Day War and China exploded its first hydrogen bomb. The same was true of 1981: there was little to report on the space front, except that in April, the space shuttle Columbia landed without incident after a three-day maiden voyage; in June, the Israelis claimed to have the technology to build an atom bomb.

There are problems with these figures. They give no indication of the quality of individual report or even of how they were followed up. Some of my predecessors tried to categorise the reports under such random headings as 'satellites', 'aircraft lights' or even the tantalising 'unknown'. At least some of these groupings appeared to have been based on guesswork as opposed to logical, detached investigation of specific sightings. And worse, there seemed to be no consistent approach in the definition of a UFO report. If a family of four observe the same thing in the sky, is that one sighting, or four? It may well be that a statistician would reject the figures entirely, as a thirty-six-year span does not give the chronological sweep necessary to ascertain trends and patterns. Perhaps in a century's time, a story will emerge from the statistics. But then, perhaps in a century's time we will have solved the UFO mystery altogether.

The biggest problem, then, lies in what the figures do not say. Are the 8,890 sightings since 1959 merely the tip of the iceberg? Here, I am on surer ground. The UFO lobby, who have followed this matter more closely than any other organisation over the last few years, believe that approximately 95 per cent of all UFO sightings are never reported at all. The estimates suggest that

13 million people worldwide have seen UFOs. Why do they not come forward?

One reason is that they are unsure of who to report them to. For many people, reading this might be the first indication they've had that anybody in the Ministry of Defence looks at UFO reports. It would be impracticable, not to mention undesirable, if the Ministry of Defence touted for custom in this area. Similarly, the various private groups, such as BUFORA, are less high-profile than one might imagine. Their journal, *UFO Times*, is not likely to be on the shelves of many newsagents. However, the other big UK UFO group, Quest International, have just started to market their publication, *UFO Magazine* through newsagents, so perhaps this situation is slowly changing.

Even when people do pluck up the courage to come forward, it is difficult to see the whole picture because there is no central depository for such reports: Britain possesses no database for UFO information. Some people rang or wrote to me with their evidence; others will have contacted a local UFO research group. Still others will have gone to the police, or civil airports. And many, perhaps the majority, will recount their stories, sheepishly, after a few pints at the local. These reports lie all over the country, scattered, dissociated from one another and ultimately forgotten.

Another major factor is the fear of ridicule. The general attitude to UFOs and those who claim to have seen them is one of scepticism. The articles carried by the press are invariably tongue-in-cheek, and you don't have to resort to the famous *Sunday Sport* headlines – 'HOW TO TELL IF YOUR MUM-IN-LAW IS AN ALIEN', 'UFO BUM STOLE MY KNICKERS', 'PET-FANCYING ALIENS BEAM UP 26 ELEPHANTS' – to catch the flavour of it. Even a supposedly sober national, the *Daily Mail*, preceded what was actually a straightforward piece of reporting with the headline: 'LITTLE GREEN MEN OR BIG GREEN DOLLARS?' (28 March 1995). And television is little better. Even serious and conscientious programmes such as the *Network First* programme in which I participated in 1994 cannot resist the dramatic skies, sinister music and weird camera angles. Michael Aspel's *Strange But True?* is guiltier still of the corny special-effects syndrome, although its reportage is usually accurate. This approach is likely to deter many witnesses, especially those in positions of responsibility for whom public ridicule would mean the end of their careers. And it is just such people – pilots, police officers, forces personnel at all levels – who make excellent witnesses, because they are experienced, and trained to be good observers and to remain calm in a situation which might terrify you or me. It does not bode well for those on high who have admitted to seeing UFOs that the two most famous examples from the United States are Jimmy Carter and Ronald Reagan.

So what sort of people do submit UFO reports? Who are this vocal minority who are prepared to stand up and be counted? They come from all walks of life, both sexes, all ages. Most of them – and this is what made their stories so convincing for me – came forward tentatively, embarrassed, and sorry for taking up my time. The vast majority did not believe in alien civilisations and wanted to avoid publicity at all costs, and to keep away from civilian UFO groups. Without the lure of money or limelight, it is difficult to see why they would have reported their experiences unless their accounts are genuine.

I had always believed, along with millions of others, that UFOs were saucer-shaped (the media's mangling of Kenneth Arnold's description in 1947 has a lot to answer for). In fact, UFOs come in all shapes and sizes. In the MOD files one description emerged again and again, and from totally independent sources. It was a huge triangle, hanging silently in the air, hovering like some vast bird of prey, then vanishing within seconds at incredible speed.

These were no aircraft lights or weather balloons, and hoaxing on this scale was out of the question. There is no doubt in my mind that I was reading about something real.

I formed the view that UFOs were potentially the most important issue currently facing the human race, and that the military would be in the front line if I was right. Predictably, my bosses did not share this view. The consensus seemed to be, for whatever reason, that we should not delve too deeply. I was amazed. I believed I had clear evidence that craft of unknown origin were demonstrating a technology apparently far in advance of our own and were using it to penetrate our airspace. Our radar could only rarely detect them, and even when they could, it seemed highly unlikely that our aircraft and missiles would be able to stop them. Yet some of my superiors appeared to laugh the matter off. And when they realised that I was serious, and they stopped laughing, I was told to drop certain lines of inquiry.

But I was not alone in believing that something bizarre was going on, something beyond human experience and something hostile.

ATTITUDES

There can be few subjects other than ufology for which government policy is dictated so much by attitudes and so little by facts or hard evidence. And many of these attitudes have been created by the media.

Ever since Kenneth Arnold's UFO sighting, the media have had a torrid affair with the UFO. This could and should have been a good thing: a constant stream of UFO stories taken seriously, reported seriously and backed by serious editorial comment would almost certainly have led to the subject being treated by politicians with the gravity they reserve for politics, scientists their science, and so on. In the past, the power of the press has been mighty indeed. In its heyday, *The Times* had the capacity to topple governments. Only recently the Prime Minister has been said to be annoyed at the bias of the BBC – the Blair Broadcasting Corporation, as he called it. The media revolution is upon us. We are blasted by news on the half-hour, every half-hour. The Gulf War was given coverage for a solid twenty-four hours a day. The joke ran that there were more reporters in the desert than troops. And in the lulls between the crashing of Scud missiles, geriatric generals were wheeled in front of the cameras to give us their speculative view on what might happen next.

But the media, which has so much power to help and support, took the easy option with UFOs. What sells newspapers? Sensationalism. And what could be more sensational than the notion of little green men from Mars? Constantly, the most absurd claims are highlighted while more reasonable accounts are ignored. Where is the excitement in a small white light over a Scottish loch, which might be lens flare anyway, in comparison with the story of Dolly Newland, who told the *Daily Sport* that she was descended from a race of aliens who had first visited earth millenia ago? They were, she said, shy and invisible, and some of them lived in her attic.

The problem is that because of the inherent strangeness of the subject, it is prone to ridicule and the temptation for a journalist to fill a few columns with a lighthearted piece about aliens is often too much to resist.

Recently, however, there have been encouraging signs that this dismissively jocular approach is beginning to change. In Britain, the satellite television channel Sky TV has featured many programmes and news articles on UFOs, thanks largely to the enthusiasm of producer Geoff Baron. The series *UFOs – No Defence Significance?*, which Baron created, featured a number of cases and questioned the Ministry of Defence's insistence that no sightings reported to date had any defence implications. Sky 1 has also screened other UFO series, such as *Sightings* and *Unsolved Mysteries*.

In 1994, another British television producer, Lawrence Moore, put together a landmark documentary for Central Television which was shown in all ITV regions in January 1995. The programme, part of the prestigious *Network First* series, was one of the few to look with a serious and open mind at the UFO phenomenon. This documentary concentrated on first-hand eyewitness accounts and showed some remarkable UFO footage. Moore and his researcher, Livia Russell, included interviews with Congressman Steven Schiff of New Mexico, who is determined to get to the bottom of the Roswell incident, which took place in his state; senior officers of the former Soviet Union, who have themselves had some very close encounters; and former Chief of the Defence Staff Lord Hill-Norton.

The Ministry of Defence was asked to take part in the making of this programme. Such requests were not unusual, but up to that point they had always been declined, a sort of knee-jerk reaction born of the Cold War and the need to distance ourselves from sensational headlines and scurrilous reporting. However, as this was clearly to be a sensible programme, I spoke to my bosses at the ministry and managed to persuade them that it would be a good idea for us to explain our role on camera and to lay to rest a few misconceptions. There is nothing more guaranteed to convince the 'conspiracy' lobby that we have something to hide than the age-old 'no comment' response. Here was a chance to put across accurate statements about our policy and views. It was time to put the record straight.

The opportunity came on 25 April 1994. Billed, perhaps slightly tongue-in-cheek, as 'the man from the ministry', I was interviewed by Lawrence Moore himself. I freely admitted that many of the cases on file cannot be explained today in conventional scientific terms.

I suspect – and hope – that the *Network First* programme will have generated more serious debate on the UFO phenomenon than any other. The interest of a government department lends the whole thing an air of acceptance and respectability which encourage honesty and openness, and may prompt people who have sightings and reports of their own but are reluctant to seek out civilian UFO groups to share their information.

Two other major series with a paranormal theme have only recently been screened. *Schofield's Quest* was an interactive series of programmes covering a plethora of themes, UFO sightings among them, and viewers were encouraged to ring the studio with their own accounts. Michael Aspel's *Strange But True?* focused on everything from reincarnation to spontaneous human combustion. Two of the programmes in the series concentrated on the sighting in Bonnybridge, Scotland (dealt with in Chapter 4) and the notorious incident in Rendlesham Forest, which we shall address fully in Chapter 8. Although the series is a little too kitsch, with Aspel narrating from a shadowy Gothic library, and witnesses interviewed against a backdrop of dramatic, menacing light, the accounts themselves are faithful to the originals and reconstructions were used only to clarify particular incidents.

In November 1994, BBC 2's *Horizon* devoted an entire episode to the phenomenon of alien abduction. The presenter, Dr Susan Blackmore, a healthily sceptical psychologist from the University of the West of England, interviewed Budd Hopkins, who has dealt with 1500 abductees in depth over a period of years; John Mack, Professor of Psychiatry at Harvard Medical School; and Dr Michael Persinger, who deliberately stimulates the temporal lobes in the brain in an attempt to create effects similar to those reported by abductees. During the programme Dr Blackmore underwent Dr Persinger's experiment, and the action of electrodes on her brain produced an unpleasant and frightening sensation of being physically manipulated by an entity she couldn't quite make out. She was frightened and felt as if she were floating – a classic combination reported by those who claim to have been abducted. Even so, the findings were less conclusive than it was hoped they might be. The abiding image for me was an abductee's defenceless and terrified pronouncement on the 'Greys' she believed had taken her several times from her bedroom – 'I don't like them. I don't like them at all.'

And there the list of serious programmes dedicated to the UFO phenomenon ends. It is to be hoped that respected Media figures like Geoff Baron and Lawrence Moore continue their investigative work and that their influence extends to more of the mainstream media. At the moment, however, they are exceptions to the rule, just whistlers in the wind.

Oddly, at local level, the media tend to do better, perhaps because local incidents, being closer to home for both journalists and their readers and audiences, create more interest and demand to be taken more seriously. Newspaper articles on UFO sightings are invariably more detailed and often they are followed up in the next edition by letters confirming or elaborating upon the incident. Taken together, the mountain of evidence can be overwhelming. On a national scale, stories are all too often seen in isolation. The only people who can take an overview are the dedicated ufologists who subscribe to specialist press-cutting services and so receive a more complete picture.

I was keen to make use of the media whenever I could. I spoke to journalists at every opportunity, patiently spelling out the ministry's role and views or discussing particular sightings. Officially, it is the ministry's press office that handles contact with the media, but the problem with this arrangement was that there was a great deal of background information the press office had no need to know. This was particularly true of individual cases, where it was likely that only two of us knew the facts – the witness, who might have avoided publicity like the plague, and me. So I was given special dispensation to deal with the media direct. I tried to show that we were open-minded, prepared to look at the evidence, and in this way I built up a good rapport with the press, civilian UFO groups and the public generally, and was able to counter some of the adverse press the ministry had got over the years. If the truth were out there, I wanted to be part of it, and as word spread, more and more people contacted me as a result of articles they had read. The press cuttings began to multiply.

At this stage one interview was authorised by my Head of Division for the December 1992 Edition of *Focus*, the ministry's in-house magazine, which was read conscientiously by everybody from the newest administrative assistant to senior officials and defence ministers. Just as the majority of the public had no idea that my post existed, neither, it seemed, did large numbers of my own colleagues. Clearly, not everyone studied the MOD directory as thoroughly as I had. *Focus* was planning a regular feature on unusual jobs within the department and mine became the first in the series. 'Nick issued a general invitation,' wrote its author, Doreen Porter, 'to anyone who has any sort of evidence about UFO sightings to make it available to him.' The article generated considerable interest and resulted in phone calls from people who wanted to know more. The only drawback was that the publication of my photograph led to strange and furtive glances in my direction as I walked the corridors of power.

One of the major influences on the public's attitude to UFOs is science fiction. It is fascinating how this genre, via books, film and television, has reflected – or perhaps has itself shaped – people's views over the last century. It was probably Jules Verne in France and H.G. Wells in this country who together created the concept of voyages beyond Earth, although the seventeenth-century swordsman, poet and scientist Cyrano de Bergerac also has a claim through his work on human visits to the Moon. Verne's *Journey to the Centre of the Earth* (1864), *From Earth to the Moon* (1865) and *Twenty Thousand Leagues Under the Sea* (1870) captured the mood of his generation and it is interesting that the celluloid versions of two of these stories were equally popular in the 1950s, the first full decade in which UFO sightings were reported.

Whereas Verne wrote in the heyday of Victorian smugness and complacency, his disciple Wells belongs to the more uncertain and doom-laden Edwardian era. With uncanny prescience, Wells foresaw chemical warfare, aerial combat, genetic engineering and the exhaustion of the world's resources. Verne's aliens are usually either human in form or incredibly backward, enabling humans to control and manipulate them. Wells's, on the other hand, are technologically advanced, and their intent hostile, as in *The War of the Worlds* (1898).

In Britain, the appalling reality of the First World War, with its 'scientific' weapons of terror – the aeroplane, the tank, the submarine and gas – led to a decline in the fad for science fiction, but the genre flourished in the United States, where direct experience of the war had been minimal. *The Thrill Book* of 1919 and *Amazing Stories* of 1926 were popular partworks that soon had an avid readership. *Science Wonder Stories*, *Air Wonder Stories* and *Astounding Stories*, although they sound hopelessly naïve today, had a huge following and virtually created the 'bug-eyed monster' from a distant planet. As science fact established that no planet within our solar system seemed capable of sustaining life, the range of the rockets simply increased or alien abilities extended so that extraterrestrials could visit us. Perhaps as an antidote to the slump and the pessimism of the 1930s, America produced superheroes equally at home in space and on earth: Buck Rogers, Flash Gordon and Superman.

The 1950s witnessed an upsurge in alien invasion films, mostly from the States. *Invasion of the Body Snatchers* (1956) was arguably the best in a whole rash of similar black-and-whites, their titles only slightly less lurid than their poster billing: 'From out of space – came hordes of green monsters!', 'Time was running out for the human race', 'It! From Beyond Space'.

In the 1960s, a whole generation grew up on this side of the Atlantic with television. *Dr Who*, whose protagonist was able to travel through time and space and shift his shape to accommodate seven different leading actors, became a cult show way beyond the early limitations of the Daleks and the confines of the studio. From the States, much more sinister, and more in keeping with the concept of ruthless, insidious aliens was the ABC/Quinn Martin production *The Invaders*, starring Roy Thinnes. Gravel-voiced William Conrad read the introduction: 'It began in a deserted diner and a man too long without sleep . . .' Architect David Vincent was to endure forty-three episodes with hardly anyone but him believing that there were aliens undermining American civilisation. The hand of McCarthy and his communist witch-hunters is apparent in this series, and indeed in various films of the 1950s, including *Invasion of the Body Snatchers*.

The 1970s and 1980s produced an altogether more benign message. In *Close Encounters of the Third Kind* and *E.T.*, the technology is superior, but the intent is kindly. And over the last three decades, successive generations of the *Starship Enterprise* have boldy gone into our hearts and minds.

It has been argued that since the appeal of science fiction is so strong, fulfilling as it does the needs of those with wanderlust, those who seek escape, we ought by now to have a population of believers who accept that life beyond our solar system is not only possible but a palpable fact. But people are rather more discerning than film-makers would have us believe. In short, they know their fact from their fiction. The film of Whitley Strieber's book *Communion* (1990), starring Christopher Walken, which is at times genuinely frightening, was not a box-office hit. 'On December 25, 1985,' ran the poster blurb, 'Whitley Strieber had a dream . . . Months later he made the most shocking discovery of his life. Now, you will discover it.' People didn't; they stayed away. And if *Alien* (1979) gripped, it was not because a generation was filled with wonder at the vastness of space, but because they wanted to see that thing erupting from John Hurt's chest. As Les Keyser says in *Hollywood in the Seventies*, 'Don't close your eyes or it will get you.'

So much for science fiction, but when it comes to UFOs, who thinks what? As we have seen, the media's general approach is to trivialise or to exploit. Most politicians will not touch the subject with a bargepole. They can afford to be lambasted by their opponents and the press – not only does that go with the territory, many of them positively thrive on it – but the only kind of publicity they shrink from is that which leads to ridicule. They cannot afford to become figures of fun. Such is the nature of the UFO controversy that very few MPs have willingly joined in any aspect of the debate.

A dilemma arises, however, when MPs are asked by their constituents to raise questions with the appropriate government department. I was often called upon to draft responses for defence ministers who had received such enquiries. It was noticeable that MPs would often bend over backwards to distance themselves from the UFO debate, debunking it as ridiculous and a waste of time.

There are three establishment figures, however, who have been prepared to bear the sniggers and whispers and for that they should be applauded. The first is Major Sir Patrick Wall, who took an active interest in the Rendlesham Forest case of 1980. Sir Patrick, who was Conservative MP for Humberside, spent more than thirty years in the Commons pushing the cause of serious UFO research at every conceivable opportunity. He pressurised the Ministry of Defence and, as a consultant to NATO at the height of the Cold War, was directly and closely involved in matters of national security. Sir Patrick's interest in the subject has not waned. In 1989 he became the president of

BUFORA and is an internationally known expert on the UFO phenomenon.

Another politician connected with the debate was the late Brinsley Le Poer Trench, Earl of Clancarty. A UFO researcher and author, Lord Clancarty was involved at various times with two leading UFO organisations, Contact International and BUFORA. He was the driving force behind the House of Lords debate on the subject in January 1979. There was a huge amount of interest in this, and although the general tone of the speeches was lighthearted, some serious points were made, and the fact that Hansard, the official record of parliamentary proceedings, sold out almost immediately speaks volumes for the attention the topic attracted. As a direct result of the debate, Lord Clancarty went on to set up a UFO study group in the House of Lords. Unfortunately, it is now no longer functioning.

Lord Hill-Norton, former chief of the defence staff, has already been mentioned and his vociferous comments carry a great deal of weight.

I had only one opportunity to talk directly to a politician on the subject of UFOs, and that was on 3 August 1992, when the under-secretary of state for defence, Lord Cranborne, came to our offices. His visit was essentially a walkabout, an opportunity the for viscount to meet those who worked under him, but he was clearly fascinated by the briefing I gave him and astonished at the number of reports we received. This was probably one of the few occasions ever when a British Defence Minister received any briefing on the UFO phenomenon.

The attitudes of the civil service are mixed. Most of my predecessors had written bland standard letters in response to enquiries on UFOs. Because the UFO desk officer is to all intents and purposes a 'squad of one', his or her views are seen, inevitably, as the official line. Because these views vary, some people have pointed to this as an example of an inconsistency on the part of the ministry, the fog of a cover up. The implication perhaps is that UFO desk officers are lone agents, mavericks who do as they like. Of course, this is not so. Supervision is minimal, but I was always aware that my bosses kept a very close eye on me and indeed they made no secret of their disapproval of some of my initiatives. Having said that, there was a unique occasion when my head of division came hurtling into my office brandishing a sheaf of papers on which he had plotted locations, times and estimates of an astonishing rash of UFO sightings that occurred on the night of 30–31 March 1993. But his level of interest was never to be repeated, and it never came remotely within reach of that of Ralph Noyes, who had worn his shoes back in the days of Defence Secretariat 8.

The attitude of the military was perhaps the most surprising of all. Traditionally, the armed forces are seen as hidebound; ultra-conservative and slow to accept charge. In civilian circles, the myth of the stiff-necked automaton, trained to act without thought, to kill without conscience, still abounds. I therefore fully expected the RAF personnel to be dismissive of UFOs. They weren't. On the contrary, most of them were astonishingly open-minded. One reason for this might well be that the RAF is more alive to the potential threat of a superior technology than the other services. After all, if there were ever to be a hostile action from a UFO, it would be the fighters of the RAF that would be deployed to engage it. If underestimating your enemy is a sin in the military world, failing even to acknowledge their existence is a cardinal one.

Another practical reason for the approach of the RAF is simply that many pilots have themselves seen UFOs. Pilots past and present have admitted to me in numerous off-the-record conversations that they have witnessed things in the skies, in all lights and weather, and at all times of the day and night, that they cannot explain. Two of them were station commanders at RAF bases. Such people are expert witnesses. They know a weather balloon when they see one, and are trained in recognition techniques, and reports from such sources are worth taking seriously. It is unfortunate, then, that on an official basis such reports are almost non-existent. The fear of ridicule is strong, and it is odd, bearing in mind the cultural history of the past half-century, that more reports are now coming out of the former Soviet Union's air force than we are currently likely to find in the 'enlightened' West.

What do the scientists say? Surely, if anyone were to pressure for a serious, in-depth study of the UFO phenomenon, it would be this group. Sadly, this is not the case, for science has achieved an orthodoxy and an establishment of its own, and it is a shame that Patrick Moore, one of the best-loved astronomers of our time, who regularly reaches the public via television, should be convinced that there is nothing out there. It is deeply ironic that the breed of narrow-minded scientists who scoffed at Rutherford and Einstein still laugh mockingly at the likes of Vallée. It is the very freedom of the spirit of inquiry they have championed that in the past pushed forward the frontiers of science. But science is a fickle mistress and it reflects the spirit of the age. Was it only in 1969 that Neil Armstrong stepped out of the Eagle, Apollo 11's lunar module, with the words, 'That's one small step for a man, one giant leap for mankind'? It seems an eternity ago. And the breadth and the vision and the hope of the 1960s have given way to the gloom and doom of the 1990s in a way reflective of the generation gap of Jules Verne and H.G. Wells. Now, we are obsessed with pollution and global warming and acid rain. We are too engrossed with what is happening at our feet to look up at the stars. And the bald fact is that scientists have a living to earn. Grants are not given to cranks; giant chemical companies do not employ what they may perceive as the lunatic fringe. Scientists, like most of us, go where the money is – into weapons research, chemicals and medicines, computers and genetic engineering. Space and aerospace projects, less extreme than they were thirty years ago, deal soberly with the art of the possible, with the here and now.

UFO research has no place in all this. With the exception of a few small grants from UFO groups or interested benefactors, there is no money. The pity of it all is obvious. Laying aside for a moment study for its own sake – 'to seek out new worlds' – if even a few of the UFO claims are true, then the financial rewards of developing our own advanced technology based on 'theirs' would be immense.

Three men stand out as exceptions to the otherwise closed book of conventional science: Jacques Vallée, the late J. Allen Hynek and John Mack. Frenchman Dr Vallée is oddly, not given a separate entry in John Spencer's otherwise comprehensive *UFO Encyclopedia*. He is a parapsychologist and astrophysicist who pursues the link between physical and psychic phenomena. Are the aliens of today the fairies and trolls of yesterday? This approach is considered too cranky by orthodox scientists, who accept none of the hypotheses in Vallée's *Dimensions*. The reputation of Dr Hynek is enormous, even several years after his death. John Spencer credits him with being 'perhaps the single most significant figure in the study of UFOs over the past forty-odd years'. Professor of astronomy at Northwestern University in Evanston, Illinois, in America, he was employed by the United States Air Force in 1948 to look into the sudden and rapidly increasing rash of UFO sightings. Over a twenty-year period, he was the American government's scientific consultant to two of the three major UFO research projects – Sign and Blue Book. When Blue Book closed down in 1969, Hynek, convinced that the phenomenon was genuine, set up the Center for UFO Studies (CUFOS), one of the first such groups in the world. On his death in 1986, the foundation was given his name. Researcher Hilary Evans has pointed to Hynek's invaluable skill:

'Almost single-handed he showed how UFO research, though it might not constitute a science in its own right, could and should be conducted on a scientific principle.' No one has taken his place, and the whole field in America – and indeed in the rest of the world – is now beset by personal bickering and rivalry.

What of the UFO researchers themselves? Most of those I have met – the best of them, people like Timothy Good and John Spencer, are the key figures in research today – have been honest, open-minded people, prepared to spend their own time and money in their search for the truth; a truth which affects us all. Their patient and quiet operational methods are thorough and commendable. What is refreshing about these people is that they have not brought down the shutters of bigotry and unreason. They are the first to admit they do not have all the answers.

Unfortunately, the highly emotive and controversial nature of the subject makes it inevitable that a certain lunatic fringe is drawn to it. As is often the case, this fringe tends to shout the loudest and hog more of the limelight than it actually merits. Because of the actions of a few eccentrics, the world of ufology has become very political. The groups proliferate and get bogged down in petty squabbles and protracted controversies about the authenticity of documents, or become paranoid about the existence of 'agents provocateurs', sent by some vague agency, in their midst. One such group member was convinced that aliens could read her mind and did so on a regular basis. Only by wearing a particular hat with a metal top could she deflect their telepathic powers. Another insisted that every set of conventional aircraft lights he saw in the night sky were those of a UFO, and fellow researchers could not persuade him otherwise. If ufologists could bury their differences and present a more united front to the public, then perhaps they could command the respect and influence most of them deserve.

There are distinct signs now that some factions in ufology

are becoming more militant in their attitude towards official reaction to UFOs and thus to officialdom itself. This partly stems from a growing belief that the British government, like many others, is involved in a conspiracy of silence over the UFO phenomenon. As early as 1958, London taxi-driver George King's Aetherius Society campaigned with placards demanding that Harold Macmillan's government 'end the saucer silence'. 'Why the silence in the air force?' the placards wanted to know. 'This is your chance to demand the truth.' More recently, respected UFO writers such as Jenny Randles and eminent men like Lord Hill-Norton have added their voices to the same questions. It may well be that another reason for the increased stridency of various civilian UFO groups is a sense of frustration that the truth they have been seeking for nearly fifty years is 'just around the corner', and has not yet materialised.

In America a group called Operation Right to Know has organised a number of demonstrations outside the White House and the Pentagon. It has a United Kingdom branch, and the groups in both countries co-ordinated a united day of action on 23 May 1994. Bemused members of the public going about their business along Whitehall were bombarded with leaflets about UFOs and a small delegation headed by the campaign's leader, John Holman, met me in Main Building and handed over a document stating their position. The leaflets they distributed for a second day of action on 20 March 1995 quoted the *Network First* programme. In particular, they demanded action on the Rendlesham Forest incident. Their message read:

> The worldwide quest for the truth about military knowledge on the UFO issue is gaining momentum, and we invite you to join us. This issue is not an issue of UK national defence. Common sense dictates that the MOD has known this for at least fifty years, ever since pilots

filed UFO reports during the Second World War. This quest has nothing to do with believing or not believing in extraterrestrial intelligence; it is simply a quest for the truth. We ask that military establishments worldwide share with the people of the world all they know and understand about UFOs.

You can help this effort by first educating yourself on the subject. Begin to read the books, go to the conferences, watch the videos and generally 'get on' the information network! Make yourself aware!

The whole episode was typical of my uphill struggle with the ministry. John Holman organised his demonstration with sophistication and played it by the book. The whole area around Whitehall is ringed with tight security, IRA rockets notwithstanding, and Holman had followed the regulations to the letter. He had contacted the police well in advance telling them exactly what he intended to do and how many people were likely to turn up for the demo. He telephoned me, also giving plenty of notice, to make sure that I could meet him and accept his petition. When I told my head of division about this, however, merely as a matter of courtesy, his reply surprised me. It wasn't appropriate, he said, to meet demonstrators at all. If a petition must be accepted on behalf of the ministry, let a receptionist take it. When I pointed out, perhaps a little naïvely, that people have a right to protest and governments a duty to listen, he was still unswayed. Only when I explained how suspicious it would look if I failed to arrive, having promised to meet the delegates, did he relent. The image of officials skulking behind drawn blinds is precisely the negative one that the department had projected for so long. A photo opportunity like this was not only good publicity for Operation Right to Know but I couldn't see that it would do us any harm, either.

I breathed a sigh of relief when my arguments won the day, but Holman's petition was only one signpost in the long three-year road to UFO *glasnost*. I was never actively blocked by my superiors, but there were times when things were made very difficult for me; times when I was quite deliberately given special one-off tasks to divert me from a UFO case. At the end of my tour of duty, there were certainly those who were happy to see the UFO desk being run by somebody else. To the debunkers and sceptics of the world, whoever they may be, my farewell message was 'Minds are like parachutes; they only work properly when they are open.'

It is difficult to guage whether groups such as Operation Right to Know will achieve anything in terms of a change of attitude. Their demonstrations received some publicity, but the mainstream UFO lobby, while supporting some of the campaign's aims, distanced itself from the actions of the splinter group that day. It may be that in the long view all it did was to reinforce the idea that most people involved with UFOs are cranks.

What of the people? The largest and ultimately the most important group whose attitudes we should consider is the general public. Assailed as they are by trivialisation of the subject by the media, and otherwise left in the dark because of an almost total absence of comment from anyone in authority, it would not be surprising if their response were one of indifference at best, dismissal at worst. In my experience, though, this is far from true. The few polls that have been conducted show that more than 50 per cent of the public believe in the extraterrestrial nature of some UFOs and that a significant percentage have actually seen an aerial object that they could not explain.

Try it yourself. Discuss the subject with any group of people at random – friends, colleagues, the man on the Clapham omnibus – and it is astonishing how prevalent belief and acceptance are.

Recently I carried out this experiment with three strangers. All believed in the existence of extraterrestrial craft and two had seen UFOs. Thanks to the media, however much they scoff, people are much better informed and more sophisticated than our leaders would like to think. Whitley Strieber's *Communion* and Budd Hopkins's *Intruders* topped the bestseller lists in America, and Timothy Good's *Above Top Secret* did likewise in Britain. Knowledge that was once confined to the most single-minded UFO researcher is now, slowly, gaining ground with a wider audience.

One thing is certain in the 1990s – questions are being asked. The powers that be had better start finding some answers.

INVESTIGATION

The system is there, but it doesn't work. In theory, any member of the public can simply pick up the phone and report a UFO sighting to the UFO desk officer in Whitehall. In practice what happens is that instead those people will invariably contact their local police station, civil airport or nearest RAF base. Each of these institutions has a written procedure. There is a pro-forma document on which the date and time of the particular sighting is recorded, as well as a description of what was seen. The papers are then bundled up and sent to Secretariat (Air Staff) at the MOD.

Unfortunately, when I took over as desk officer this apparently simple operation had broken down. People who should have forwarded forms hadn't done so. Most embarrassingly and frustratingly, some of those who received UFO reports from the public had no idea that there was official interest at all and tended to lump all UFO reports under the vague and unhelpful heading of hoax or crank calls. Reports were often not being passed to the ministry at all.

One of my first initiatives was to update the entire reporting system. There is still a good deal of controversy about the procedure, and it is a commonly held belief among ufologists that two separate forms exist, one for members of the public and the other for people in positions of authority – police officers, pilots, the military, and so on. The implication is that the 'them' and 'us' approach is necessary to perpetuate whatever cover-up the government is operating. The implication is that the public's reports are binned or filed out of harm's way, whereas the 'authoritative' information is somehow treated differently. I am totally unaware of any such system. There should now be only one form in use – mine – to be used by anybody and everybody. A copy of it can be found in Appendix 2.

What actually happens is something like this: a report is lodged by a member of the public at, say, a London police station. The appropriate form is filled in, usually by a desk sergeant at the dictation of the witness. How seriously this job is taken depends on the officer's personality and training. The report is then posted or faxed (if it is made at an airbase it will be signalled or telexed) to Secretariat (Air Staff). The drawback here is that the desk is not manned twenty-four hours a day, so reports made outside office hours will probably be sent via the London Air Traffic Control Centre at RAF West Drayton in Middlesex. Up-to-the-minute sightings can then be partially verified by the radar facilities there. If a member of the public phones the MOD's switchboard out of hours, he or she will be put through automatically to the permanently staffed Air Force Operations Room, where details of the sighting will be recorded, and forwarded to Secretariat (Air Staff) the next day. The problem is easy to see: with so many different people and procedures involved, confusion can quickly arise; indeed, stories of secret departments spring from such situations.

It quickly became obvious to me that my predecessors had adopted a variety of practices to deal with UFO reports. Under the rules by which all civil servants operate, all letters from the public must be answered, unless they specifically state that no reply is required. The exception to this is the 'blacklisted' individual, someone who is a persistent letter-writer – 'Appalled of Tunbridge Wells' – whose previous letters have already been answered and all points covered. Some UFO reports, however, had obviously simply been filed and forgotten, and I wasn't happy about this. Most of these had been made to third parties such as the police, but anyone who had taken the trouble to offer information deserved at the very least a friendly letter explaining government policy on the subject. I have included an example of the sort of response I made in Appendix 3. I felt that this approach appropriately reflected the aim of John Major's Citizens' Charter.

My letters of reply did two things. They spelled out the ministry's official policy – that we were interested only in matters of defence or threat – and they also provided details of the national UFO organisations (see Appendix 4) and encouraged witnesses to contact them. Filing away reports would achieve nothing, and I knew that various UFO groups would kill for the details offered. This approach at least created an opportunity for sightings which would otherwise be known only to the ministry to become public knowledge. If a witness chose not to contact a UFO group – and there were certainly those who wanted nothing to do with them in the mistaken belief that they were all run by cranks – then obviously there was nothing I could do, for I could not breach witness confidentiality. Most of the people who contacted me wanted no publicity – they certainly didn't want the paparazzi on their doorsteps along with the morning milk – so I could not divulge individuals' names to UFO organisations. This code of integrity had on occasion been broken. One man had written to the ministry before my time to report a light low in the sky which he thought might have been an aircraft in trouble. A few days later two decidedly odd ufologists turned up on his doorstep, rambling about flying saucers and aliens. The witness was less than enchanted. Confidentiality is vital if people are to be encouraged to report sightings of UFOs.

My evaluation of the cases I received depended on the individual report. Sometimes the information was just too vague and it was impossible to draw any firm conclusions. Where the details were clearer, I could often find a logical explanation. Was there military activity in the area, perhaps involving low-flying aircraft? Few people are familiar with, say, a Tornado GR1 at close quarters. These aircraft travel very fast, hurtling out of the cloud without warning, and they disappear just as quickly. Was there an astronomical explanation for a sighting? A phone call to the Royal Observatory at Greenwich could confirm this. And then there was RAF Fylingdales. Fylingdales provides early warning of attack from ballistic missiles and also tracks satellites and space debris, the thousands of tons of metal floating about above the Earth's atmosphere that are the litter of forty years of space exploration. Their equipment is sensitive enough to locate an object one foot square hundreds of miles away in space. Fylingdales could tell me if there were any satellite orbits likely to be visible from earth or a re-entry that might cause some spectacular light show. Radar returns from any of the regular RAF bases dotted around the country might also provide a possible explanation for a sighting.

The basic principle of radar is that radio waves are emitted from a transmitter, bounce off solid objects and are picked up on a receiver, giving the little green 'blips' on the screen familiar now to movie-watchers all over the world. A continuous watch is kept on our airspace using ground-based and airborne radar systems. In America, there has recently been an attempt to avoid use of the term UFO and all its oddball connotations by introducing RDA (radar-detected anomaly) and VOA (visually observed anomaly). Not surprisingly, neither has caught on. In

Britain, the Ministry of Defence is experimenting with the equally uninspiring Unidentified Aerial Phenomenon.

Until recently, any object attempting to penetrate our airspace would be detected. The advent of stealth technology, however, has lessened the likelihood of that. Assuming that aliens, if they exist, can reach us, then they are likely to have a far higher level of technology than ours and therefore it must be assumed that they would have got round the little problem of radar very early on.

Much is made of UFO sightings backed by radar evidence, because radar is one of those safe, understandable technologies we have come to trust. I once travelled in the cockpit of the hovercraft that runs from Portsmouth to Ryde in the Isle of Wight, and the pilot showed me a tiny blip on his screen. 'There he is,' he said, pointing through the windscreen, 'That's the blip – that chap digging for bait at the water's edge.' With such a refined system, we feel secure. In fact, as with everything else, no radar system is infallible and there are examples of returns that do not correlate with reality. The screen shows a solid object where there is none. These 'angels' or ghost returns can be the result of two radar systems interfering with each other or of unusual meteorological conditions, which can cause a radio wave to bounce off dense air and pick up a geological feature, such as a coastline, recording its position as though it were in mid-air. This effect is known as anomalous propagation (anaprop). The most famous example of it is an incident in the Cold War when West German radar operators picked up what was assumed to be an aircraft moving towards their airspace from the east. Their own aircraft were scrambled, but the fighters could see nothing – until, that is, they swooped low enough to duck under the cloud over which the radio blip was flashing. The blip was a harmless train, travelling along the track it used every day. The radar had bounced the image into the sky. Bizarrely enough, a flock of birds can generate a radar return, which will disappear as the flock disperses.

A surprisingly large number of angels are picked up all the time by radar systems all over the world. In America, they are called 'uncorrelated targets'. If they do not satisfy the conditions of an aircraft or missile trajectory, they are merely written off as a glitch in the system. This is at best questionable, and at worst it could be lethal. What we are doing in effect is discarding all data that does not fit our own preconceptions, rather in the way that orthodox science rejects the alien. If humanity does not have the technology to travel at many thousands of miles an hour, then it must be impossible. This is blinkered madness. In *The UFO Experience: A Scientific Inquiry*, J. Allen Hynek lists ten cases of radar-visual sightings, from 6 December 1952 to 13 January 1967 and from Lakenheath in Sussex to Albuquerque in New Mexico. A total of forty-nine people saw the various UFOs and the individual sightings lasted from five minutes to one and a half hours. Hynek quotes from Project Blue Book, the United States Air Force's official investigation into the UFO phenomenon from 1952 to 1969. Although Hynek was the project's scientific adviser, it is clear from what he has written that he was very unhappy with its findings. On 13 February 1957, at Lincoln Air Force Base, Nebraska:

> Objects were visually observed by three control operators and by the director of operations . . . Objects were observed on radar by NCOIC and GCA operators (two separate radar installations). The objects were observed for a period of three to five minutes . . . The individual objects were about five to six miles behind an airliner and moving twice as fast . . . One of the objects broke in two and another made a 180-degree turn . . . Visual estimation of the size was impossible, but the radar operator stated

that the blip on his scope was about the same size as that received from a B-47. The objects appeared to stand still and then speed up and rush away.

The Blue Book's solutions? 'Probable balloons', and 'Probable aircraft'. Hynek makes no comment on the fatuousness of this, probably because he was speechless. No balloon ever made can move faster than an airliner, and no aircraft ever built has the facility to break itself in two. Interestingly, the concept of the clash of the two radar systems, which might have caused an anaprop, was not even considered.

I had a personal experience that illustrates how common it is for 'experts' to think only in terms of familiar parameters. I was talking about radar sightings of UFOs to a military officer who told me that radar operators often picked up objects travelling in a straight line at speeds of several thousand miles an hour. These were automatically classed as meteorites. The officer had asked why this assumption was made. The official answer? 'Because they travel so fast.'

This is a disturbing situation. If a blip appears briefly on a radar screen and disappears, it is classified as a ghost return, an 'angel'. If an object sails overhead, in a straight line and at lightning speed, it's assumed to be a meteorite. Clearly, not every single anomaly can be looked into, with fighter aircraft on standby twenty-four hours a day, 365 days a year, ready to scramble to investigate every weather balloon or flock of geese. However, the danger is clearly there, and it is a very real chink in our armour. If there is anybody out there, and if they are a hostile force, wouldn't they know exactly how to operate their craft to confuse our radar? To throw us just those comforting messages we expect to find?

Ground radar is particularly prone to interference known as 'ground clutter' – tall buildings and trees can register on a radar screen. But skilled, experienced operators will recognise the patterns, know a spurious return from a real one – won't they? There is in fact a world of difference between air-traffic control radars and those used by military air defence. They are looking for different things in different places and therefore have different capabilities. Radars can be programmed to look for certain objects and to reject others. If you were looking exclusively for a fast jet, you'd probably use a radar which ignores the echo of any object moving at less than 100mph. Radars are not even switched on all the time, and while some are monitored visually, others transfer their data on to videotape. Such tapes are usually kept for only a few days and then wiped, ready for reuse. Is there any alien information that was briefly in the possession of a radar base somewhere in Britain before it was erased? Who knows?

One of the first things I decided to do when I took over the UFO desk was to see whether there was a geographical distribution pattern to the sightings that had been reported to us. I was fielding questions like, 'How many reports did you get from Scotland last year?' or 'Are there more UFOs seen in the countryside as opposed to the towns?' Incredibly, perhaps, none of my predecessors had sought to harness this line of inquiry or to plot a map. If every single UFO sighting had been along an arrow-straight line, we would have been none the wiser. I went back to 1990, hauled out the files and drew my maps. Disappointingly, they reveal no stunning information. As might be expected, clusters of sightings tend to occur over densely populated areas because here there are more people around to witness any anomaly. I released these maps to the national UFO groups, who were rather suspicious at first, unused as they were to any help from the ministry. There also were some raised eyebrows in Secretariat (Air Staff).

As I said earlier, evaluation of written reports of UFO sightings can be a difficult business. Vague hints at what someone may have seen are really impossible to work from. Fred Whiting of the Fund for UFO Research summed it up superbly in the *Network First* programme I've already discussed. 'Stories of crashed saucers [or any UFO phenomenon] were twice-told tales. "I have a friend who has a cousin who has an uncle whose barber says he knows someone who heard something . . ."' Important sightings are those backed up with photographs or, better still, videos. The popularity of the camcorder has increased the ranks of amateur film-makers, and indeed a number of good-quality UFO videos have come to light recently. Such data can be analysed scientifically by the Ministry of Defence.

Of course, it is possible, as it always was, to fake it. The adage that the camera cannot lie was disproved almost as soon as it was invented. In the 1850s, an era when table-rapping and séances were new and exciting parlour games, the desire to catch a ghost on film was so powerful that some unscrupulous photographers and 'ghost-hunters' produced bogus 'spirit photographs'. In most cases, these were studio portraits cut out and pasted on to another photograph to suggest the disembodied spirits of the dead float-ing around in the ether. To disguise the join, little wreaths of cotton wool were glued on and the whole scissors-and-paste job rephotographed. The irony was that such was the exposure time necessary for mid-nineteenth-century photographic plates, the fraudsters really needn't have gone to such trouble. Absolute stillness was required of the sitters for anything up to seven minutes. Clearly, no one told that to the little dog photographed in 1916 by Arthur Springer, a Scotland Yard detective. While two ladies and their maid took tea on the lawn of their house at Tingewick, Buckinghamshire, a dog turned up and moved its head and tail as the photograph was being taken. The result was a 'ghost' dog, apparently materialising or dematerialising before the lens of the camera. Such accidental ghosts abound in early photography.

While the nineteenth-century fakes are laughably obvious to the modern eye, as photographic technology developed, so too did the sophistication of bogus images. Inevitably, photographs of UFOs have always been prey to both allegations of trickery and 'accidental' special effects not unlike that of the Tingewick dog. In March 1967, Robert Rinker, a field technician at a weather station high on snow-capped Chalk Mountain in Colorado, took a series of photographs of the station. When he had the film developed, the image of an unidentified disc with a clear rim hurtling through the sky had appeared. Rinker had seen nothing when he took the photos, yet here was the evidence. The image appears translucent and blurred, however, in contrast to the static scenery, and is almost certainly an example of lens flare, a reflection of light on the camera lens.

John Spencer cites as the earliest known photograph of UFOs the picture taken at the Zacatecas Observatory in Mexico by astronomer José Bonilla on 12 August 1883. A number of witnesses reported discs crossing the sun on that day and the next.

The two photographs taken in 1950 over a farm near McMinville, Oregon have withstood all modern analytical attempts to prove them fraudulent. On 11 May of that year, the farmer's wife, Mrs Trent saw a huge disc flying towards her. Her husband managed to get two photographs before the object disappeared. The otherwise sceptical Condon Committee, a research group working for the United States Air Force between 1966 and 1969, was genuinely puzzled by these pictures:

> This is one of the few UFO reports in which all factors investigated, geometric, psychological and physical, appear to be consistent with the assertion that an extraordinary flying object, silvery, metallic, disc-shaped, tens

of metres in diameter and evidently artificial, flew within sight of two witnesses.

Certainly modern computer analysis has found no wires or other obvious evidence of fakery with the Trent photographs. But perhaps we would do well to remember that the famous Cottingley Fairies – the photographs of two Edwardian girls playing with fairies at the bottom of their garden – were never in fact exposed as photographic fraud: the trick only came to light because one of the girls involved admitted to the hoax years later.

The most spectacular recent UFO photographs are those taken by Ed Walters, a no-nonsense architect from Gulf Breeze, Pensacola, Florida, in 1987 and 1988. What makes them unique is that they support a close-encounter incident which may have involved abduction. In November 1987 Walters took five shots of a UFO which emitted a blue shaft of light that lifted him off the ground. Further photographs were taken over a six-month period. Walters used an elaborate set-up involving two ordinary cameras and a four-lens, three-dimensional camera to record the sightings as clearly and in as much detail as possible. Inevitably, the case stirred up a hornet's nest in the States, and reactions to it have ranged from the totally convinced to the resolutely sceptical.

Gulf Breeze is either a brilliant hoax on a scale never before attempted or Walters' alien craft are real.

Annoyingly, there is no central repository for photographic and video evidence of UFOs. Ed Walters sent his photographs to the local newspaper, partly because another eyewitness to the incident was the editor's mother. Others have sent their photographs to the police, to UFO groups and just occasionally to the Ministry of Defence. But the rest of the iceberg is, I suspect, languishing in drawers and cupboards in people's homes, to be brought out now and again to offer friends something more intriguing than the holiday snaps. When I started actively seeking out material of this kind, I was bombarded with photographs, videos, even soil samples – exactly the sort of evidence I needed. If I wasn't technically capable of analysing all this data, it didn't matter – the ministry is full of experts, and I always knew a man (or woman) who could.

Most sightings, having been analysed in a variety of ways, turn out to be perfectly explainable in a logical, natural way. A jumbo jet, coming in to land at night, will usually display standard red and green navigation lights, a red, flashing anti-collision light and in some cases flashing white strobe lights, as well as a bright landing light. Someone living near an airport would see these light patterns all the time, but an irregular observer might be alarmed. This is even more likely if the aircraft is travelling towards the witness. The noise alone can be terrifying, and when the aircraft swings right or left, the impression is of an unnatural change in course; an illusion that the craft was hovering and has moved off at greater speed. Military aircraft, with a different light pattern and greater manoeuvrability, can be even more disturbing. Yet some people are not prepared to accept a calming, rational explanation of what they have seen. I remember one woman ringing me to say that she and her boyfriend had seen red and green flashing lights in the sky over her home. I asked where she lived and she said, 'near Heathrow.' When I politely suggested that their encounter may have been aircraft lights, her boyfriend was adamant: 'That's no plane.'

Other common visual phenomena associated with UFOs are meteors and fireballs. A meteor is a piece of dust or rock which occasionally enters the Earth's atmosphere and burns up in the heat. The result is usually a brilliant flash of light, although large examples, meteorites, will be solid enough to reach the ground, the biggest of them forming craters. Most meteors are the size of a dust-speck and are to all intents and purposes invisible.

The visible ones are often seen by many people. They travel downwards due to gravity and usually give off a white light, which lasts for only a few seconds. If your UFO turns out to be one of these natural phenomena, it's worth remembering that collectors are prepared to pay a lot of money for meteorites and astronomy departments at universities would certainly appreciate being told of any sightings in their area. Fireballs are more spectacular, larger and brighter than meteors, and their colours vary. Some are bright enough to be seen in daylight and I spent many a phone call explaining to people that what they had seen could still be a fireball, even if it was coloured.

Satellites or satellite debris re-entering the Earth's atmosphere also generate UFO reports. Since the era of Sputnik 1 in November 1957, we have been firing missiles into space and many of them are still there, each slowly decaying and falling increasingly closer to Earth. RAF Fylingdales tracks about 7,000 items of space debris every day. Of these, six or seven re-enter the atmosphere in any given twenty-four-hour period. Some of them, trailing light, will be seen and registered by an eagle-eyed, curious or frightened observer as a UFO.

There is a well-rehearsed catalogue of other natural phenomena regularly reported as UFOs, occasionally even by trained observers. The planet Venus is well known for this. Known to the ancient world as Phosphorus or Hesperus, the morning and evening star, it is the brightest of all planets seen from Earth. Viewed from a moving vehicle, especially through a screen of trees, Venus appears to hover and exhibits the blue-white light so often associated with UFO experiences.

Aircraft seen during the day, especially from odd angles, give rise to all sorts of reports. The triangle of the stealth bomber is a new and classic example, but anything unexpected can account for suspected sightings. The vision of a Lancaster bomber over Warwickshire in the summer of 1991 was a bizarre one for me, even though I knew exactly what it was. It merited at least a double-take, and for an instant, thoughts of a time-warp ran through my brain. The range and colour of high-altitude kites, hot-air balloons and iridescent, sun-reflecting helium balloons are also apt to confuse. A weather balloon was, of course, the 'official' explanation for the debris found at Roswell. Flocks of birds, especially when seen in an odd light, such as sunset, can have a very strange appearance to the uninitiated, but the oddest illusions can be caused by lenticular clouds. These rare formations are disc-shaped, and because of the pattern of their vapour, appear metallic grey in colour.

Recently, the increasing use of sophisticated lasers and search-lights in advertising explains some of the reports I have received. They typically fire beams high into the night sky which are reflected downwards and give the effect of bright discs chasing each other. Pop concerts use them constantly and I've even known a new nightclub to invest in this kind of *son et lumière* for its opening night. I remember once staying with a friend at a univer-sity hall of residence in central London and being woken at about two in the morning as the entire room was bathed in light. With images from *Communion* and *Close Encounters of the Third Kind* going through my head, I staggered to the window only to find that British Telecom were testing the searchlights with which they planned to illuminate the BT Tower the following night in a publicity stunt to advertise the new London telephone codes.

Richard Branson's Virgin Lightship, used for sightseeing trips and as an advertising platform, is another culprit. Companies buy advertising space on the airship's sides and have it flown over the country. By night, as well as carrying the usual battery of lights all aircraft must display, it is illuminated from the inside, giving it the appearance of the classic cigar-shaped or saucer-shaped UFO, depending on the angle from which it is observed.

The most controversial natural phenomenon sometimes used

to explain UFO sightings is ball lightning, although ball lightning itself is not a proven phenomenon, and to explain one unknown with another is decidedly unscientific. British researcher Hilary Evans believes that most spheres of light seen in the sky can be explained by ball lightning – *if* it exists. 'Ball lightning,' he says in *Frontiers of Reality*, 'is most commonly seen in the form of a short-lived . . . luminous mass, generally spherical in shape . . . It is frequently but not invariably seen in association with electrical storms.' He quotes a number of instances of ball lightning entering houses and appearing to 'chase' humans, as in the case of Mrs Matthews of Philadelphia, who in 1960 saw 'a huge red ball of fire' enter her living room with a sizzling sound. It burned her scalp and her hair fell out. Many examples of this sort of energy have been observed over the Norwegian fjords, but the only film which might show the phenomenon is that taken in January 1973 by Peter Day, who saw an orange ball of light in the sky between Thame and Aylesbury on the Oxfordshire-Buckinghamshire border. It was about three-quarters of a mile from him and at an estimated height of 2,000ft. A frame-by-frame analysis of Day's footage shows that when the image disappears, the trees nearest to it seem to be bending sharply, as though rocked by an explosion. Two intriguing explanations have been offered. One is that the peculiar appearance of the trees was caused by camera-shake, the other that the whole glow was caused by an air-force jet dumping fuel. In fact there was a plane crash in the area that day, but it was accurately recorded as taking place a quarter of an hour after Day's sighting. In a way, the whole episode is typical of so many UFO sightings. The explanation may be ball lightning, or a fireball. Then again, it could be an air-force jet, or something more exotic.

And in all these examples of natural phenomena that can be mistaken for UFOs, let's not forget the humble low-flying, unusually shaped aircraft. Lincolnshire is a county studded with airbases, both American and British. RAF Waddington is the home of early-warning Sentry aircraft, which have a large saucer-shaped radome mounted on the rear of the fuselage. At night they look spectacular, as the base's community relations officer can confirm. One night she was driving past the perimeter fence with a red Metro in front of her. She glanced up to see a Sentry flying in to land. When she looked down at the road again, she had to slam on her brakes. The red Metro was lying at a crazy angle in a ditch. When the driver was helped out, he was rambling incoherently about flying saucers and aliens coming to get him.

It is generally acknowledged that something like 90 to 95 per cent of all UFO sightings can be explained in conventional terms, and this is certainly borne out by my experience. Yet allowing for the fact that an estimated 13 million people have seen 'something', at least 650,000 sightings worldwide remain unexplained. All the Ministry of Defence can say about these sightings is that it keeps an open mind. I suppose this is a fancy way of saying that we have no idea what the objects reported might be. The ministry's position has always been that, to date, no evidence of any threat to the United Kingdom has been found. It would be more accurate to say that there is no evidence that an overtly hostile act has taken place in our skies – yet. There are some, of course, who dispute this: there may be no evidence of threat, but neither is there evidence that a very real phenomenon like UFOs is harmless.

Hundreds of cases; dozens of files; thousands of words. I can only scratch the surface. But to provide a flavour of the sharp end of ufology, my work on the inside, let us look at some of the individual cases with which I dealt. For reasons of witness confidentiality, I have not used names unless they have already been made public elsewhere. The following selection has been made to show the full range of cases I handled – explained and unexplained; mysterious, hilarious and terrifying.

Case 1: Capital

There is usually a time-lag – hours, days, sometimes weeks – between a sighting and the point when a witness decides to contact someone 'official'. In the Capital case, things were rather more immediate. The call came from Capital Radio's headquarters in Euston, and the voice on the other end of the line was very excited. The caller was staring out of his window, giving me a running commentary on a UFO about to land in Regent's Park. He was gabbling, his words jumbled, hysteria in his voice; a man on the edge. 'It's almost down . . . it looks a bit like – like a big kite, but it can't be. It's down! It's down! My God, people are gathering round it . . .' There was a pause. The voice seemed less strained, less panicked. 'It can't be a kite, can it? Oh. The people are putting it back in a box. It is a kite. Sorry for having wasted your time.'

He hung up. God knows what agonies he had gone through in those few mad minutes. God knows how much he'll cringe at the memory of it from time to time.

Case 2: Waterloo

Thousands of people cross Waterloo Bridge over the Thames every working day. One of them rang me in 1992 to tell me of a sighting witnessed by hundreds. It was about five in the afternoon and he was crossing the bridge when he suddenly stopped dead on the pavement. A brightly coloured object was hovering over the brown of the river, just yards away from him. Then it burst away, in sharp spurts of speed, an erratic flight pattern impossible for an aircraft.

This was bizarre, for the object must have been seen by hundreds of people on that bridge as it hovered over one of the most densely populated cities on Earth, yet there was no corroborative evidence. Did it constitute a threat? It was right here, in the capital, a scenario that H.G. Wells might have envisaged. It was as though it never happened. The irony was that this incident took place only a few hundred yards from the Ministry of Defence. A file from 1990 showed that shortly before I took over the UFO job, a number of civil servants from Main Building in Whitehall had reported seeing a UFO from their office windows in a separate incident. A mysterious bright light had been observed hovering just above the cloud cover. No explanation was ever found.

Case 3: Fire in the Sky

The county of Herefordshire abuts the line of defence known as Offa's Dyke, built in the eighth century to keep the marauding Welsh out of King Offa's Mercia. In this idyllic part of the English countryside, late in the afternoon of 9 December 1991, as the light faded and temperatures dropped after a day of winter sunshine, several dozen people saw a fiery glow in the sky. It was several thousand feet up; so high, in fact, that it was also witnessed in neighbouring counties. Some witnesses said that the glow was preceded by a guttural roar and it was the noise that had made them instinctively look up in the first place. The glow had lasted for only a few seconds.

I spent most of the morning of 10 December plotting the various sightings on a map. I could not plot a straight line, but it was clear from the reports that the various witnesses were describing the same thing. I took an unusual step: deciding to risk whatever flak came my way from my superiors, I rang two leading civilian UFO groups, BUFORA and Quest International, and suggested that we exchanged data and co-operated on this sighting. Both organisations were wary at first, but I told them that we should all be working towards the same end – to discover the truth about UFOs. I gave them the information I had on the Herefordshire incident, and they reciprocated. The reports tied in. Beyond a shadow of a doubt, something out of the ordinary had happened in those winter skies.

My first line of attack was to assume that the UFO was a fireball. The noise factor pretty well ruled this out, because fireballs are silent. I rang the Royal Observatory at Greenwich, who confirmed this and added that they were unaware of any fireballs or freak atmospheric conditions over Herefordshire on the day in question.

My next guess led to a line of inquiry which solved the mystery. On the afternoon of 9 December an American F-111 jet from RAF Upper Heyford in Oxfordshire had been on a routine flight over the area when it was recalled to base because of deteriorating weather conditions. The runway at the base was already icing up and air traffic control wanted all aircraft back before the situation worsened. As a precaution, the pilot had jettisoned some of his fuel to minimise the risk of an explosion in the event of a bad landing. The roar witnesses heard was the sound of the jet fuel being ignited by the afterburners of the aircraft, which left a spectacular fiery trail as it streaked across the sky to produce the momentary glow they saw. The flightpath of the aircraft fitted the locations of the sightings. It was nice to get to the bottom of a UFO sighting for once.

I rang BUFORA and Quest and contacted all the witnesses who had been in touch with me. An unexciting case? Perhaps, but it illustrates two points. First, that the vast majority of UFO sightings do have rational explanations; secondly, and perhaps more importantly, how co-operation between the ministry and the UFO groups can produce smooth, accurate results. This was the start of many exchanges of information which marked my three years in office. Everyone I contacted was grateful for it: witnesses, genuinely alarmed at the fire in the sky, had their minds put at rest, and the UFO groups were able to stamp this one 'Case solved' and concentrate their efforts elsewhere.

Case 4: Visitors

This case predates my time as UFO desk officer, but it is a good example of the humorous side of the job.

One day an old man heard a strange noise in the distance. It was foggy, but out of his window he could just make out lights flashing a hundred feet or so above a nearby field. What looked like a laser beam, a shaft of white light, suddenly hit the ground from the hovering object. A rope was lowered and figures in bulky suits and helmets dropped silently down it before deploying themselves in the field. Terrified, the witness still had the presence of mind to phone the police. 'Aliens,' he told the desk sergeant, 'invading. In the field below my house.' The police, while not perhaps convinced of the old man's explanation, thought the call serious enough to take a look.

The explanation was rational enough. The lights were those of an army helicopter, the 'laser beam' was the craft's searchlight and the spacesuits and helmets standard special forces gear. This was a routine wargame for the special forces, but for all sorts of obvious reasons, no one had told the hapless locals.

Perhaps the rope gave it away: would a superior race, capable of travelling through light years of space, descend from their craft at the end of an earthly rope? Why not? We use lasers and ropes in the same ambit of our technology. The old man had taken no chances, and he was right not to do so.

Case 5: The One That Got Away

Rollesby is one of the Norfolk Broads, a few miles from Great Yarmouth on the coast. As in the rest of the county, the land is flat and on a clear day, the visibility good. On 23 October 1993, three men out fishing on the broad – Bill Deuters, Stephen Farrow and Mark Wilkins – decided to abandon their day's sport as the wind was picking up and it was getting cold. They were packing up their gear in their open boat in the middle of the water when Steve saw a bright silver light in the sky. He shouted to the others, who all agreed it was hanging there motionless at a considerable height. Bill was carrying his camcorder, which he used to record the day's catch. He filmed the object for several seconds before it moved silently off into the distance.

When they watched the video, the image was incredible. The small silver light distorted as the lens zoomed in, becoming a diamond shape, glowing orange. The lower section was darker than the top. The recording was shown on morning television. I was contacted by Brian Bruce, a friend of the three fishermen, some months later. Brian had also gone to the *Mail on Sunday* and the newspaper and I carried out various inquiries independently. I was sufficiently impressed by Brian and the video to instigate a full-blown investigation.

The erratic flight pattern of the object ruled out a planet like Venus, because it had moved away (many stationary UFOs turn out to be planets). It likewise ruled out at least civilian aircraft, which cannot 'hover' in the way this object did. Military aircraft are a possibility, especially Harriers, which are specifically designed to manoeuvre in that way. But the RAF bases confirmed that there had been no military aircraft over Rollesby Broad that day. Weather balloons are often made of reflective silver material and powerful gusts of wind (remember, the wind had been rising) might well blow them off course quickly. There is a balloon-launching site near Rollesby, but no launch had been made on 23 October. So it was not a star, not a plane, not a balloon. This looked promising. The *Mail on Sunday* sent the video to the labs at Panasonic UK and their spokesman, Simon Nash, offered an explanation for the orange diamond. A similar object had been filmed over the Black Sea and shown on Russian television three months earlier, a recording which also produced the orange diamond. The shape proved to be a reflection of the camcorder's iris, which automatically regulates the amount of light reaching the lens. When I saw the iris and compared it with the image in the sky, it was obvious. We had a match.

The Rollesby case is a fascinating example of how our own technology can hamper attempts to verify a UFO sighting. But though the orange diamond could be identified, the silver light was another matter. Simon Nash says: 'The image at the beginning of the tape is quite unusual and can't be explained by normal camera technology. It could be reflection from a plane' – except of course that at Rollesby, it couldn't have been – 'or other light source'. Whatever the three fishermen saw in the sky over Rollesby that day, it couldn't be explained in rational terms.

Case 6: 'Fear not, Zacharias . . .'

In the early hours of 29 October 1993, just six days after the Rollesby Broad incident, something took place at St Austell in Cornwall which I was utterly at a loss to explain. The witness was a young naval cadet from the prestigious Britannia Royal Naval College at Dartmouth, forty miles away. The cadet, referred to as 'Charles' in an interview with UFO researcher Doug Cooper, who had twenty-twenty vision and was trained in careful observation, experienced what ufologists call a close encounter of the third, and perhaps even of the fourth kind. He saw a bright object glowing eerily in the sky over nearby houses as it hovered silently over a sports field behind his home. In this position its shape was clearly that of a disc and it appeared solid, with a battery of different-coloured lights and three protrusions on its underside. The top seemed to turn in an anti-clockwise direction. Echoing the story of the appearance of angels to Zacharias, or Mary and Joseph in the New Testament, the witness claimed that he received telepathic messages of greeting, telling him not to be afraid. The craft's lights had by this time gone out and it hovered in front of a set of goalposts eighty yards from him. Similar reports, in which a potentially terrifying experience is modified by a sense of calm and wellbeing, have been made by abductees across the world. A large bird, presumably a rook or crow, flew close to the object, then plummeted to the ground. A bright light glowed on the underside of the craft and it shot vertically upward at great speed.

Charles ran to wake his family. They saw the bird on the ground, but no sign of the craft. Even the bird had gone by seven the next morning. The cadet was confused by what he had seen – perhaps due to the feeling of disorientation other abductees have described. He reported the incident to the local police at Launceston the next day. They in turn contacted me and put the cadet in touch with local ufologist Doug Cooper, who phoned me to discuss the case. The cadet had also told his superiors at the naval college about his experience. They allegedly told him to keep quiet. Doug Cooper obviously believed that this in itself implied some cover-up – the same sort of message relayed to witnesses, military and civilian, at Roswell – but I suspected that the advice was well meant, designed to shield the cadet from the ridicule of colleagues. In any event, no one from the college spoke to me. The sighting was clear enough, and the large bird at least was witnessed by several people. I was not able to come up with any explanation, and neither was anyone else.

Case 7: Craigluscar

Craigluscar Reservoir lies below Craigluscar Hill, rising 744ft above sea-level, between Loch Leven and the Firth of Forth. The M90 is no more than five miles away, crossing the firth to Dunfermline and Cowdenbeath. In February 1994, forty-three-year-old Ian Macpherson, a retired civil servant, was walking along the banks of the reservoir, his camera in hand. Macpherson is an artist and he takes photographs of local landscapes on which to base his paintings. As he strolled along, he was suddenly aware of an odd humming noise, quite unlike anything he'd heard before. He looked up and saw something coming in low over the dark waters. It was huge, several hundred feet in diameter, disc-shaped and metallic, with lights on its rim. It descended until it was completely stationary, hovering a hundred feet or so above the water.

He watched this object for a full fifteen minutes, fascinated, until it began to slowly move off. Suddenly, it accelerated away at incredible speed, many times faster than a jet aircraft, and vanished in a couple of seconds.

During this sighting, Ian Macpherson felt oddly disorientated. He found this sensation impossible to explain, but he was sure he had never felt it before. It was as though he were paralysed, not only unable to use his camera, but unaware even that he had a camera with him, although he was holding it in his hand all the time. As the object began to move, Macpherson lost the strange feeling that had gripped him and managed to get two photographs of the retreating craft. The first, which I have seen, shows a frisbee-shaped object in the sky; the second, taken only a second or two later, merely a dot in the distance.

Macpherson went to the *Scottish Daily Record*, who contacted me. He had no ulterior motive: he received no money from the paper, or from anybody else for that matter, and in fact the whole experience has been very unsettling for him. For some time afterwards, he would wake up in an armchair in the middle of the night, with no recollection of how he got there. Some may talk of abduction. Ian Macpherson himself thought he was standing beside a reservoir for fifteen minutes, but was he?

I carried out the usual tests. No radar blips; no weather balloons; no aircraft in the vicinity. The photographs Ian took have been analysed, and there is no evidence of fakery. Either Craigluscar was a highly ingenious and rather motiveless hoax, or . . . The ministry's official verdict is 'Unexplained'.

Case 8: Bonnybridge

Fifteen miles as the crow flies from Craigluscar, beyond Falkirk in central Scotland, lies the town of Bonnybridge. The area is a 'ufocal', a term defined by expert Jenny Randles as 'the name given to a place where more UFO events than chance should allow seem to occur'. Warminster in Wiltshire is usually cited as the country's best-known ufocal. It may be that Bonnybridge has a reasonable claim to second place. Certainly between 1992 and 1994 some 8,000 reports were made by local inhabitants. It is a classic example of the way the reporting system fails, that only two or three of these ever reached my desk. The details of these reports were vague, with nothing to indicate whether or not the object seen was the huge, triangular-shaped craft that many swore was terrorising the local population.

Local councillor Billy Buchanan held a meeting to discuss the sightings. Hundreds turned up and television crews appeared from as far afield as America and Japan. Oddly, the only media who stayed away were our own. I wanted to go to Bonnybridge to see the situation for myself, but this was not permitted. Key figures in the UFO lobby rang me. What was our view on the sightings? What on earth was the ministry going to do? Sheepishly, all I could do was tell them that we simply did not have the raw data. People might have been talking to the foreign press, but they were not talking to us.

A real and natural concern still exists in the area. Strange things were happening but the government didn't seem to care and even the media did not want to know. To the people of Bonnybridge, I can only apologise. Like them, I have no idea what is going on in the skies over their town.

If there was ever a case for tightening up the reporting system, Bonnybridge is it.

Case 9: Terror in the Quantocks

The Quantock Hills, with Wills Neck as their highest point, lie in Somerset between the Vale of Taunton Deane and the sea. In 1992 I received a letter from a woman whose husband had been walking there four years earlier, intent on photographing the lovely scenery. The sky was clear, the air still. This is one of those cases where the time lapse could be unfortunate, yet even so the woman's memory was vivid and so was that of her husband. He had heard a deep rumbling sound, ahead of him and above, and saw a huge black craft moving towards him, its body saucer-shaped, but with two bat-like wings, one on each side. It hovered for about five minutes, close enough for the witness to see that the main fuselage had two decks and a dome on top. He could even make out a small figure, wearing some kind of helmet, through the windows on one of the decks. The craft flew directly overhead, no more than fifty feet above the land. Instinctively, he threw himself to the ground, and as the shadow passed over him, he felt a burning sensation. When he got home, he discovered that his clothes had been singed.

Over the next two years, the witness's health deteriorated. Like Antônio Villas-Boas, the first known abductee (in 1957, he claimed to have had sex with a female alien), the Quantocks man found it difficult to eat and experienced waves of extreme nausea from time to time. He also had severe pain in his head and back. Perhaps unfortunately, the witness told his GP the story of the black craft and the doctor immediately suspected psychosomatic symptoms and mental illness.

The witness's wife was terrified that he was suffering from radiation sickness and would die unless somebody could help. Radiation sickness is highly unpleasant. Ionising radiation, such as gamma, X-rays and ultraviolet, can cause nausea, vomiting, hair loss, diarrhoea, headaches, tiredness, the lowering of resistance to infection and skin burns. The problem for doctors is that many of these symptoms have other causes too. Only a GP of some vision and sympathy would make the necessary connection in the case of the Quantocks man.

It was clear from the lady's letter that she and her husband wanted no publicity. They simply needed help and treatment and were desperate. Her husband had lost his job and she feared he would lose his life. My bosses were not keen on proactive investigations, but I could not ignore this cry for help. If I was unable to intervene directly – this man's health had no implications for the defence of the realm (though I would dispute that) – at least I now had the contacts who could. I shared my concerns with BUFORA, who agreed that the main priority was to save the witness's life and that the couple's fears were not overstating the case. One of their top researchers, Ken Phillips, intervened with the witness's doctor, having contacted Dr Rima Laibow of New York, from the organisation TREAT (Treatment and Research into Experienced Anomalous Trauma). The man's medical records are, quite rightly, confidential. That said, I am aware that he was treated, and recovered.

No explanation was ever found for that black craft over the Quantocks. Perhaps the man who had seen it while walking there would rather it stayed that way.

THE CROP CIRCLE MYSTERY

As far as we can tell, the phenomenon of crop circles started in Westbury, Wiltshire in the August of 1980. To the south lies Warminster, the most concentrated ufocal in the country, and to the east, across the rolling expanse of Salisbury Plain, the army training area and one of the Ministry of Defence danger zones, dotted with red waving flags and rutted with the snaking tracks of tanks.

Three circles had appeared in the corn below the Hill of the White Horse and nobody, least of all the *Wiltshire Times*, which carried the story, could explain how they got there. Certainly there was talk of a prank, along the lines of the speculation about the Devil's footprints found travelling up vertical walls and over rooftops in the Devon snow in the winter of 1855 (and no one has ever proved how that was done, either), but there were those who drew immediate parallels with the Warminster 'thing'.

In 1965, Gordon Faulkner photographed a disc-shaped UFO over the army town and the tabloids published the picture gleefully. For ten years, thanks largely to the enthusiasm of local ufologist Arthur Shuttlewood, Warminster was the UFO centre of the world. A whole culture, heralding the so-called New Age, was born among the young skywatchers who spent their time communing with the cosmos on Starr and Cradle Hills. The whole thing got a little out of hand, with hoaxes perpetrated all over the place, and a great deal of nonsense spouted. It was still the early days of ufology, and mistakes of methodology were made. For some, who rejected the existence of the Warminster 'thing' with its lights and sounds and possible abductions, the exposure of the hoaxes was the end of the whole controversy. But rather as the detection of fraud by the Fox sisters in Hydesville, New York in 1848 spelled not the end but the beginning of Spiritualism, so the incidents at Warminster heralded a new dawn. And perhaps crop circles were part of it.

Local Wiltshire ufologists consulted atmospheric physicist Dr Terence Meaden, who came to the conclusion that the strange circles of flattened corn, with their distinctive swirling pattern, were caused by fluke summer whirlwinds. The problem with this theory is that the whirlwind must have been incredibly localised and stationary and indeed, Meaden admitted that he had never seen anything like it before.

There was a precedent for the circles. Possibly the earliest recorded example is the 'Mowing Devil' in Hertfordshire in August 1678, but the description of that circle is vague and may have more to do with the old religion, the spirit of the corn and the belief in fairies and their rings than with the physical and photographed phenomena of today. In 1966, one of the most unusual UFO sightings was made in Tully, Queensland, Australia by a farmworker. He saw a craft rise from the ground, but there is no mention of his having seen it land. When he went to investigate, the reeds in the swampy area from which the craft had risen were flattened in a circle. Other circles were found, and a consensus grew among ufologists that these were 'saucer nests' or 'UFO landing nests'. Ralph Noyes is not a devotee of this theory. In the introduction to *The Crop Circle Enigma* he points to other UFO landing traces which feature scorched earth and depressions in rock a foot or more deep. For him, the extraordinary, complex and beautiful designs which dominated the 1980s – singletons, doublets, triplets, quadruplets, triple-ringers, Celtic crosses, swathed circles and swastikas – had to be something very different. And as the shapes became ever more convoluted, as though Nature was trying to outdo herself to impress the hordes of crop-watchers who camped in Wiltshire and Hampshire and never once saw a circle being created; as satellite circles appeared at points of the compass and singletons were tailed and ringers were spurred, Terence Meaden clung doggedly, with all the tenacity of orthodox science, to his whirlwind theory.

By 1983, the very complexity and diversity of the patterns had given rise to a general acceptance that they were elaborate hoaxes. That was the year when a national newspaper allegedly created its own circle in an attempt to set up a tabloid rival. Supposedly someone was paid by the paper to hoax the quintuplet at Bratton, Wiltshire, but the whole scam misfired.

It might have been silly season for the press, but there were plenty of exotic theories. Colin Andrews and Pat Delgado arrived on the scene. Their famous sentence offering a comprehensive description of crop circles is quoted wherever cerealogists (as experts in the field are known) meet. They believe that whatever causes the phenomenon, it is:

> a silent, short-duration, strong, contrarotative, damage- free flattening, swirling, whorl- and vein-forming, swathing, stem-bending, horizontal-growth-inducing, non-growth-interfering, straight path-forming, plant-extracting, total

darkness-operating, gap-seeking, superimposing, circle-grouping, weather condition-free, extraneous marks-free, topographically conditionless, worldwide operative force.

Many of these prerequisites have now been challenged or disproved entirely, but at the time, it was a brave stab at describing the indescribable. The basis of Andrews' and Delgado's theory – that the circles were formed by some as yet unknown earth energy – was elaborated upon later when they formed a group called Circles Phenomenon Research. Their book *Circular Evidence* was an international bestseller. In it, they put forward the hypothesis that the Earth energies might be manipulated by an unknown intelligence. Extraterrestrial forces were one possible explanation.

Still Terence Meaden didn't give up. He had seen over 200 circles by the middle of the 1980s. Their size ranged from 9ft to 90ft in diameter and the corn was flattened by a massive force of at least 40kg. Meaden's problem was the complexity of the design. No whirlwind, however unusual, could have created the extraordinary pictogram at East Kennet near the ancient burial mound of Silbury Hill. So was born the plasma vortex theory. An ordinary wind vortex (whirlwind), not uncommon on the hot, windless days of a Wiltshire summer, might in some cases become ionised, leading to the formation of a plasma, an almost solid area of electrified air. The plasma, and its resulting electromagnetic field, might cause all sorts of patterns in the crops. They are little understood by scientists, as Pat Delgado discovered when he spoke to a reporter from the *Winchester Gazette*. 'We are so disgusted that Dr Meaden is so adamant that the rings are caused by whirlwinds that we don't want anything to do with him,' the journalist declared. 'We rang Met. 9, the intelligence department of the Meterological Office, and they fell on the floor laughing at his theory.'

Scientists who are not rolling on the floor believe that plasmas may be connected in some way with ball lightning. Professor Yoshi-Hiko Ohtsuki of Japan has conducted research into the strange swirling dust patterns that were discovered on the Tokyo underground. In his laboratory, he has created plasma balls in a microwave. When they come into contact with the powder he has sprinkled over the chamber floor, the produce a whorl/circle effect. A team of Japanese scientists came to Wiltshire to investigate the crop circles, immediately conferring upon the phenomenon a mainstream, academic, scientific status that ufology has never been able to provide.

There have been reports of lights in the night sky in connection with crop circles. In 1985 five such lights were seen matching the quincunx formation which was to appear in the corn the next day. Most are yellow and pulsating. One resembled a huge funfair wheel. Meaden was not dismayed. If he was right about plasma, and if plasma is connected with ball lightning, the resultant glow might well be taken in the darkness for a craft's landing lights.

One imponderable which was never properly addressed was why had no one seen a crop circle before 1980, and why the decade saw such a proliferation of them. If Meaden's theories are correct, they would have been universal, a regular feature of country life for centuries, like rainbows or will-o'-the-wisp. And what was it about Wiltshire? Ralph Noyes, writing in 1990, was wary of the notion of a worldwide phenomenon. The evidence, he said, had not been published. But the Tully episode in Queensland in 1966 and the appearance of singletons, again in Australia, in 1989 would seem to leave the matter in no doubt. In the 1980s, the counter-argument ran that Wiltshire was simply the area being focused upon; for whatever reason, the press were being selective in their reporting. Indeed, circles have appeared all over Britain (I have seen a small singleton below Carisbrooke Castle in the Isle of Wight), and as for their sudden occurrence in 1980, many senior citizens have now come forward to say that they remember them from their youth, but in those days there was no interest in them and no one to report them to. Historical research is now in progress to find other examples like the Mowing Devil, and until the quest is over, a question-mark continues to hang over the historicity of crop circles.

The Ministry of Defence was drawn into the crop circle debate for the first time in 1985. A farmer had found a spectacular quintuplet on his land and telephoned the local army air corps base at Middle Wallop in Hampshire to ask them what they were up to. They were not in fact up to anything. Lt-Col Edgecombe, who investigated the matter, was mystified, but attended a meeting of crop circle researchers to give his views. Someone had suggested that the circles might be caused by the downwash from the rotor-blades of an army helicopter. Lt-Col Edgecombe was able to explain that the downwash could not cause such effects. He also informed the meeting that he had photographed the formation from a helicopter and had submitted his photographs and a report to Secretariat (Air Staff).

The UFO connection with crop circles has never gone away, despite the vortex/Earth energy/hoax theories of various cerealogists. And in an indirect way, it loomed now over the involvement of the army. The conspiracy theorists had a field day. Here was a senior officer in the British army, as much a figure of the establishment as anyone they were ever likely to get, taking a very close interest in a phenomenon previously associated (like UFOs themselves) with joky media reports and odd people in anoraks. Wild rumours began to circulate: space-based laser weapons were being tested – though why on farmers' fields, where the results would become public knowledge, and not on the ministry's private land was never explained; centres of the circles had been tested and found to be crackling with radioactivity; Margaret Thatcher, the Prime Minister, had asked for a full report on the circles and ministers were seen hurrying into Number 10, looking grim and strained, with barely a nod to the usual knot of paparazzi.

It was true that researchers had carried out soil and crop analyses from within formations, but the results were contradictory and inconclusive. The laser-weapon theory was nonsense, and the high-level meeting at Number 10 never happened. But the speculation continued. Wiltshire is crowded with army bases, and aerial activity over the county is an everyday occurrence. People began to notice that the military were paying particular attention to the circles. Not just army air corps helicopters, but giant Hercules transport aircraft from RAF Lyneham were buzzing them. Something was going on. Most of these stories came probably from the lunatic fringe of the UFO lobby who are obsessed with cover-ups and Men in Black. There was no remit for the army to fly the circles, but military pilots are human like everyone else and just as curious. They had a rare opportunity we groundlings lack: the chance to fly directly overhead some of the most beautiful and intriguing mysteries of our time. No doubt there are some spectacular photographs in aircrews' family albums or on some crew-room walls. No doubt, too, the formations were useful landmarks for navigators, in the monotonous expanse of Wiltshire.

In the event, Colonel Edgecombe's report was filed, along with other public correspondence, and the ministry offered no formal guidance. In 1985 the phenomenon was (or appeared to be) only five years old, and there was certainly no reason why, before Colonel Edgecombe's intervention, the ministry should have become involved at all. But now we were involved. If crops were being flattened in what increasingly appeared to be an unnatural way, then surely some unknown physical force was connected with them? The force, powerful as it was, might yet have significant defence implications. My bosses, of course, disagreed. I had to watch and wait.

The circles continued to evolve, and every summer, in the dearth of news occasioned by the recess of Parliament, the media filled space with their fascinating formations. Terence Meaden had predicted 'satellites', that is, smaller circles surrounding a large one, but surely it wasn't possible for Celtic crosses to be the result of plasma vortex? In the summer of 1990, the most spectacular of all pictograms appeared in a field near the little Wiltshire village of Alton Barnes, too small to be shown on most average road maps. Here was a Mecca for crop circle researchers and proof at last as far as Andrews and Delgado were concerned that only unknown and intelligent forces could create formations like this. They came, throughout that summer, from the ends of the world – ufologists, cerealogists and New Age travellers – who never strayed very far from the ley-lines that cross the south-west, between the shrines of Glastonbury and Stonehenge. Where the 1960s had brought 'skywatches' by enthusiastic ufologists, 1990 saw 'cropwatches', bevies of hopeful, determined people camping in the Vale of Pewsey or on the edge of Salisbury Plain, hoping to witness the formation of a circle.

One potentially ominous development was that farmers had seen the bandwagon and leaped on it with alacrity. The charge was usually £1 a head for entrance to the circles, and one farmer reputedly made £5,000 in a weekend, significantly outweighing the loss in revenue caused by damage to the crop itself. Eyebrows were raised, suspicion festered. Perhaps the writing was already on the wall.

In the summer of 1990 came Operation Blackbird. It may be that nearly a thousand circles appeared that year, adding 'scrolls' and 'dumb-bells' to an already staggering array of formations. To those who had come to believe that the Earth itself was transmitting arcane, cryptic messages to us, perhaps with some reference to ecology, the urgency seemed to increase. Andrews and Delgado organised the biggest cropwatch to date, but it became a media circus. Despite the sophisticated array of cameras, including infra-red, a circle was formed under the cropwatchers' noses during the night of 25 July. In the centre of the circle, however, were six occult board games, designed perhaps to implicate New Agers or occultists. It was clearly a hoax, and Andrews and Delgado had been set up. The question was, by whom?

Some continued to point the finger at the army, who had the manpower and probably the technology to create circles quickly in the dark. Cerealogists and ufologists blamed each other and amid the chaos cynical reporters shook their heads and laughed as they took their photographs and wandered away, and the Sunday newspapers decided that all circles were hoaxes. A man named Fred Day said he'd been making them since he was eleven. In 1990 he was fifty-nine. The *Mail on Sunday* carried a double-page spread on how to create your own crop circle. As circle expert George Wingfield has pointed out, 'Such facile reasoning demonstrated little else but the idiocy of certain journalists.'

Andrews and Delgado were undeterred. They spotted the hoax quickly, not just because of the 'planted' evidence of the board games, but because the formation was very crude. Terence Meaden and many other cerealogists can also generally tell a hoaxed circle from the real thing.

The following year a dazzling pictogram appeared near Barbury Castle, and the new complexity of shapes produced names like 'The Brain', 'The Snail' and 'The Dolphin'. Perhaps the most astonishing of all was 'The Mandelbrot Set', a design first generated on a computer and used in 'chaos mathematics'. It was named after Benoit Mandelbrot, a Polish-born American scientist who has coined the term 'fractal geometry' to describe 'self-similar' shapes

– a motif that repeats itself indefinitely, each time smaller. On a computer, fractals are used particularly to display geographical or biological processes such as coastal erosion or the development of plants. The theory of chaos mathematics, or chaology, deals with chaotic systems, for example an oil rig buffeted by ever-changing and unpredictable (hence chaotic) wave action.

Colin Andrews showed photographs of the Wiltshire circles to Hopi Native Americans. They simply said 'Mother is crying.' This reinforced the opinion of the 'greens' that the Earth was in distress. Archaeologist Michael Green had come to a similar conclusion the previous year when a symbol appearing to depict the Great Earth Mother, Gaia, was formed in the corn at Cheesefoot Head in Hampshire.

On 7 and 8 September, a conference (characteristically dubbed 'cornference' by the media) was held, fittingly at Glastonbury, as one of the great ley-line and mystic centres of the country, with associations with King Arthur and Druidic Earth power. Most of the well-known figures in crop circle research were there, but as the conference drew to a close, there were rumours of impending disaster.

On 9 September, *Today* carried a front-page story which put hoaxing on an altogether higher plane. Two Southampton men in their sixties, Doug Bower and Dave Chorley, claimed to have hoaxed most of the circles which had appeared. They actually began, they said, in 1978 and were rather disappointed that it took two years for anyone to notice them. Their methods were simple but effective. Sights fastened to their caps to ensure the symmetry of the circles and straight lines, planks to flatten the crops and ropes attached to a central pole to create the radius of the circle.

Doug had been staying in Australia when the incident in Tully, Queensland had hit the papers there and farmers down under began to make 'UFO nests' as a practical joke. What was their motivation, *Today* wanted to know. It was great to laugh at the so-called experts they had fooled, said Doug and Dave, with their talk of plasma vortices, helicopter downdraughts, Celtic symbolism and the weeping of the great Earth Mother. It was also just very nice to while away an hour or two in a summer field under an August moon, when the ears of corn stand silver in the night.

Today called in Pat Delgado to authenticate a circle. In a quote that was to come back to haunt him, he said that no human could have been responsible for it. If he was right, that didn't say very much for Doug and Dave, who had made the circle for the newspaper to prove a point. Conspiracy theorists leaped to the fore. The whole thing was a con: Doug and Dave clearly worked for the intelligence services as some sort of latter-day agents provocateurs. They still thought the army was up to something. But the bubble had burst and the faithful began to trickle away.

Neither did Terence Meaden escape. Still content with the plasma vortex theory, he happily accepted an invitation to take part in Channel 4's *Equinox* series. In the documentary, screened in October 1991, he proclaimed genuine a circle which had been hoaxed by a group called the Wessex Sceptics. Meaden, so sure of his ability to tell real circles from the fabricated versions, was devastated.

The love affair between the media and the public and crop circles died that October. And yet many questions remain. A few key figures in crop circle research had been caught out in spectacular fashion, but does this undermine the entire phenomenon? What about the Mowing Devil of 1678? Could Doug, Dave and the Wessex Sceptics be responsible for the thousands of formations which have occurred? What about the mysterious lights and trilling sounds which some witnesses have observed in fields where circles had formed by the morning? What about those dust circles in the Japanese underground?

I recently wrote a paper in which I outlined my own views on the subject. I say my own views, because in 1991, before the bubble burst, I had scores of letters asking what government policy was on the circles. The reply to a question tabled in Parliament two years earlier spelled out exactly what my reply had to be: 'The Ministry of Defence is not conducting any inquiries into the origins of flattened circular areas of crops.' To this day, the government has no policy on crop circles, despite the continued proliferation of them in the summers of 1992, 1993, 1994 and 1995. The basic theories in my paper can be summed up as follows:

Theory 1: The Hoaxers

I have no doubt that many of the circles and even more complex formations are hoaxed. From Piltdown Man to the Hitler Diaries, it is in the nature of some people to con others and in the nature of others to be conned. Some of us simply want to believe, in the same way as we want to believe in the Yeti or the Loch Ness Monster. In my own field of UFO research, the risk of material being fabricated in many ways, from the stories of fantasy-prone individuals to faked photographs, is high. But the experts are usually right, despite the embarrassment of Delgado and Meaden. A faked circle's edges are rough, where the 'genuine' ones are smooth. In hoaxes, the stalks of the corn are usually broken; in a 'real' circle they are swirled flat. A number of the 'real' circles are dowsable (that is, they respond to a dowsing stick); bogus ones are generally not. Most significantly of all, some of the crops from 'genuine' circles allegedly show distinct cellular changes when analysed; crops from hoaxed circles do not. We should perhaps be grateful to Doug and Dave, because they have cleared away the cranks and the media. If all circles are faked, why are they still being created, four years after the exposure of the hoax? What would be the point?

Consider too, the complexities of hoaxing. As Ralph Noyes says, 'What pantechnicon of skilful technicians has succeeded for eleven years in rushing about Wessex and, latterly, other parts of the country, not to mention the wider world, without ever being detected, even in the most public areas?' Hoaxers have to work at night, without lights, and are usually in a hurry. They have to avoid full moons. They can't afford to wake farm dogs or even sleeping cattle. They must keep an eagle eye out for shotgun-toting farmers, intent on scaring off trespassers. They must dodge the infra-red lenses of diehard cropwatchers. And yet despite having to contend with all this, they have far exceeded the results of competitions to create crop circles, carried out in broad daylight with all the time in the world.

Theory 2: Meteorology

Terence Meaden's plasma vortex theory was drawn up when the stationary whirlwind without debris clearly didn't fit the bill. Despite the experiments of Japanese science and the peculiarities of Wiltshire winds, the first time I saw a pictogram, I knew that meteorology wasn't the answer. Orthodox science dismisses UFOs on the grounds that they can't be real, because humanity is incapable of such astonishing technology. So it is with circles: they cannot be supernatural, because orthodox science doesn't recognise the supernatural. They must therefore be natural. I am not so sure.

Theory 3: Earth Energy

The Earth's magnetic field, it has been suggested, contains

an energy that flows in definite paths, usually straight. These ley-lines, as they are called, can be detected by the more psychic or spiritually aware of us. Early hominids, more animal than human, in their quest for food and survival, were probably more attuned to the Earth, the great Mother, than we are today. A large number of crop circles have appeared near ancient burial mounds and sites that were sacred to our ancestors. No fewer than twelve ley-lines converge on Stonehenge and some of the most extraordinary circles of 1988 were found very close to Silbury Hill, the largest artificial hill in Europe. Is it an accident that the shape of most crop formations is identical to that of the standing stones at Stonehenge, Avebury and elsewhere? They reflect the shape of the sun, the giver of life.

Wilhelm Reich and Trevor James Constable have produced between them the orgone theory. Orgone is alleged to be a form of organic radiation, emitted from all life forms. Some say it can accumulate in the ground, close to sources of natural Earth energy; others believe it can build up in the air and may itself evolve into a life form rather like a huge amoeba. The theory contends that it is this orgone energy which, on contact with crops, either from above or below, produces the circles.

Theory 4: The Living Earth

If, as some assert, the Earth itself is alive, and stones have spirits and trees scream silently when they are felled, then, this theory runs, the circles could be messages of some kind intended to shake humanity out of its hedonistic, destructive complacency. Certainly, the appearance of circles in increasing numbers and complexity from 1980 coincided with the period in which scientists were warning of ecological disaster on an unprecedented scale and the message seemed to be getting through to ordinary people for the first time. This would be in line with the Hopi observation that 'Mother is crying.' Crying perhaps for the rainforests, the ozone layer, and the other harm being done by her destructive children.

Theory 5: Extraterrestrials

There can no longer be many ufologists, even the die-hards, who cling to the Queensland theory that the circles are UFO nests. The saucers would be weird indeed if the pictograms are their imprint in the corn. However, the designs could still be extraterrestrial in origin, perhaps made by an energy beam or remote-controlled probe. Again, assuming the existence of alien beings and their ability to reach us, the creation of beautiful and mysterious patterns, the flattening of the crop without damage and the cellular changes would all conceivably be within the scope of alien technology.

The purpose of extraterrestrial circles, the explanation goes, is to communicate with us, just as early humans did with each other through pictograms and symbols. To ensure smooth storylines and familiarity among readers and filmgoers, science fiction has conveniently assumed that aliens can speak pretty good English, but we need not be so naïve. Indeed, official attempts are now being made to contact other civilisations in our universe. NASA, for example, transmits radio signals, unmistakably artificial ones such as sequences of prime numbers so that alien cultures cannot assume they are 'natural' in configuration, and binary code sequences which, when decoded into black and white components, take on the crude figure of a human being. The frequencies used are quiet, to avoid confusion with signals naturally emitted by pulsars and other stellar objects.

Perhaps someone or something is using our fields in the same way in an attempt to contact us. The corn is a blank canvas. Etch on it patterns which are unmistakably artificial, and, as humans attempt to explain them away naturally, scientifically, make them more and more complex so that they *cannot* be dismissed, either as plasma vortices or hoaxes. Mathematics, they say, is the only universal language. If this is so, is it possible that extraterrestrials would use a form of mathematics to communicate with us?

Benoit Mandelbrot devised a shape on an IBM computer as a representation of the concept of infinity. An exact replica of that shape appeared in a cornfield in England in 1993. Coincidence? A hoax by a team of university professors? Or something less earthly? And what of the quintuplets, one large circle surrounded by four smaller ones. Could the message be as simple as something like, 'We come from a star with four planets'? 'Our planet has four moons'? Or perhaps, 'We come from the fourth planet of *this* star. We come from Mars.'

I have only once stood inside a crop circle. It was August 1993, when an ultra-sceptical friend and I visited a formation near Calne in Wiltshire. The circle was symmetrical, beautiful and, I would have thought, difficult to fake. I looked at the people inside with us, standing in that weird shape in a field of golden corn under a blue sky. There were New Age women with braided hair and beads, holding babies. There was a man photographing the formation with a camera mounted on a long pole. There was a dowser with a quivering rod explaining the energy forms he was detecting to his companion. Finally, and perhaps inevitably, there were some American tourists. Perhaps, I thought, it didn't matter whether the formation was genuine or not. And if it was genuine, perhaps it didn't really matter how it had been created. What was important was that everyone there was having a good time. Whoever or whatever had made that pattern in the corn, he, she or it had brought a little joy to all of us who stood within the corn walls of that formation, watching and wondering.

M ilk Hill is in Wiltshire. Near it stood one of the most frequently photographed of the crop pictograms and near it lies the fields worked by farm worker Leon Besant, who for months had been telling his family strange tales of a shining object that passed his tractor one day at high speed.

Imagination? Reflection from a passing vehicle? A seagull lit by the sun? Perhaps any of these. Except that the shining object was filmed quite independently by Steven Alexander in July 1990. It is clearly metallic, clearly under intelligent control.

And it appears to be circling the area of the pictogram.

SLAUGHTER OF THE
INNOCENTS

The year 1967 was a record one for UFO sightings. It was also the year when the mutilations started. In September, a mare called Lady was found dead in a field on a Colorado ranch near Mont Blanca in the San Luis Valley. The animal's flesh had been ripped from the neck backwards along the body, yet there was no blood on the ground. There were no signs of a struggle and no tracks indicating who or what might be responsible. An autopsy revealed that the cuts on the horse's body had been caused by something that generated huge amounts of heat, which could only have be a laser. And some of the mare's internal organs had been removed. There were burn marks found nearby, which showed traces of radioactivity.

Just as UFO sightings before 1967 are sporadic and the records have not always survived, so we have no idea whether animal mutilations of this type occurred earlier. Perhaps they weren't reported at all; certainly, they didn't make the headlines, unlike the death of Lady, the Colorado mare. But as Kenneth Arnold's 'saucer' sighting in 1947 first led to a public awareness of the UFO phenomenon, so Lady's slaughter created an awareness that something was going on, in Colorado at least. Reports multiplied, reaching a peak during the 1970s – and not just in America, but all over the world. Horses, sheep and cattle were the most common targets, but most of the examples have certain common denominators: despite horrific mutilations, there was no blood on the ground; internal organs had been removed and, perhaps most significant of all, so had the genitalia, irrespective of the animal's sex.

The scale of the problem remains unknown. Unlike the UFO phenomenon itself, which has its extremist cranks and is thus newsworthy; unlike crop circles, which have a natural beauty and charm irrespective of how they are made, the mutilation of animals is abhorrent. Most of the coverage of it lies in local newspaper libraries and UFO literature. There is no central register. As with UFO sightings, it may well be that what has been reported is merely the tip of the iceberg.

Where reports are made, the first port of call is usually the police. Animals are valuable to farmers and cherished by families as pets, particularly among the British, who pride themselves on being a nation of animal-lovers. In the States, of course, the likelihood of animals being attacked by predators is greater than it is in Britain. Laying aside for the moment the possible existence of Surrey pumas and their ilk, our natural predators are the fox, birds of prey and, in remote parts of Scotland, the wildcat. A strong horse or cow need have no fear of any of these, although sheep, especially lambs, have been taken by all of them as well as by dogs. The United States has the coyote, cougar, wolverine, bear and a larger range of birds of prey than we do, all of which pose more of a threat to both pets and livestock.

Naturally farmers have lost their stock to predators for centuries, but the peculiar characteristics of these slaughters had never been seen before. Most predators go for the throat, or sometimes the hindquarters, while chasing a running prey.

They do not kill for sport but to eat, and in most cases little except the head and the odd bone is left after their meal. Many of the carcasses of the mutilated animals were found intact. The usual predators and scavengers seem to have left them alone. Normally a crow, for instance, will peck out the eyes of a dead lamb before starting to tear flesh from the body, but no such damage was evident in these corpses. Even maggots were absent. The blowflies that feed on rotting carcasses and lay the eggs which develop into maggots – hundreds of thousands of them per carcass, which continue to feed on the flesh while they develop – were avoiding the mutilated animals. All this flies in the face of nature and suggests that some other, unknown, factor is at work. Most astonishing of all was the precision used to mutilate the animals and the absence of blood. A predator rips with its jaws or claws, leaving blood and entrails scattered over at least a small area around the kill.

If predators were not responsible, the police surmised, what about Satanic cults? The old religion which predates Christianity involved appeasing the Lord of Darkness, by whatever name he was known by different generations. The notion of animal and even human sacrifice is common to many primitive cultures and despite the growth and spread of Christianity, has never disappeared altogether. When the press is not ridiculing another UFO experience in the silly season, they occasionally find evidence of ritual Satanic abuse – sheeps' hearts on altars, white chickens slaughtered on the lawn, the Devil at work in the Orkneys and even on a Rochdale council estate. Slaughtered animals were just another grim piece of evidence of some nauseating sect. And America, of course, has more of those per square inch than any other country.

Rewards were offered, investigations launched. They yielded nothing. Not even Satanists, for all the diabolical help they may have received at their Sabbats, were able to stab or cut up animals without drawing blood, and no goat-horned cult leader seemed to have access to a laser.

Here police inspiration came to an end. Others were more inventive, more lateral in their thinking. In the States, much of the research into animal mutilations has been carried out by television producer Linda Moulton Howe. Her book *An Alien Harvest* carried scores of interviews in an attempt to provide a solution. She has spoken to ranchers and farmers who reported mutilations, veterinary experts who have examined carcasses and police officers charged with investigating the phenomenon. Some of her findings seem to point towards some sort of government involvement. One theory runs that some animals were exposed to – indeed deliberately used to test – biochemical weapons by the government forces. Ms Howe's other findings also claim government involvement with UFOs.

In several instances, silent, black helicopters have been seen circling over areas where mutilations have occurred in a sinister echo of the vultures that normally fly over carrion. These helicopters have been sighted in greatest numbers in the infamous Area 51, near Groom Lake in Nevada (see Chapter 10). Here, it is rumoured, the United States government is testing and flying recovered alien craft. The black helicopters, so the story runs, are actually extraterrestrial craft (hence the lack of engine noise) disguised as earthly choppers in order to allay the fears of the public. There is also a slightly less hysterical claim that the helicopters are made in the USA, but use reverse-engineered technology from crashed alien craft.

In their book *Alien Animals*, British researchers Janet and Colin Bord cite a number of instances in which there seems to be a link between animals and UFOs. Reports of various sightings of UFOs in America and South Africa also mention a black dog, for centuries a sign of death or impending doom. In a spate of animal mutilations in Puerto Rico between February and July

1975, owners heard loud screechings and what sounded like the flapping of gigantic wings in the dark. In an astonishing case in the Rocky Mountains, again in 1975, just about every conceivable alien phenomenon occurred in a single incident. Cattle mutilations were accompanied by an untraceable humming sound, in the sky and on the ground, 'entities' inside and outside ranch houses, disembodied voices – even a Bigfoot-type animal snuffling through woods nearby. The Bords raise the legitimate question of whether blood is the real link, and whether it might be tied in with the human abduction experiences which now abound.

One woman who spoke to Linda Moulton Howe was Judy Doraty, from Houston, Texas, who underwent an extraordinary experience in May 1973. Under regression hypnosis Judy remembered having seen bright lights through the windscreen of her car one night and, in a classic example of the abduction experience, being floated on to a craft of some sort by creatures with large heads and black, wraparound eyes – Greys. What made her memories even more bizarre was that she saw a calf being floated on to the craft at the same time, as though the Greys were seeking to examine more than one life form. In a later regression session, she remembered the Greys dissecting the animal.

There are drawbacks to regression hypnosis, not least that the repression of will involved can lead the subject to 'remember' what he or she thinks the examiner wants to hear. However, if Judy Doraty is right, if the whole issue of alien abduction is reality, rather than the temporal lobe disorientation claimed by orthodox science, then why should humans be the only creatures to be abducted? Isn't it likely that aliens will be as fascinated by cattle, sheep and horses as they are by us? For nearly 1,500 years, thanks to the ignorance of early doctors with inflated reputations, like Galen, it was assumed that animal and human skeletons were identical anyway. British researcher Jenny

Randles in her *UFO Study: A Handbook for Enthusiasts*, discusses 'animal disturbance' and claims that dogs, cats, horses and cattle are particularly susceptible to UFO presence, showing a range of symptoms from trembling to what in humans would be called acute depression. Some dogs' personalities have altered so totally after their experiences that they have had to be destroyed. It is possible that they are sensitive to ultrasonic vibrations which we miss entirely. The animals Jenny Randles cites are those most familiar to humans, with which many of us share our daily lives, and we are more aware of their behaviour. It may well be that other animals whose habits are less familiar are affected too.

What are we to make of the sexual mutilation of animals? The abduction of Antônio Villas-Boas in October 1957 led to the closest encounter ever – he twice had sex with an alien woman with crimson pubic hair – but many abductees refer to medical and sexual examinations – investigations of the navel, rectum and vagina, and so on. This has led to speculation about some alien attempt to mate with humans in order to create a hybrid creature, but one might also draw the conclusion that if abduction stories are simply the rationalisation of some deep sexual psychosis (notice how like an unborn baby a typical description of a Grey sounds), then inevitably there is going to be a lot of discussion about genitals. If there is a genetic experiment underway, then why should it be confined to humans?

We have no evidence at the moment of human mutilations, although many who undergo the most dramatic abduction experiences tell of physical pain followed by vomiting as well as psychological trauma. Is this lack of mutilation simply a matter of differentiation – that as a higher species we are not subjected to it, perhaps because, whether we realise it or not, we can communicate with aliens? Or is it, as some allege, that the world's governments have done a deal with extraterrestrials and are tacitly allowing animal mutilations to take place as part of whatever technological exchange has been worked out – a deal whereby animals may be mutilated and killed as long as humans are only temporarily abducted and returned alive?

There are, however, researchers who hint darkly at human mutilation and of course, the vast number of missing persons worldwide provides millions of potential candidates. In America and Europe, where figures are kept, the list of missing persons is frightening; elsewhere, where there are no such records or they are woefully incomplete, the true picture is probably horrific. For every crazy, mixed-up teenager who runs away and refuses to contact family and friends again, how many cannot do so because they met, not a human murderer, but a small, grey figure with huge, black, insect-like eyes?

In 1993 the animal mutilation problem reached Britain. All over the south of England there was an outbreak of attacks on horses. Families were shocked and distressed to find their pets lying in paddocks with their genitals slashed. The police assumed that the culprit must be a pervert, someone not unlike the strange anti-hero of Peter Schaffer's *Equus*. I find it rather disturbing that so many people are prepared to believe a human being capable of this sort of crime and yet do not even consider the possibility that something else – something alien – might be responsible. That said, it should be stressed that this case did not have the hallmarks of a 'typical' mutilation and the culprit here – although not elsewhere – is likely to be human.

In my official capacity I had no remit to investigate mutilations at all. The link between ufology and mutilations is obscure, and little discussed outside the States. Consequently I received no mutilation reports from the public during my three years as UFO officer, and nor would I have expected to. However, ufologists who were aware of the link did send reports to me. My official line had to be that mutilations were a matter for the police or perhaps the Ministry of Agriculture, Fisheries and Food (MAFF).

Privately, I was becoming deeply concerned that if aliens could sneak in under our defences, single out and mutilate animals in the most horrific way, then the Ministry of Defence did indeed have a problem on its hands.

One of the letters I received on a UFO sighting came from someone who happened to work for MAFF. He suggested we meet for lunch, since his office was just along Whitehall from mine. MAFF have a network of veterinary experts at local level, who, while not directly employed by the ministry, carry out various tasks for them. My contact made a number of discreet inquiries of these experts and they admitted to having unsolved cases on their books. It *was* happening here.

B odmin Moor is a large, wild area of north-east Cornwall, formed by the four towns of Camelford and Launceston in the north and Liskeard and Bodmin itself in the south. The rolling landscape is scattered with huge boulders, some, like the Cheesewring and the Hurlers stone circle, associated with ancient Celtic legends. This is the lair of the 'Beast of Bodmin'.

For several years now, local farmers have been losing lambs and calves to the beast. The London *Evening Standard* recently carried an item suggesting that the legendary Beast of Exmoor (which may or may not be the same animal) might have slaughtered twenty-two lambs belonging to farmer Bruce Owen on his remote farm at Simonsbath, Somerset. The farm is over fifty miles away from Bodmin Moor, but big cats can cover that distance easily, and, like aliens, presumably, do not recognise county boundaries. A number of people claim to have seen the predator, almost exclusively at night, and the assumption is that it is a wildcat of some sort, perhaps a lynx, panther or puma. Similar cats are believed to exist in Surrey, Nottingham and the Isle of Wight – in fact, there are now very few counties that do not possess one – and 1994 was a prolific year for sightings. Indeed, some wag adapted the term used for a rash of UFO sightings, a flap, and dubbed this year a cat flap. The *Fortean Times* has listings of several hundred incidents, all gleaned from local papers.

There is nothing native about a lynx, panther or puma in Cornwall, and even though it is widely believed that these are natural animals which have escaped from a zoo or were originally exotic pets, it is odd not only that has one not been caught, but that even attempts to photograph them have not been particularly successful.

What most people who have seen the beast remember is the eyes, which are large and intense. Abductees have similar memories – alien eyes are large and almond-shaped, and some have likened them to those of a cat. One theory about aliens is that they are adept at changing their shapes, to mimic the appearance of terrestrial creatures, though often out of place in a given habitat. The concept of shape-shifting is not a new one – it has been part of various cultural myths since the dawn of time. Perhaps the best-known shape-shifters are vampires and werewolves, both of which are fierce predators, and most myths and legends have their roots in reality . . .

Late in 1994 there were two waves of sightings of lions roaming the country. This had happened before – in the mid- to late 1970s, a number of zoo animals, including lions, were seen at large, but these were all known to have escaped captivity and their freedom was short-lived. This was not the case in 1994. There are actually very few lions in British zoos, and they are all registered. The regulations governing the ownership of exotic pets were also tightened up in the late 1970s. No lion was reported missing, yet dozens of apparently reliable witnesses claimed to have seen one. One of the most recent sightings occurred in a small village near Hartlepool, Cleveland; the other was over a hundred miles away, in Basingstoke, Hampshire. So what is the explanation? Did those witnesses actually see a shape-shifting alien, or an alien able to project, telepathically, the image of a lion? And if one day we should find humans who have been mutilated, will it be assumed that a lion or the Beast of Bodmin is responsible when the real culprit is an extraterrestrial?

Perhaps the oddest thing about the victims of the beast is that the injuries inflicted have not been consistent with the teeth and claws of animals such as pumas or panthers. Such improbable mutilations have not been confined to the land, either. More than thirty seals were washed up on the beaches of Orkney with their heads missing. The animals' skins were intact and the bodies healthy. A post-mortem carried out by the Scottish Society for the Prevention of Cruelty to Animals found that decapitation had been carried out with a very sharp knife, almost surgically. The lack of serrations on the throats rules out sharks or killer whales, whose rows of teeth leave a ragged wound. The only explanation I have heard put forward for this is that local fishermen, anxious to protect their livelihood by saving fish stocks, had performed an illegal cull, shooting the seals in the head and decapitating them to disguise the cause of death. The fishermen concerned vigorously denied such accusations and indeed, such an exercise seems a rather convoluted solution. When Tony Dodd, director of investigations for Quest International, made enquiries, he was told that locals had seen UFOs over the islands in the days before the seals were washed up.

In another incident, thousands of dead sea birds were washed up on the east coast. This time there was no mutilation, and no apparent cause of death at all. In these ecology-conscious days it is all too easy to automatically blame pollution. But no detailed analysis was ever carried out into the death of these sea birds and the only other plausible theory – which seems to me rather limp – is that some sort of population explosion had occurred among the birds and that, unable to feed adequately on dwindling stocks of fish, thousands of them had simply starved.

Strangely, the National Farmers' Union has no records of any strange animal deaths. Likewise, the National Veterinary College, obviously out of touch with some of its members, has never heard of any mutilated corpses either aside from the horse ripper crimes which involved instances of mutilation to horses genitalia. These attacks were believed to be the work of a sexual pervert. One reason for this is under-reporting. In the case of attacks on livestock, insurance companies will not pay out on a claim that animals have been slaughtered by 'alien big cats' (so-called because they are alien to the UK, although the name may be apt for other reasons) on the dubious grounds that they do not exist. Farmers therefore record attacks as the work of large dogs, and vets, not knowing of any alternative, go along with this explanation.

Urgent study of the mutilation problem is needed, first to assess its true extent and then to try to provide a solution to the mystery. The only organisation centrally involved at present is the Ministry of Agriculture, Fisheries and Food, and they have no database of cases. Instead, like too many UFO sightings, reports are probably filed away in the memory banks of some computer. However, in the Summer of 1994, the MAFF, pressurised by increasing sightings of out-of-place wild animals and the increasing loss of farmers' livestock, agreed to carry out an examination on the available evidence.

The results were predictably inconclusive, but the study was the first, tentative step towards stopping this horrific slaughter of the innocents.

THE REAL X-FILES

'The truth is out there, Scully.' *The X-Files* has become a cult show in both America and in Britain. Each week a pair of agents, Fox Mulder and Dana Scully, tackle cases the Federal Bureau of Investigation would not normally handle on the Bureau's behalf. To date the duo have tangled with ghosts, werewolves and aliens. In fact UFO sightings and alien abductions are frequently featured and form the main focus of Mulder's obsession – his own sister was abducted by aliens when they were children. The official file was simply headed 'Missing'.

The series is purportedly based on fact and its creator, Chris Carter, claims to have spoken, unofficially of course, to government agents who have seen the real X-Files. The Central Intelligence Agency and the Defense Intelligence Agency have used psychics in their own intelligence-gathering operations (police forces certainly have, famously in the case of Albert de Salvo, the Boston Strangler, in 1964). It is also alleged that the CIA has a small department tasked with the job of studying a range of paranormal subjects such as telekinesis, the movement of objects by 'supernatural' means, to see if they have a useful application for the military or intelligence networks.

I became the butt of MOD humour when I was the UFO desk officer. People began to call me Spooky – Mulder's nickname in *The X-Files*, and walking down Whitehall corridors, I would occasionally hear someone whistling the haunting theme of the programme, or that sequence of notes from *Close Encounters of the Third Kind*. I'm not sure how much I could identify myself with Mulder, an obsessive maverick whose operations are constantly under threat of being closed down by his bosses. And I don't think I quite share Mulder's paranoia – his computer password is 'Trust NO 1.' However, it must be said that insofar as Fox 'Spooky' Mulder had a counterpart in Britain, I was it, and the files at my disposal in Secretariat (Air Staff) were probably the nearest thing the British government has to X-Files. One of these in particular would have done the television series proud. This was the Ministry of Defence file I opened on cases involving contact with alien beings, some examples of which are reproduced here.

Case 1: Aliens on the Estate

'I am writing to you today with extraordinary news; there are aliens on my estate.'

The letter was signed and an address provided. The estate was on Merseyside and it had, the writer believed, become the focus of a hostile alien takeover. Here I was plunged into something that sounded like a plot from a B-movie sci-fi film of the 1950s. The estate had, it seemed, become the bridgehead for an invasion, but the details in the letter were infuriatingly vague. It was not clear, for instance, whether the aliens had assumed human form or whether they were invisible. Some kind of oppressive presence was at work, even if the witness was unable to identify it specifically. He sent a photograph to the Ministry of Defence which purported to show aliens. The photograph was returned, with thanks, advising its owner that the objects in the picture were crows. Shape-shifting? Alien animals? Who knows.

This case occurred before my time, and I have not seen the photograph, nor was I able to contact the witness. It would be easy to write it off as a hoax or self-delusion, and many did. If something doesn't fit our conception of reality, our tendency is to consign it to the bar-room joke or the asylum.

But something on Merseyside terrified this man. I wonder if we shall ever know what it was?

Case 2: The Go-Between

A poltergeist is a noisy spirit and this case exhibited many of the classic properties associated with a haunting of this kind. It involved a series of events, linked in a common purpose, which occurred over a number of years. Poltergeist activity is so common and so well-attested that very few would now persist in pouring upon it the scorn that used to be standard. Its cause is unknown, but the focus of much poltergeist activity seems to be teenage children, as though the energy hurtling through them as they reach puberty needs to find an altogether more robust outlet than the human body.

The witness in this case experienced typical poltergeist phenomena, such as unlocked doors refusing to open, as well as less common ones. In the midst of a green cloud of gas, transparent slug-like entities appeared to him. Terrified, the witness shot one of them with an air-gun and the creature dissolved into nothingness. As the years passed, and the witness became more able to cope with the recurring appearance of these entities, he began to receive telepathic messages from them. There was an alien presence here on Earth and it wanted to open some sort of dialogue with the human race. The witness's role was to act as an intermediary, a kind of roving ambassador, between us and the aliens. Unfortunately, there had been a setback: the benign aliens of his youth had been destroyed by others whose motives were far more hostile.

Claims of this type – people being chosen to act as go-betweens – are quite common. For centuries, clairvoyants and 'sensitives' have professed themselves able to bridge the gulf between this world and the next, and the same claims have been made for the ability to link this world with alien civilisations. London taxi-driver 'Sir' George King, founder of the Aetherius Society, declared that in May 1954, after years of practising yoga and meditation, he heard a voice saying 'Prepare yourself – you are about to become the voice of Interplanetary Parliament.' This voice, said King, was not psychic but physical, and it told him that other planets were home to technologically superior 'masters' who were concerned about the welfare of humans. Eight days later, an Indian swami walked through a locked door to tell King how to establish proper telepathic contact with Venusians. 'Quite soon after,' wrote King 'I was able to tune in and receive, telephatically, information which was relayed over millions of miles of etheric space.'

Case 3: The Alien Witness

This case is possibly unique among the files of Secretariat (Air Staff). The letter was allegedly written by an alien. This is the story she told. She was a member of a tall, beautiful, benevolent species which was in conflict with another, small, unpleasant and grey in colour. They came from a planet or organisation – the exact nature of the organism is unclear – called Spectra and the witness had been captured by them.

Using secret powers, she had escaped and fled to Earth, to relative safety.

Her story reads like a fantasy. The concept of two superpowers locked in grim and endless combat, though it has Earthbound Cold War echoes, is also the stuff of science fiction, from Milton's 'Paradise Lost' – 'There was war in Heaven' – to Gene Roddenberry's *Star Trek* – 'Klingons on the starboard bow.' The racial types described in the letter are also familiar: the cold, hostile Greys who feature in most abduction memories and the friendlier Nordics, who have been involved in close encounters, but not generally in abductions.

Fanciful as this might all sound, the interesting point to note is that the letter was written to the Ministry of Defence some time before the accounts of Greys and Nordics first appeared in popular literature. Is it possible that some elements of this story are true? Was the woman herself an abductee, perhaps unable to come to terms with her experience? And was wrapping up her anger in a fantasy of her own making her way of fighting back against her kidnappers?

Case 4: Alien Mechanics

The scene is a railway yard in the middle of the night, where a man is sleeping rough. His sleep is disturbed by an alien craft in trouble. It has landed in a goods siding and is being repaired by two crew members. The witness crawls as close as he dares to watch the aliens tinkering with their machine, noisily revving it up. But they see him, paralyse him with a beam of light and capture him. They release him before leaving in their repaired craft.

Again, sceptics will cry 'Delusion, hoax, dream.' What was this witness doing sleeping rough in a railway yard? Was he a drug addict, an alcoholic? Was the craft a Harley-Davidson and the 'aliens' merely bikers? Any or all of this is possible as an explanation. Yet if so, why write the letter? It takes paranoia or some other form of psychosis of considerable power to impel people to contact governments about an experience they believe they have had.

It could be a straightforward hoax, of course, but what is interesting about this account is the odd twist of detail so often missing from reports, perhaps because witnesses are afraid to commit to paper points which do not fit accepted norms. Virtually all references to abductions mention a beam of light, but few of them refer to a noise of the type heard in that railway yard. A 'low hum', a 'trilling sound', are the phrases encountees tend to use: they do not usually describe anything as mundane as the revving of a machine. Was it possible, this witness theorised, that aliens deliberately use railway tracks so that should they be heard by a human, he or she would simply assume that the engine noise was that of a train?

Case 5: A Classic Road Abduction

Two women, a mother and daughter, were driving on a lonely road late at night. They both saw a light in the sky which they couldn't explain and they felt odd, confused and disorientated. When they got home, it was much later than it should have been. And that night, and for many nights to come, they both had strange and disturbing dreams. A figure they described as alien, though not necessarily extraterrestrial, was doing something unpleasant to them, but they couldn't say precisely what.

This case from the MOD's X-Files bears all the hallmarks of a classic 'road abduction' story: a lonely highway, without witnesses; a bright light in the sky; a feeling of disorientation;

the concept of 'missing time'. It reads like an experience with the Greys, first and most dramatically recounted under hypnosis by Betty and Barney Hill. This incident took place after the Hills' experiences, but nevertheless predates the time when such stories became widely known. It was clear from the letter that neither woman had any real knowledge of the UFO phenomenon. Regression hypnosis, that two-edged sword, might have unlocked their memories, but perhaps there are memories best left alone.

What are we to make of such cases? In none of them was there an obvious motive for a hoax, and only one of the five – the last – received any publicity. Even that was limited and arose merely because the women concerned contacted a UFO group, and they neither sought nor received any payment. The sole motive I could see was that the witnesses thought the Ministry of Defence ought to know about their experiences and perhaps take action, or that they felt a need to talk to someone about a traumatic, even terrifying, event.

In all cases except the last, my predecessors took the decision not to reply to the witnesses' letters. In Case 5, a short standard response was sent, outlining our policy on UFOs and suggesting that the women consulted a doctor. The witnesses' reply to this was, needless to say, blistering. The ministry was not keeping its collective mind open. It wasn't even treating the witnesses with the dignity and respect they deserved. The right approach is undoubtedly that of Budd Hopkins: to find out what happened is only the secondary aim; the first is to help the witness.

A number of people telephoned me in the belief that they might have been abducted. My replies to their questions were always honest, open and, I hope, helpful. I told them what I knew of the various theories that exist; I explained the pros and cons of regression hypnosis and cautioned them about the lunatic fringe of the UFO lobby who might well have their own agenda. I warned of the dangers of seeking publicity. To stand up to the scorn of the media – and the neighbours – they would need broad shoulders indeed. I never pushed my contacts into a decision: all I did was to place before them the options so that they could proceed – or not – with all the relevant information at their disposal. Crucially, if I had my doubts about the physical or mental health of a witness, I would try to steer them towards appropriate professionals rather than towards ufologists.

The witnesses to whom I spoke were deeply troubled people who had clearly undergone some sort of genuine trauma; whether or not that trauma involved alien abduction is not for me to say.

Of course, the cranks do exist, and I had my fair share of them. One regular caller – from Australia – claimed that he was an alien. 'I can prove there's an extraterrestrial presence . . . I am an alien and I have been living among you for many years.' I asked him if he had any proof of his origins, the ignition keys to his spaceship, perhaps, or a beer can with the Alpha Centauri label. Strangely enough, he didn't. Another man insisted that everybody in his town had become aliens and that they were invading his back garden. Paranoia was evident in his every word, but still I tried to be patient, spending hours on the phone explaining, calming, rationalising. My colleagues said I shouldn't talk to these people, that they were mad. I disagreed: whatever delusions they were suffering from, the fear was real and they needed help. I was always afraid that a curt, officious 'Good morning' would add to their troubles and perhaps even push them over the edge. I am not a trained counsellor; I just used courtesy, patience and common sense.

I took the unprecedented step of releasing the five cases outlined above to the national UFO groups, deleting names, dates, places and any other information which might have given clues to the identity of the witnesses and lead to unwelcome publicity. This was not a popular move in some quarters, but it paid off, opening up a dialogue with BUFORA and Quest International and creating the atmosphere of trust and openness which I had tried so hard to foster.

Now that I have left Secretariat (Air Staff) I have no idea whether the 'X-Files' are still used for the purpose I intended, as a means of drawing together all close encounter reports so that analysis and in-depth research could be carried out. What I do know is that, whatever has happened to them, the 'X-Files' are fascinating, charting as they do events at the very edge of human experience.

These were my X-Files; I had felt that such close encounter cases were so important that they needed to be isolated from the more usual UFO sightings. And yet one question kept occurring to me: where were the rest of the cases? Ufologists had long argued that the ministry ought to have received a fair number of such cases, in roughly the same proportion as they did, when expressed as a percentage of the total number of sightings reported. They had a point. And yet, over the years, the ministry had consistently denied having received any reports of what might be classified as a possible alien abduction.

Some people simply thought we were lying, and saw this as part of a wider cover-up. They believed we kept these cases under wraps for fear of alarming the public. I generally have little time for such theories, and suggested that my predecessors had simply been in error. Perhaps such cases had just been filed away along with ordinary reports . . . perhaps material had been accidentally destroyed.

And yet. And yet, in moments of doubt, I began to identify more and more with my alter-ego, Fox Mulder. He had found himself thwarted in his X-File investigations not just by the closed minds who always sneer at the paranormal, but by more powerful forces with more sinister motives; people who seemed to know what was going on, in situations where Fox was only groping in the dark, albeit with the best of intentions.

The UFO lobby thought I was in a similar position to Fox Mulder. They accepted that I was being straight with them, and that I was as interested as they were in getting at the truth. On the other hand, many of them seemed convinced that more powerful forces stood behind me, unseen, but ready to make a move if I ever got too close.

Could it be that somewhere within the cavernous bowels of Main Building (or Rudloe Manor, often alleged to be the centre of official British study of UFOs) there lurk more X-Files? Could the UFO lobby be correct in their assertion that there must be material which even I couldn't access? If so, where is all this material? Who has it, and why are they keeping it under wraps? Why was it kept from me, when it could have been a crucial piece of the puzzle? If I had access to more good cases and hard data I could have come closer to forming a definitive assessment of the situation.

Of course, all this is speculation, and I never came across anything more suspicious than the odd radar that seemed to have been 'down for repairs' at a crucial moment, when it might have corroborated a key sighting, or the occasional missing file. But these are the sorts of quirks and errors that plague every organisation. Aren't they?

THE REAL UFOs

The late 1980s was a busy time for Belgian UFO researchers. Sightings were coming in from all over the country in increasing numbers, from civilians, police, the military. So numerous did they become that as a result of public pressure a procedure was instituted whereby the police force immediately contacted air force radar controllers if any significant sightings occurred. There was a flurry of activity on 29 November and 2 December 1989, which led to the scrambling of intercepting jet fighters.

The Belgian air force consists of 12,100 personnel. It has four squadrons of F-16 fighter/ground-attack aircraft and two of F-16 fighters. It operates a similar system to all other NATO countries in that it keeps a small number of jets and pilots, known as the Quick Reaction Alert, on standby in case of trouble. These jets are supported by a complex ground radar system which has a range of over 300km and is capable of reaching 3km up into the air.

On 2 December the sightings came from Liège, the largest Walloon-speaking city in the country, which straddles the confluence of the River Ourthe and the Meuse. The radar controller contacted by the gendarmerie could see a blip on his screen which looked as though it might match the visual sightings and two F-16s were scrambled to investigate. They were in the air within five minutes, but the search proved fruitless. As they approached the target area, the object disappeared from the screen.

A second sighting occurred later in the Hasselt area, forty miles to the north of Liège near Maastricht in Limbourg. This time there was no radar trace, but the Belgian air-traffic controllers were in no mood to take chances. When the F-16s arrived there appeared to be a laser show in progress. Thereafter it was decided that there were to be no scramblings without radar confirmation.

Then, on the night of 30–31 March 1990, everything went haywire. No definitive number has ever been quoted for the sightings that occurred that night all over Belgium and north Germany. UFO groups put forward a tentative figure of 2,600, and I have not seen this denied anywhere by official sources. But even assuming that every single sighting was reported, which I very much doubt, and comparing the British figure for reported sightings of 209 for the entire year, something sensational was going on in the skies over northern Europe that night.

Most of the descriptions submitted to the gendarmerie – and indeed the incidents personally witnessed by the gendarmerie – featured coloured lights. A high proportion of witnesses saw these lights in a triangular formation on the underside of a huge craft which hovered over villages and towns at low altitudes and was very clearly visible from the ground. The speed of the triangle varied: some reports spoke of 30 to 40mph – slow even for a car; others described a hovering motion followed by a disappearance at incredibly high speed, several times faster than a jet. An F-16 can travel at about 1,100mph and many of the witnesses were used to seeing these aircraft in flight. They were adamant that no plane belonging to any known air force could have caught that triangle.

Most of the sightings were centred on the Wavre area, to the south of Brussels. The local gendarmcric contacted the NATO radar stations at Semmerzake and Glons, which had both simultaneously picked up unexplained blips on their screens. The sector commander of the NATO air defence system authorised the scrambling of the Quick Reaction Alert and two F-16s were airborne in minutes. Their radars locked on to the target they were chasing, which appeared on their screens. Each time they vectored closer, however, the radar lock was broken, as though the object were taking evasive action. The speed at which it was moving defied belief. At one point it dropped 1,300m in one second, an observation which matched the eyewitness reports from the ground. At under 200m from the ground the trace vanished completely from all five radar screens tracking it. The aerial chase had lasted seventy-five minutes.

Actual interception of the object was probably impossible. The night of 30 March was clear, which meant that many stars were visible and the pinpointing of specific light sources would be difficult. F-16 radar screens tend to share one affinity with orthodox scientists: they filter out and ignore slow-moving or stationary targets on the assumption that they will not be jets. The pilots had no way, therefore, of using their own radar to close in on the object once it had slowed down or stopped.

Witnesses from the ground at Petit-Rosière reported that the object lost the intensity of its lights and faded into invisibility on the arrival of the F-16s. This is either an unbelievable coincidence, or the craft was deliberately evading them and therefore under intelligent control. The F-16 pilots thought they were chasing real craft, and the air force top brass seemed to agree. The Belgian air force chief of operations, Colonel (now General) Wilfried De Brouwer, commented, 'There was a logic in the movements of the UFO.'

What was the official view of the Belgian government? My

contacts with them elicited the conclusion that a structured craft had flown over Belgium that night at varying speeds and heights. They had no idea what the object was, and would dearly love to find out. This view was the essence of defence minister Guy Coëme's statement to the Belgian parliament.

The implications of the Belgian case are frightening. A structured craft flew over Belgian airspace, clearly observed from the ground and on radar, but it evaded the fastest, most sophisticated aircraft they possessed. They had, in effect, been powerless. What if that triangle, whatever it was, had been hostile? Whether extraterrestrial or very much of this earth, what if it had started dropping bombs?

On 31 March 1993, three years to the day after the Belgium incident, I arrived at work at 9am as usual to find that there had been a major wave of UFO sightings in Britain the previous night, with many police and military witnesses.

The first call came from a constable in the Devonshire Constabulary. He and his colleague had been on routine patrol in their car the night before and had seen a UFO. He was the first police witness I had come across directly, and I remember listening particularly carefully to what he had to say. This was not Joe Public, but an observer trained to be calm and rational and meticulous in compiling detailed reports. What was more, the fact that this was a double sighting gave it an even stronger authenticity.

The constable was often on duty at night so he was used to all the sights and sounds of the darkness: the hoot of an owl in the woods beyond the stationary patrol car; the barking of a dog; the ghostly appearance of trees on the roadside when headlights dapple their branches. But what he and his colleague had seen was like nothing they had come across before. This was no shooting star, no meteor. Two bright lights, together with a third fainter one, were flying in perfect formation ahead of vapour trails. I probed carefully over the phone. From what he told me about their colour and movement, they were clearly not aircraft lights. Similarly, they were not fireballs. They were simply unidentifiable.

As the morning wore on, the calls came in thick and fast. Other people had seen the three lights, two bright, one fainter, in the same perfect formation. The pattern began to ring bells. The police report suggested three craft in some sort of squadron, but could the three lights be the Belgian triangle – three lights on one unidentified craft? Some of the reports described the lights travelling at high speeds, others talked of a virtual hover. There were references to a high altitude as well as statements putting the lights low in the sky. Colourful experiences like this produce excitement, and excited people don't always make good witnesses. Even so, the pattern that was emerging was the same as that in Belgium three years earlier. Could we be looking at the same astonishing, chameleon craft? The uncanny anniversary date wouldn't go away and the hairs on my scalp started to prickle.

I knew better than to jump to conclusions. Orthodox science has done that and come up empty-handed. Other planets do not have the 'right' proportion of oxygen, hydrogen or carbon, and are therefore incapable of sustaining life. That contention is highly questionable as a hypothesis. The UFO extremists have made similar quantum leaps. Betty and Barney Hill claimed to have been abducted by aliens, therefore aliens are among us. I could not afford to be so dogmatic. As the government's sole UFO official, alone at my desk, I had to keep an open mind.

Most sightings had occurred between 1 and 1.30am, with a particular concentration at 1.10. Either the triangle had been over our skies for half an hour or it had appeared briefly at 1.10 and the other reported times were only approximations. Having established a vague timing for the appearance of the lights, I needed to co-ordinate the sightings on a map, to mark each with a time, height (if that could be ascertained) and compass bearing. The resulting pattern did not give me the straight line I'd hoped for, but the sightings were concentrated, over Devon, Cornwall, Somerset and Wales. There were sporadic reports, too, from the Midlands and even Yorkshire. If all the sightings were of the same object, then it was zigzagging in a random pattern through our skies at incredibly high speed.

By lunchtime it became obvious that I was right at the centre of the biggest wave of UFO sightings ever reported in Britain. As if to confirm this, the initial police report said that officers all over Devon and Cornwall had seen the lights. And I knew from experience that still more witnesses would never come forward. At that time of night, most people would of course have been in bed, so the number of sightings would be reduced accordingly, but even so, I estimated that several hundred people had seen something extraordinary. And the sightings were not confined to mainland Britain. Other reports reached me from the Irish Republic, and in the days that followed I heard of sightings in France, and, significantly, Belgium.

Not surprisingly, the UFO groups were also swamped with calls. BUFORA and Quest International contacted me – this case transcended any past differences between us and the communication channels that had been established paid off. Anxious not to be accused of favouritism, I exchanged information with any group or researcher who asked. No one group or individual – least of all me – had the whole picture, but the pieces of the jigsaw were increasing in number and a clearer overview of the night's events was now possible. I hope I don't sound too much like Colonel Blimp when I say that, if a threat to the security of my country was at stake, then I was going to do my damnedest to sort it out. That was my job.

An important report came in from a military patrol guarding RAF Cosford near Wolverhampton in the West Midlands. This was dynamite. An unidentified craft in any British airspace was threatening enough, but over a high security military establishment? There was better to come. One of the sightings in Wales was from a man with vast experience of aviation and mathematics. He had watched the object flying low over the coast near Haverfordwest in Pembrokeshire and had timed its passage between two points on the shoreline whose distance from each other he knew. From that information he was able to calculate its speed at that point to be about 1,100mph an hour – the same, at that moment at least – as the top speed of an F-16.

In Rugeley, Staffordshire, five members of the same family saw a huge diamond-shaped object flying steadily over their heads. They estimated its height at less than 300m and the diameter of the craft was about 200m. They also reported a low, humming sound of the frequency you'd experience standing in front of the speakers at a pop concert, feeling the sound waves passing through your body. It wasn't pleasant, but they decided to jump in the car and follow it anyway. Either they lost the UFO, or it lost them; either way, the chase was unsuccessful. They thought it was going to land in a field beyond the road because it was flying so low. They screeched to a halt by the gate, but when they clambered out, the craft had gone. They saw nothing after that. They were disappointed, but perhaps they had had a lucky escape.

Perhaps the most interesting report came from RAF Shawbury in Shropshire, to the north of Shrewsbury. The meteorological officer there saw the most astonishing sight of that whole amazing night. An object in the sky, at first stationary, moved erratically towards him at a speed of several hundred miles an hour. At one point it fired a beam of light at the ground, which swept the countryside from left to right, as though it were looking for something in the fields and hedgerows. The sighting was not a second's glimpse, but lasted for five minutes, long enough for the witness to estimate the size of the craft to be about that of a Jumbo jet. But as he and I knew, Jumbo jets don't hover and they don't scan the countryside with searchlights. He heard the same low frequency hum the family from Rugeley had heard.

What could I say to this man? He was a trained observer, considerably more familiar with the night sky than I was. A patronising lecture on aircraft lights seen from unusual angles seemed wholly out of place. On the phone I agreed with him that there was only one conclusion: whatever he had seen was unknown. What I didn't discuss with him was the fear I felt at his description of that probing beam searching the fields. It implied intelligent occupants of the craft, and it also implied that they might be searching for what is usually in the fields on a mild, spring night – cattle.

I carried out my usual checks, looking for the explicable, hunting for the mundane. I needed to cover my own back, to be ready for the media deluge. What were the ministry's answers? There was no unusual civil or military aircraft activity that night that came remotely close to fitting anything that had been seen. There were no weather balloons in the area of the densest sightings and no unusual planetary activity, said the Royal Observatory at Greenwich

Then RAF Fylingdales came up with something. It confirmed that debris from a Russian rocket, Cosmos 2238, had re-entered Earth's atmosphere that night and might just have been visible from the United Kingdom. So that was it, the doubters said, orthodox science had triumphed again. But of course, it hadn't. A piece of re-entering space debris would burn up, like a meteor, and produce a flaming trail which would last only seconds. This couldn't account for the five-minute sighting from RAF Shawbury or the low hum heard there and in Rugeley; neither would it be seen flying low over the coast near Haverfordwest, because the debris didn't come down anywhere near Britain; neither can a piece of even the smallest space debris hover – it falls with the speed dictated by gravity.

I took an unprecedented step and ordered a number of radar tapes to be impounded and sent to me. As these tapes are usually wiped for reuse, it was important to work fast. There were a few returns which fitted the times and locations when sightings were made and after several hours of scouring the standard VHS videos I could isolate and identify these. At first, the results were disappointing. The blips faded in and out all night, like ghosts in the morning light. RAF radar experts explained these conventionally enough. Ground clutter, they said, tall trees picked up now and again around one particular radar head. But the frustration turned to fear: there were too many visual sightings, and the reports were from witnesses too trustworthy to ignore. Whatever it was that zigzagged Britain on 30 and 31 March 1993, that probed our fields and raced our cars, it was not picked up by radar. And consequently, with no radar track to set the procedure in motion, we hadn't even got our aircraft into the air. Was this the same triangle that had been seen over Belgium three years earlier? And could it now evade radar altogether?

Over the coming weeks I tried to find an explanation, but every avenue led nowhere. Whatever it was had come and gone. It was time to take the whole problem 'upstairs'. Frankly, I didn't hold out much hope that my bosses would listen. As I have said, my hands-on approach and my firm views that we were facing in UFOs a genuine phenomenon that needed serious and urgent research had not met with popularity in Secretariat (Air Staff). Subtlety was the key word, I felt. I drew up a carefully constructed report of the 30–31 March sightings and sent it to my head of division. I deliberately avoided the emotive word 'UFO', inspirer of prejudices, and opted instead for 'uncorrelated target' and 'unknown craft'. Government bureaucracies are sometimes accused of inventing jargon for the sake of it, but here I felt it was necessary, it paid off. The report was passed up the chain of command until it reached the assistant chief of the air staff himself.

Simultaneously, I contacted the American embassy and asked them whether an unusual prototype aircraft of American con-struction was operating over Britain and might explain the various sightings. There had been rumours for months in the corridors of power that an aircraft called Aurora, which would make the Stealth bomber look like a Sopwith Pup, was in production. There had been consistent denials everywhere, however. A high-tech, radar-evading craft capable of great speeds and manoeuvrability, the sort of machine Clint Eastwood flies in *Firefox*, belonged to fiction. Aurora, we were told, did not exist. The Americans were as nonplussed as we and the Belgians were by the sightings.

The assistant chief of the air staff noted my report – there was little else he could do. By now I had tried all possible lines of inquiry. There were no other avenues left.

So the official findings (mine) read: 'Type of craft – unknown; origin of craft – unknown; motive of occupants – unknown.' And, although it appears nowhere in the official documentation, I would have to add: 'Conclusion – unsatisfactory.'

The 30–31 March sightings brought about a marked change in my own attitude. I would play no further part in bland platitudes about UFOs being 'of no defence significance'. I sensed that some of my colleagues thought UFOs were only of defence significance if they aimed laser beams at cities. But any craft, conventional or otherwise, that can do what that triangle did is of *extreme* defence significance in itself. Our radar couldn't trace it, our jets wouldn't be able to catch it. We can all thank our God – or our lucky stars

– that whatever it was it was not, on that particular occasion, anyway, hostile.

Over and over again, I pondered the significance of the date. The odds against such a phenomenon occurring coincidentally on the same night three years apart are high. That suggests that the date was not random, but was deliberately chosen and planned. Furthermore, it was chosen by an intelligence fully familiar with human frailties. Newspaper reports of incidents occurring that night would run on 1 April, the day when every national and many provincial papers carry an April Fool story. Who was going to take these stories seriously? Predictably, only the UFO community ran articles and asked questions, and followed up as best they could. The public at large just smiled wryly over their breakfast cereal. Isn't this exactly the reaction an alien force might hope to achieve by capitalising on a time when the world is unreceptive, when everyone expects bizarre stories and dismisses them out of hand? It was absolutely the best date to choose to minimise the risk that any sightings might be taken seriously.

And something else rang bells for me, too. It wasn't just the date, the precise three-year gap since Belgium, it was that business of the Russian rocket re-entry. A similar re-entry had happened on the same night as another dramatic sighting. But it wasn't over Belgium. It was here, near Woodbridge in Suffolk, at a place called Rendlesham Forest.

Rendlesham lies between the Rivers Deben and Alde, a straggling tract of mixed deciduous and coniferous forest framed by the joint RAF/USAF airbase at Woodbridge and the neighbouring military base at Bentwaters, three miles away (curiously, a scene of UFO activity in 1956). Woodbridge was, in the days of the Cold War, one of the busiest airfields in the country. As such, it was a high-security area and any nearby activity was closely monitored by the commander and personnel of the base. Following the break-up of the former Soviet Union, these bases were closed down and sold off.

At three in the morning on 27 December 1980, two security patrolmen on their routine tour of the camp perimeter saw bright lights among the trees of Rendlesham Forest. Their first assumption was that an aircraft might have overshot or misjudged the runway and been forced into the trees, although they had heard no noise. They asked permission to investigate beyond the camp gates, which was duly granted.

In the forest it soon became clear that the object was no aircraft. They encountered a metallic, traingular craft, unlike anything they had ever seen before. Two nights later, the object returned and a larger team, led by the deputy base commander, Lt-Col Charles Halt, went out to investigate. They too had a strange sighting. The text of Halt's subsequent report can be found in Appendix 5 in this book. The tape-recording of the search in those trees is now available to the public, courtesy of Quest International. Called 'The Halt Package', the eighteen-minute tape is accompanied by news-clippings, official documents and correspondence from both sides of the Atlantic. Unfortunately, key evidence from that Suffolk night is missing, and without it, what actually happened in Rendlesham Forest is destined to remain a mystery.

Halt and a number of his men have given interviews to the media. As the deputy base commander told Michael Aspel's *Strange But True?* programme in 1994, 'I knew there was something there, but I was also convinced there was a logical explanation.' Halt and four of his men advanced into the forest, leaving the remainder in the vicinity of the powerful light-alls that had been brought up to illuminate the scene. Their equipment behaved strangely. Although the tape-recorder, Geiger counter

This beautiful crop circle pattern appeared at Avebury, Wiltshire, in August 1994. The small dots in the formation are people.

A rare photograph depicting 'foo fighters' - luminous objects seen by Allied and Axis pilots during the Second World War. (*right*)

This spectacular photograph of lenticular clouds illustrates how natural phenomena are some-times misidentified as UFOs. (*bottom left*)

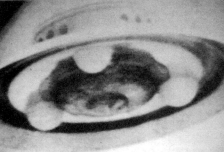

A 'Venusian scout ship' photographed by George Adamski in 1952 (*above*)

A spectacular photograph showing a high-domed disc, taken by George Stock above New Jersey, USA, in 1952. *(top left)*

The Trindade UFO: Taken on 16 January 1958, by the Brazilian Navy at Trindade Island in the south Atlantic Ocean. The photographs are regarded by many as authentic, and have passed several critical examinations. This shot shows the disc moving slowly over the mountains and contains an inset with enlargement. *(bottom 1st left)*

Another photo showing the famous Trindade Island UFO. There were more than fifty witnesses to this sighting. *(bottom 2nd left)*

Rudi Nagora shot an entire roll of film as this spectacular UFO descended in a 'falling leaf' motion over Deutschlandsberg, Austria on 23 May 1971. *(above)*

This remarkable photograph was taken by Eduard 'Billy' Meier in 1976.*(below)*

This photo was taken by farmer Paul Trent in McMinville, Oregon, in 1950. It was examined by Project Blue Book staff, who were unable to find an explanation.*(bottom left)*

Another shot of the McMinville UFO, in which the craft can be seen banking away from the house.*(bottom right)*

A still photograph taken from the controversial Roswell autopsy film that surfaced in 1995.

Spectacular shot of a UFO taken by Ed Walters in Gulf Breeze, Florida, in 1988.(*right*)

A huge, triangular craft photographed over Tagresk, Russia, in March 1990.(*top right*)

An official NASA enlargement of the 'Face on Mars'. NASA say it's an effect caused by a trick of the light, while some ufologists claim it's a huge artificial monument.(*middle right*)

A 'mothership' and 'scout ships' photographed by George Adamski - the most famous of the contactees - in 1951.(*bottom right*)

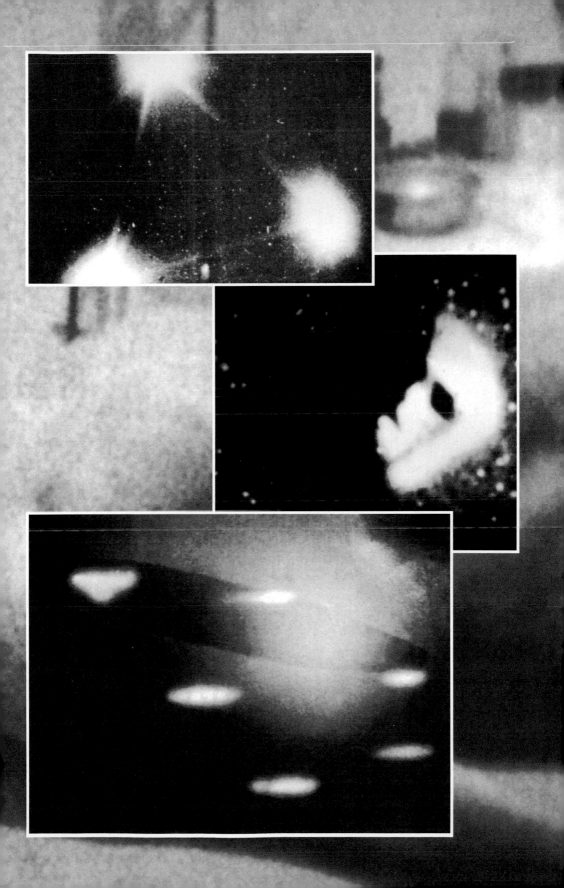

Ministry of Defence Main Building.
Secretariat (Air Staff) 2a is on the
eighth floor, overlooking Downing
Street.

The late, great Dr J Allen Hynek,
scientific adviser to Project Blue
Book.*(bottom left)*

Professor John Mack, Professor
of Psychiatry at Harvard Medical
School. His in-depth work with
abductees has convinced him of
the reality of the alien abduction
phenomenon.*(Bottom right)*

Betty and Barny Hill, whose 1961
encounter with a UFO is one of
the most famous and earliest
reports of an abduction.*(below)*

Kenneth Arnold, the pilot whose 1947 sighting marked the beginning of the modern UFO mystery.*(top)*

Operation Right to Know members outside Ministry of Defence Main Building, protesting against Government secrecy on UFOs.*(bottom)*

Artist's impression of the terrifying close encounter
witnessed by Betty Cash, Vickie Landrum and
Vickie's grandson, Colby, in December 1980.

Artist's impression of a 'grey' - the most commonly
reported type of alien, often recalled by
abductees.*(top right)*

and night-vision scope functioned perfectly, all three radio frequencies in use were prone to interference, and radios worked only intermittently. The tall light-alls used as floodlights simply refused to function at all.

It is an eerie experience listening to Halt's voice as he and his men edge their way through the undergrowth to within 150yds of the light source.

'Strange flashing red light ahead.'

'No, it's yellow.'

'Weird.'

'It's definitely coming this way.'

Halt remembered the light vividly in later years. He told Aspel's team:

> It pulsated as though it were an eye winking at you and around the edges it appeared to have molten metal dripping off it.
>
> Here I am, a senior official who routinely denies this sort of thing and diligently works to debunk them, and I'm involved in the middle of something I can't explain.

What he couldn't explain was that the moving light, now red, now yellow, suddenly exploded into three or five pieces, each of them a white light, and then disappeared altogether. Immediately, he saw three objects in the sky, like stars; except that, unlike stars, they gave off red, green and blue lights and darted in all directions in sharp, angular movements. Those to the north appeared elliptical when viewed through a power lens, but their shape changed into full circles. They were visible for two to three hours and occasionally flashed down beams of light or energy, Halt didn't know which. His scepticism had vanished. 'I was really in awe,' he confesses.

A mile away, Airman John Burroughs was with his vehicle,

still trying to repair the malfunctioning light-alls. A blue light streaked past him at head-height and the light-alls instantly came on. The light passed through the open windows of his truck and vanished into the distance. Then the light-alls went out.

Airman Larry Warren was with the another team which had left the East Gate. Aged only nineteen at the time, he is still able to pinpoint the exact spot where he saw the light, in the midst of a strange circle of mist in a field. The Cold War has gone, the USAF base has gone, but the memories remain. Warren saw the whole field, along with a huge nearby oak tree, lit by a bright light. A red ball of light approached from across the field and at first Warren thought it was an A-10 aircraft coming in to land. But it stopped over the circle of mist and exploded, without sound, without heat, into a galaxy of coloured lights. Somehow – and Warren was at a loss to explain how – the vapour of the mist and the coloured lights transformed themselves into a structured object. He estimated it was 30ft across the base and 20ft high. There was a bank of blue lights on the underside and the whole thing shone with a rainbow or mother-of-pearl effect, so bright that it was difficult to look at it directly.

Warren stayed where he was, 'glued', he said. Others, including senior officers, ran for safety, taking with them the video camera and the cine camera which had already recorded the object.

Halt's report mentions that in the calming dawn of the next day (his men had been in the woods for six hours by this time), checks were made in the vicinity of the extraordinary sightings. Three depressions 1½in. deep and 7in. in diameter were found in the soil of the woodland. That night – 29 December – Geiger counters had checked the area for radiation levels. Halt's data revealed: 'Beta/gamma readings of 0.1 milliroentgens with peak readings in the three depressions and near the centre of the triangle formed by the depressions. A nearby tree had moderate readings (.05–.07) on the side of the tree towards the depressions.' These ground readings were, claimed *Strange But True?*, twenty-five times the normal background radiation levels for the English countryside.

A cloud of secrecy hung over Rendlesham. Personnel at the base, such as Sergeant Jim Penniston, noticed unusual activity in the days that followed. Unscheduled flights came and went. Penniston was told to keep quiet and forget them. Even Halt was left in the dark. His superiors told him to submit his report to the Ministry of Defence, which he did. My predecessors do not seem to have acknowledged this and Halt, quite rightly, finds this incomprehensible. The report was forwarded to the ministry by Squadron Leader Donald Moreland, specifically to the forerunner of my department, Defence Secretariat 8. Here the trail goes cold, and it is not clear from the files what happened next. Lt-Col Halt, bewildered and angry, is still awaiting his reply from us fifteen years later.

Clifford Stone, a former US Army intelligence officer, believes he knows the origin and purpose of these mysterious flights and the reason for the total news black-out. The aircraft, ordered in by high-ranking American air force officials, carried teams of experts who collected data from the forest (probably including the invaluable film footage) and sent it direct to Washington. Whatever happened to that data and whatever conclusion was reached by the Pentagon, Halt was never told about it. He was promoted soon afterwards and has now retired.

His memo did, however, prompt a question in Parliament in Britain. The answer, essentially from the Ministry of Defence, was the usual one: that whatever happened in Rendlesham Forest, it had no defence significance. The reply did not please Lord Hill-Norton, who has consistently given his point of view on the incident. 'Either the Americans, and indeed the deputy base commander, were hallucinating, or they believed that something had landed there and they had taken photographs and records of it. In either event, it must be of interest to the defence of the United Kingdom.'

What about civilian investigation? Local people had seen lights over the forest, but they were told to keep quiet. One couple, who initially spoke to Brenda Butler and Dot Street of BUFORA, had their property surrounded by barbed wire and MOD signs forbidding entry. Gerald Harris, who lives near the base, saw lights rising and falling and zigzagging through the trees. Living where he does, he is used to aircraft lights, having seen them every night of his life for years. And in any case, the runway was in the opposite direction.

Brenda Butler and Dot Street, joined by author and ufologist Jenny Randles, pursued their inquiries with a number of witnesses. One of these was an airman who used the pseudonym of James Archer. He claimed to have been one of the first men on the scene on 27 December and to have seen an object which was triangular and had three legs. He does not mention aliens (neither does Halt's memo), but he did see unidentified shapes moving about inside the object, which, he said, did not look human. From a virtual hover, Archer saw the object shoot off at high speed – a classic description of the movement of a UFO.

Larry Warren at first used the pseudonym Art Wallace, but subsequently went public with his information. Having been given orders to surround the object glowing in the field, he saw three creatures with large heads and dark eyes (the classic description of a Grey) emerge from the craft and meet briefly with Colonel Gordon Williams, the base commander. Interestingly, Williams has never gone on record about anything to do with the Rendlesham incident. As Warren watched, a smaller triangle detached itself from the main craft and was seen in a clearing nearby. Following the incident, Warren and the rest of his team were debriefed and warned, by 'intelligence types', not to discuss what they had seen. The impression Warren formed was that at least some of the senior personnel out in the forest that night had been expecting the event. That was the reason for all the photographic equipment. The rumour was that the film taken was quickly flown to the American airbase at Ramstein in West Germany, but nothing more was heard of it.

As so often happens, the publication of a book produced more witnesses. When Brenda Butler, Dot Street and Jenny Randles wrote *Sky Crash*, among those who came forward following publication of it's first edition was Sergeant Adrian Bustinza, who not only described the object as huge and saucer-shaped, but confirmed Warren's claim that a number of photographs were taken of it.

There is confusion about Rendlesham, not least when the incidents actually happened. Witnesses' reports differ slightly, and Halt's version, written on 13 January, two weeks after the events described, makes it clear that the lights were seen in the early morning of 27 December, but then refers to the investigations carried out 'the next day' (i.e., 28 December) and beta/gamma readings taken 'the next night' (29 December).

Despite the existence now of the 'Halt Package' for UFO buffs, controversy surrounds the tape. My initial view was that it was a hoax, probably concocted by a group of USAF personnel as a joke. I put this point to a researcher and subsequently received a long letter from Jenny Randles. She believes that the tape is 100 per cent genuine and Lt-Col Halt and others have since confirmed that it is. I accept now that it is genuine, though in many ways it adds little to our understanding of what happened that night. It is fascinating to listen to, and there is no doubt that the men whose voices we hear are genuinely terrified and overawed by what they see. The tape does corroborate one comment in Halt's memo – 'At this time the animals on a nearby farm went into a frenzy.' Someone on the recording says, 'All the barnyard animals have gotten quiet now.' Other witnesses remembered the animal agitation. Was this caused by the low-frequency hum of an alien craft, or, more sinister still, does it have some connection with animal mutilations?

Despite some high-level pressure brought to bear by Lord Hill-Norton, who, it will be remembered, was a chief of the defence staff and chairman of the NATO Military Committee; and from Sir Patrick Wall MP and Ralph Noyes, who was a former head of DS8 himself, nothing concrete was done. When Halt's report became public in 1983, the media had a field day. 'UFO LANDS IN SUFFOLK' trumpeted the *News of the World* on its front page on 2 October. 'And that's official.'

There has been a steady stream of letters from the public over the years, but inevitably, fact and fiction intertwined until Rendlesham Forest became a myth. Rendlesham Forest is the British Roswell – we know that something happened, but we don't know what. I believe the Ministry of Defence squandered a major opportunity by not investigating the incident in detail at the time. The trail has now gone cold: the airbase has gone, the personnel have gone; even a great swathe of the forest has been cut down – on account, some say, of the massive radiation to the trees. Brenda Butler was unable to discover who had felled the trees or what had happened to them.

One aspect of Rendlesham has been consistently ignored by ufologists and yet, to me, it is the most tangible proof that something extraordinary happened there, and that is the radiation readings. I contacted the Defence Radiological Protection Service, attached to Haslar, the Institute of Naval Medicine in Gosport, Hampshire. Contrary to the claim made in *Strange But True?*, the readings were in fact ten times higher than normal, rather than twenty-five. They posed no threat to those present, and the military Geiger counters used were probably designed to measure much higher levels of radiation, so the scale at the lower end might have been less sensitive, making accurate readings difficult. It is also possible that the night hours were not the best time to take readings, although Halt's careful figures – 0.05 and 0.07 rather than the average of 0.06 – suggest that a great deal of precision was involved. Most ufologists have concentrated on the bizarre non-human shapes in the craft and their meeting with senior personnel. It is human nature to focus on the most dramatic and exciting aspects, and this is the stuff of contactee legend, the closest of close encounters. In comparison the actual physical proof of the radiation readings pales into relative insignificance. Yet this does not say much for the general standard of scientific research among ufologists, and does little to enhance their credibility.

So what did happen in Rendlesham Forest? There have been some quite extraordinary attempts to explain away the events described in Lt-Col Halt's report. One comes from science writer Ian Ridpath, whose theory is that the flashing, pulsating lights in the trees were actually the rotating beams from Orford Ness Lighthouse six miles away. A timing of the tape, he says, fits the rhythm of the lighthouse's circuit. He also claims that the six-mile distance would seem like only a few hundred yards at night, and as the men were moving about in the trees, the fixed light would give the impression of moving independently of them.

When Ridpath put forward this explanation in *Strange But True?*, Lt-Col Halt was, I felt, very restrained, in his rebuttal. 'A lighthouse doesn't move through a forest, doesn't explode, doesn't change shape, doesn't send down beams of light.' He might also have added that the Orford Ness Lighthouse had presumably been cheerfully emitting its beams six miles away from the airbase for years. All the personnel at Woodbridge would have seen it operating every single night.

An astronomer, John Mason, describes the re-entry of a Russian rocket that took place that night. It was this coincidence that led me to link Rendlesham with the 1993 sightings I had investigated. No doubt, as Mason contends, the re-entry was seen by many, all over south-east England, and no doubt it created a 'brilliant natural fireball' as it burned up. But, at the risk of repeating myself and paraphrasing Lt-Col Halt, a piece of space debris doesn't move through a forest, doesn't explode, doesn't change shape, doesn't send down beams of light – and doesn't last for over three hours, any more than it did over various parts of Britain in the late March of 1993. But, as in those 'April Fool' sightings, was the rocket re-entry the gap in the curtain an alien force was looking for? Did an unidentified craft slip in behind it, hoping that the re-entry would be assumed to be a single, isolated and explicable event?

Inevitably, one of the theories involved accusations of a cover-up. I have already made the comparison with Roswell, and there were those who went further by suggesting that a nuclear reactor aboard a crashed aircraft had caused the abnormally high radiation levels. I sincerely doubt whether such an accident could have been kept secret from a news-hungry media. It would not have taken much digging to get at the truth if this was some sort of English Chernobyl.

There are other more bizarre theories. My friend Liz Manning, who was brought up very close to Rendlesham Forest, told me of a local legend concerning a German pilot who was killed when his plane was shot down over Suffolk in the Second World War. Perhaps it was his ghost, said by locals to haunt the forest, that pulsated, dripped metal and shattered into pieces without noise and without heat. The indentations in the ground which Halt's men carefully measured were, said the doubters, caused by rabbits (which presumably went on to hop radioactively around Rendlesham).

More and more information about the incident is coming to light. While Charles Halt was in Britain to film *Strange But True?* he gave a lecture to ufologists and confirmed that everything in his report was true. It was not complete, however, partly because he expected full debriefing interrogations of himself and his men during which detailed information would have been provided. That, of course, never happened. He admitted in his lecture that he had seen the objects in the sky and a luminous sphere quite distinctly. He believed that both were controlled by some intelligence. That admission was a crucial one. Perhaps if he had put it in his report, the Ministry of Defence would have taken him more seriously. You never know.

Larry Warren, who returned to Suffolk in 1994 to give an interview to *Network First*, is co-writing a book on his experience, *Left at East Gate*. His co-author is Peter Robbins, who works with abduction expert Budd Hopkins.

We have no proof that an alien craft landed in Rendlesham Forest, but we have no proof that it didn't. Ex-intelligence officer Clifford Stone believes that Washington has the answer, that a highly advanced technology appeared in those Suffolk woods and that there was an intelligence involved. 'That intelligence,' says Stone, 'did not originate on earth.'

'Take me out of the story,' Larry Warren challenges, 'and you still have a story. This one will not go away.'

OFFICIAL FILES,
OFFICIAL STUDIES

Government revolves around bureaucracy. Even in the computer-literate 1990s, this effectively means paperwork. With office space at a premium and paper so bulky to store, certain documents are transferred to microfilm to save space, but an even easier solution is to destroy any that are no longer needed.

All papers, on whatever subject, are kept for at least five years. Any issue may be resurrected. A Parliamentary question triggers many hours of work: digging out the files, checking what action has already been taken, assessing what must be done next. At the end of five years, a decision must be made about what to do with 'dead' files. The process is clearly laid out in the Public Record Act, which covers the disposal or retention of files. On this point, the civil servant has to be pragmatist, politician, archivist and historian rolled into one. Will a particular file be of sufficient interest in the future to warrant its preservation? Clearly files on major policy and operational matters such as the Falklands War would come into this category. We are aware of the importance of the survival of our past now, whereas in the past documents survived haphazardly and by accident. This makes the decision to retain or destroy all the more difficult, and while mundane files will routinely be disposed of five years after the most recent paper, others will be stored to be reviewed again at a later date.

The retained files are passed to the Public Record Office at Kew, where they are made available to the public for inspection thirty years after the date of the most recent paper – the famous 'thirty-year rule'. Other papers must remain confidential for 100 years – criminal cases involving capital crimes, many Foreign and Commonwealth Office papers and, of course, many Ministry of Defence papers which deal with sensitive military and diplomatic topics.

The decision to retain a file rests with the particular branch that opened it in the first place, but there are specialist records-management divisions within government departments and of course the staff at Kew to give advice.

As we have already seen, the notion of a cover-up is very strong in many UFO circles (I shall deal with the topic fully later) and the destruction of files has given rise to a certain paranoia. What has been through the shredder? What is being deliberately hidden from us? The sad fact is that, before 1967, UFO files were not considered to be of any social or historical importance and most were destroyed. This is tragic, because now we have no information on the earliest British UFO sightings. One question often asked is why all this UFO stuff happens in America, and this lack of documentation might provide one answer. Perhaps it happened here too, but we have not kept the evidence. Only in 1967, when there was a rash of sightings and a proportionate rise in public interest, was a decision taken to retain the UFO files themselves. Before that, we are in the dark as far as actual reports are concerned. Were there 'flying saucers' sightings in 1947 that might have matched those of Kenneth Arnold? Did we liaise with the Americans? There was a UFO radar sighting by Bentwaters military base in Suffolk in 1956, but the file has gone. How did we formulate policy in the first place? When, for instance, did my own post come into being? We can answer none of these questions with confidence.

The good news is that through the sort of error that sometimes happens in any bureaucracy, or perhaps because of the interest of some forgotten archivist at the Public Record Office, a few of the ministry's earliest files escaped the fire. The references for these are listed in Appendix 6 of this book (the file numbers given are those of the Public Record Office). Anyone wanting to inspect them can go along to Kew. As they are in the public domain, they can even be photocopied – government at its most open!

In fact, most of the 1960s files are pretty unexciting. The format differs little from that of the files I used. They largely contain reports of UFO sightings together with Ministry of Defence replies offering whatever explanation seemed most rational at the time. Other papers include general exchanges of correspondence – people asking about the official position on UFOs or putting forward theories. Appended to each is the stock ministry line about the lack of evidence of a threat posed to the United Kingdom.

Easily the most interesting file from the historical perspective is PREM 11/855, which is reproduced in its entirety in Appendix 7. By 1952, Winston Churchill had had a long and extraordinary career. The failed scholar, indifferent soldier and over-the-top writer had moved on to a rollercoaster political career, but by this time in his life he was unassailable, indisputably the 'grand old man' of the twentieth century who had already enjoyed his finest hour. 'What does all this stuff about flying saucers amount to?' he asked the Air Ministry. 'What can it mean? What is the truth? Let me have a report at your convenience.' Churchill's words ring down the generations still. 'What can it mean? What is the truth?'

The rather aloof reply from the Air Ministry refers to an intelligence study carried out in 1951. Although there are no other references to this, its conclusions are set out in the reply to Churchill and do not differ widely from the sort of explanation I was giving to people while at the UFO desk. 'Known astronomical or meteorological phenomena' (meteors and meteorites, but not then, of course, space debris); 'mistaken identification of conventional aircraft, balloons, birds etc.'; 'optical illusions' (e.g., cloud formations); 'psychological delusions' (which we might, forty years on, be more inclined to be charitable about) and 'deliberate hoaxes'. What is interesting is the reference to the Americans having carried out similar investigations in 1948–9 (very shortly after Arnold's famous sighting) and having reached similar conclusions. This implies a level of liaison with the States, but it might also have been mentioned to reassure Churchill, whose mother was American and who was very popular on the other side of the Atlantic. The problem with this was that the American authorities had *not* reached similar conclusions. A 1952 CIA memorandum reported that since 1947 the Air Technical Intelligence Center had received 1500 UFO reports, 20 per cent of which remained unexplained.

The other interesting reference is to William of Occam's razor. Occam (1285–1349) propounded the theory that a simple explanation is very often the correct one, and that a complex solution should not be put forward if a simpler one is equally valid – 'Do not multiply entities beyond necessity.'

The obvious shortfall in the Air Ministry's reply is that it does not address cases that appear to defy explanation. In 1952, the most obvious were the foo fighters, the inexplicable lights that trailed Allied and Axis pilots during the Second World War. Numerous reports of these were made by Bomber and Fighter groups and certainly found their way to the Air Ministry. The reply to Churchill is not a lie *per se*, but it is selective, presumably because the whole subject had not acquired the reputation or the following it now enjoys and because the ministry considered the whole thing a waste of time. They didn't believe in little green men, so they rejected everything else as well. William of Occam has much to answer for.

If Churchill had been aware of the details contained in one of the other surviving files from this period, he would never have been palmed off with the Air Ministry's reply in the way we must presume he was. It is unfortunate that the incident occurred after Churchill had had his reply. On 19 September 1952, Flight Lieutenant J. Kilburn of 269 Squadron was standing with six RAF colleagues at the airbase at Topcliffe, between Ripon and Thirsk in Yorkshire, watching a Meteor jet fighter going through its paces. Suddenly, one of them, Flying Officer Paris,

> noticed a white object in the sky at a height between 10,000ft and 20,000ft some five miles astern of the Meteor. The object was silver in colour and circular in shape and appeared to be travelling at a much slower speed than the Meteor, but on a similar course. It maintained the slow forward speed for a few seconds before commencing to descend, swinging in a peculiar motion during descent similar to a falling sycamore leaf. This was at first thought to be a parachute or engine cowling. The Meteor, meanwhile, turned towards Dishforth and the object, while continuing its descent, appeared to follow suit.
>
> After a further few seconds, the object stopped its pendulous motion and its descent and began to rotate about its own axis. Suddenly, it accelerated at an incredible speed towards the west, turning on to a south-easterly heading before disappearing.

All this occurred in a matter of fifteen to twenty seconds. The acceleration was in excess of that of a shooting star. I have never seen such a phenomenon before. The movements of the object were not identifiable with anything I have seen in the air and the rate of acceleration was unbelieveable.

This is a classic sighting from a time before the contactee era. It was confirmed by members of the public whose reports are also in the file. Six trained pilots saw something remarkable for which there was no official explanation, and yet the matter was dropped. The silver object was apparently under intelligent control and manoeuvring in ways that our own military hardware could not hope to match. It was a clear case of something about which the Minstry of Defence should have been very concerned indeed.

As more and more of these files become available under the thirty-year rule, we shall at least be able to chart something of the history of British ufology. One word of warning to those who might wish to make a study of them: the American Freedom of Information Act has resulted in a glut of previously withheld information reaching the public domain (the report of Lt-Col Halt on the Rendlesham Forest incident is a good example). I personally applaud the fact that these documents are now available for public scrutiny, but one side-effect is the scope for forgery. Ironically, the release of genuine UFO documents has helped hoaxers by providing them with blueprints for official documents, the names of genuine departments and personnel to use and signatures to copy. This has already happened in America, and it has bogged researchers down, clouded issues and wasted a great deal of time.

Perhaps the most famous example of the controversy generated by the possibility of forgeries is the series of documents known as Majestic-12. We are still nowhere near understanding what actually happened at Roswell, New Mexico in 1947, but the consensus remains that the American government was guilty of a colossal cover-up.

The investigative committee allegedly set up by Truman to report to him personally consisted of twelve senior officials who gave the project its name, Majestic-12. They were Dr Vannevar Bush, head of the Office of Scientific Research, which had recently developed the atomic bomb; Rear Admiral Roscoe Hillenkoetter, a former director of the CIA; Lloyd Berkner, former secretary of the Joint Research and Development Board; Dr Detlev Bronk, a prominent scientist; James Forrestal, former Secretary of Defense; Gordon Gray, Truman's special assistant; Dr Jerome Hunsaker, head of the Department of Mechanical and Aeronautical Engineering at Massachusetts Institute of Technology; Dr Donald Menzel, an astronomer who was the foremost debunker of UFOs of his generation; General Robert Montague, commander of the Sandia military base at Albuquerque; Rear-Admiral Sidney Souers, secretary to the National Security Council; General Nathan Twining, commander of the Wright-Patterson Air Force Base and General Hoyt Vandenberg, director of Central Intelligence. As all these men are now dead, we have to rely solely on the surviving documentation they were alleged to have produced. It is by no means certain that these twelve were ever involved in such an organisation or indeed that the organisation itself ever existed.

The documents first came to light after an American television producer was sent a roll of film anonymously through the post. It transpired that Truman's signature at the bottom of one of the Majestic-12 documents was identical to his signature on another, totally unrelated document. Graphologists agree that no two signatures are ever identical, which makes it likely that this had simply been photocopied from the other document. We have now reached a position of bluff and double-bluff. Ten years after the first public appearance of Majestic-12, the debate is still raging on. One theory contends that the documents are totally genuine and that Roswell is probably one of many incidents the American government are keeping secret. Another has it that only some of the documents have been released ('leaked' under the Freedom of Information Act) as part of a conditioning process by which the public can slowly become acclimatised to the existence of real UFOs. Yet another is that Majestic-12 is a gloriously realised piece of disinformation, a story of crashed saucers and dead aliens so manifestly ludicrous that it has been designed to reduce the credibility of all UFO sightings. The final theory is the most obvious to non-ufologists: that UFO researchers themselves have fabricated the evidence for personal reasons. Names have even been put forward as likely culprits, and there are some indications that the forger had inside knowledge of the intelligence community. The 'official' line is that the documents were not released at all, under the Freeedom of Information Act or anything else, and are therefore complete fakes.

The motivation for the forgery of UFO documents varies, but basically the reasons are the same as those that inspire hoaxes in any other sphere of life. The first, obviously, is financial. There is undoubtedly money to be made in the field of UFO research. A convincing photograph or a gripping abduction account has led to the production of hundreds of books and films over the years. The second is to gain attention. Although virtually all of my witness contacts wanted to avoid publicity, the same cannot be said of everyone. There are those who love their moment of glory, the flash of the cameras, the sight of their names in print. Thirdly, there are genuine believers who see nothing wrong in forging the odd document to reinforce their case in an attempt to persuade others. What these people are actually doing, of course, is undermining serious scientific UFO research and putting the clock back untold years. Finally, there are the practical jokers, like Doug and Dave, who admitted to hoaxing crop circles all over southern England in the 1980s. Love 'em or hate 'em, the world is stuck with the earthly, as well as the cosmic, jokers.

One new source of valuable information has opened up in recent years. With the Soviet Union's last – benevolent – dictator, Mikhail Gorbachev, came *perestroika*, *glasnost* and ultimately the collapse of the union in 1990. As a direct result of the new openness, the former USSR has unlocked its archives, which contain some sensational UFO-related material, and allowed its citizens to speak out for the first time since Lenin offered them bread, peace and land in 1917.

In Moscow, a state-funded organisation is now researching into new propulsion systems based on UFO reports under the directorship of open-minded scientist Dr Anatoly Akimov.

General-Major Boris Suriokov told the *Network First* documentary team in 1994 that while he was flying Soviet bombers during the Second World War, his plane encountered an object that electrically charged it. Fearing an explosion, he ordered his bomber to jettison the bombs and reported the mission as a success for fear of reprisals. He drew the object for the cameras and compared it with 'a miniature sunset', but flying at great speed. It was totally unlike the anti-aircraft flashes of the time, and totally unlike anything the Russians or Americans have launched since, for that matter.

More recently, on 20 September 1977, over 170 guards and other military personnel at Petrozavodsk on the Finnish border saw a large object glowing in the sky at four o'clock in the morning. It was observed for a total of four hours, for fifteen minutes of which it appeared to rain down beams of light, before moving in the direction of Finland. Troops and police on the ground who tried to report it found that their radio frequencies were jammed and their telephones wouldn't work.

This sighting led to an exercise that no British government has ever undertaken and one which Colonel Boris Sokolov, head of the investigation team at Petrozavodsk, admitted to *Network First* was an experiment that would never be repeated either. The Soviet Ministry of Defence and the Academy of Sciences mounted an observation team of the entire Russian armed forces – over 6 million men and women, as well as civilians – to watch the skies. People covering one-sixth of the world's geographical area were on the lookout for UFOs.

Fascinating as this all is, a great deal of faked material is also coming out of the East. Living in the crippled economies of the old Warsaw Pact countries are thousands of people barely able to afford food for the table. Suddenly, along come American UFO researchers with hard cash, ready and willing to pay in dollars for information on UFOs. The temptation to satisfy the demand with the help of an old typewriter and a modicum of knowledge must be great. The results could well bog us down for years.

Invaluable though the older files are, in Britain and elsewhere, the danger of becoming too wrapped up in historical research must be avoided. Like crimes, ufological mysteries will usually either be solved straight away or not at all. As time elapses, the trail goes cold. If we are to find the answer to the UFO question it will be 'out there' in the field, so we must concentrate on the cases of the here and now rather than the faded papers of yesterday.

So would it not help if all the old files and papers were released? The UFO lobby argue that the Ministry of Defence's UFO files should be exempt from the thirty-year rule and deposited immediately in the Public Record Office. In the case of UFO reports, they say, the thirty-year rule achieves only two effects, both of them negative. First, it fosters suspicion and mistrust, and secondly, it denies good researchers the chance to follow up reports. Larry Warren was nineteen at the time of the Rendlesham Forest incident. Had his evidence been subject to the thirty-year rule, he would have been forty-nine before his account saw the light of day. So many memories, so much detail, could be lost in that time. If a particular report contains no information that could be considered classified now (irrespective of the classification applied at the time), then many see no reason why the file should not be released. Although such a move would probably not convince a die-hard conspiracy theorist (he or she would simply decide that the files had been doctored or certain crucial ones suppressed), it would go some way towards satisfying those serious ufologists who have always sought co-operation with the government. The legislation already in fact allows for a degree of flexibility on the thirty-year rule: it would not be a massive operation to take it a degree further. So runs the theory.

Another proposal which they advance is for the Ministry of Defence to release cases as they come in. By deleting the name and address of the witness to ensure confidentiality, photocopies of these reports could be sent to, say, BUFORA and Quest, perhaps on a monthly basis. The raw data could be accompanied by a survey of the ministry's activity in relation to its own follow-up and any conclusions drawn. Might we then be able to answer Winston Churchill's question?

We certainly cannot do so unless we have access to all the facts. Could there be more UFO files that have survived the orgy of destruction that many within the UFO lobby find so suspicious?

Although at the ministry I hadn't found any unexpected UFO material, I hadn't had the time to conduct anything more than a cursory search. Conspiracy theorists would tell me that hundreds of UFO files could be hidden elsewhere, away from the public gaze, and yet I felt that if there were documents still waiting to be discovered, they were probably among the hundreds of thousands of other files kept at the Public Record Office at Kew. This idea dovetailed with the suspicions of those who believed there was a cover-up; after all, the best place to hide a tree is in a forest.

I paid a visit to Kew, ostensibly to check that members of the public could access all the files I claimed were in the public domain, but I was also curious to see whether there were any clues to the existence of other files.

My visit proved very interesting. Even though I was armed with references for the files I wanted to see, it took some time to retrieve them. I certainly pitied anyone who turned up without the numbers to try to track down any material on UFOs. They would be in for an uphill slog.

If the files are there, how did it happen? Remember that disposing of files is a difficult business; desk officers will send files to specialist archive sections within their own departments, with recommendations about their ultimate disposal. They consequently lose sight of old files, and may not be directly involved with their fate. Add to this the confusion that can arise from the differing titles a file can be given. Modern ufologists expect them all be marked 'UFOs', but life is not that simple. The term 'UFO' would not have been used in the late 1940s, for example, when 'flying saucer' would have been the norm. Other more bland terms might have been invented by civil servants or military officers anxious not to be seen as cranks: 'Miscellaneous breaches of the UK Air Defence Region', or 'anomalous radar returns', perhaps. UFO reports might be tucked away inside files on more general topics, such as security alerts, or in the routine log books kept by military bases to record any noteworthy incidents. Specific events might be placed on separate files, with a title like 'Incident at Rendlesham Forest, December 1980'.

Given these factors, it is not inconceivable that there are UFO files somewhere in the system that I never saw. What they contain, I can only guess at, but it is my hope that we might yet salvage material from the early days of the UFO mystery, when analyses were undertaken, when liaison with the Americans occurred, and when Prime Ministers were interested enough to ask what it all meant.

The United States of America has more UFO activity than any other country – or at least, more of it is reported. America has a proportionately greater number of civilian UFO groups than anywhere else in the world, which ensures a higher level of coverage of the subject than is the case in other countries. There is perhaps something in the American psyche which enables people to accept the extraterrestrial hypothesis more readily than any other nationality. Every phase of ufology had its first airing in America: Kenneth Arnold's sighting led to the 'saucer' concept; George Adamski was the first contactee, Betty and Barney Hill the first abductees to report their experience. It is almost, as John Spencer says in *The UFO Encyclopedia*, as if the world waits for an American go-ahead before similar incidents occur elsewhere. Even Britain's most celebrated encounter, at Rendlesham Forest, involved Americans.

The American government has carried out a number of official studies into UFOs. The motives behind this have been questioned. To some, it is simply a matter of genuine curiosity and uncertainty about the multiplicity of reports of ghost aircraft, foo fighters and flying saucers. To others, particularly after the Roswell experience, official interest was born out of the sure knowledge that UFOs were real, that they were extraterrestrial craft and they needed to be investigated, thoroughly and urgently. In a sense, however the motive doesn't matter – it is the methodology and the results of such studies that are all-important.

The United States Air Force study of UFOs began just two months after Roswell, in September 1947. This developed into Project Sign, at the time nicknamed Project Saucer, whose headquarters were at the Wright–Patterson Air Force Base in Dayton, Ohio (the supposed final depository for whatever it was that crashed near Roswell). Setting the pattern that has come to plague much UFO study over the years, Project Sign was dogged by controversy and three distinct camps emerged. One group believed that UFOs were foreign aircraft or reconnaissance devices, probably from the USSR – after all, Churchill's 'Iron Curtain' was only a year old. The second rejected the whole concept, rather as the British Air Ministry was to do in response to the Prime Minister's memo in 1952, and recited the usual chorus of birds, clouds, weather balloons and hoaxes. The third group came to believe that UFOs were in fact extraterrestrial craft. This faction produced a paper, 'Estimate of the Situation', and passed it up the chain of command to the top brass at the Pentagon. The report went to General Hoyt S. Vandenberg, allegedly a member of Majestic-12, who had, by 1948, become US Air Force chief of staff. He classified the document 'Top Secret'.

'Estimate of the Situation' was rejected by the Pentagon, and it soon became clear that Project Sign was so bogged down with internal bickerings that it was pointless carrying on. In a last attempt to break the deadlock, the air force sought the views of the wider scientific community. One of the key figures here was Dr Donald Menzel, professor of astronomy at Harvard University, who, in keeping with the vast majority of astronomers worldwide, spoke out strongly against the extraterrestrial hypothesis. To Menzel, UFO reports were either hoaxes, psychological delusions or mirages. This rationale was woefully inadequate, but the influence of a Harvard professor was enormous and the orthodox scientific community closed ranks against anyone who put forward anything more exotic. Furthermore, it should be remembered that Menzel himself was alleged to be a member of Majestic-12, and is now known to have had a lengthy association with the CIA and the National Security Agency. Before it was wound up, Sign's last report, in February 1949, claimed that 20 per cent of reported cases were unexplained. Its remaining members urged a full-blown investigation into UFOs.

Instead, they got Project Grudge. The name itself speaks volumes for the attitude of its members, and indeed there was a distinct lack of enthusiasm among the personnel brought in to staff the project. True, there was no trace of the dissent that had plagued Sign, but that was because the united front was now one of unalloyed scepticism. Blinkers and preconceptions were the order of the day, with military personnel reports being accepted in favour of civilian or maverick scientific ones. Despite the fact that Grudge received 23 per cent more reports of UFOs than Sign, its final recommendation was that the UFO study should be reduced in terms of time, personnel and money. All the unexplained reports were listed under the dismissive heading of 'Psychological'.

Conspiracy theorists found the change of official attitude from Sign to Grudge – projects that were less than a year apart – inexplicable. Unless, of course, Grudge was simply a puppet, and behind the scenes a terrified Pentagon was frantically working to cope with what were, after all, genuine alien sightings. Whatever the truth, the United States Air Force's investigation went into its third phase in 1952 under the codename Project Blue Book. Unlike its predecessors, this one ran and ran – it wasn't finally closed down until 1969 – and unlike Sign and Grudge, its profile was high. Its first chief was Edward Ruppelt of Air Force Intelligence, who had not yet, it seems, gone over to the debunkers. Instead, still working at the Wright–Patterson Air Force Base, he instituted new scientific techniques and appointed open-minded Dr J. Allen Hynek as chief scientific adviser. Hynek had worked on Project Sign, but played no real part in Project Grudge.

It was this very vigour, however, that gave rise to the chief criticism of Blue Book. It seemed to many that the unexciting cases were being rigorously pursued, with careful follow-ups, interviews with witnesses, and so on, at the expense of the more bizarre incidents, which were labelled 'Unidentified' or 'Insufficient Data'. Yet it was precisely these cases that Blue Book had been set up to clarify, and therefore they should have been subject to the greatest scrutiny.

Appendix 8 of this book lists the official sightings reported to the United States Air Force between 1947 and 1965. The huge boost in 1952 (from 169 to 1,501 cases) marks Ruppelt's time as co-ordinator of Blue Book, but the percentage of unidentified cases swings wildly, from 20 per cent in 1952 to 1.4 per cent in 1957. The average for this period is 6.4 per cent, a figure which accords broadly with the British estimation of today. I am wary of using any Blue Book statistics, as I do not believe that, in later years, cases were investigated in a thorough or open-minded way, but the bottom line is this: the American Air Force admitted that a total of 646 sightings (and remember, these are likely to be only the tip of the iceberg) were unexplainable by rational means.

Ruppelt left the air force in 1953 and subsequently published some extraordinary information in his 1956 book *The Report on Unidentified Flying Objects*. Perhaps because of pressure from the forces or government circles, he later 'slept with the enemy', modifying his earlier findings. He died of a heart attack in 1960.

In the late 1950s and early 1960s, Blue Book became less and less open-minded and more akin to Project Grudge. In fact, its debunking activities were now so effective that the team's enlightened elements, like Hynek, could not persuade NASA or any other research organisation to take on the data they had amassed. The scientific establishment did not want to know. In 1965, however, a new wave of sightings led to the formation of an independent scientific team which first met in February 1966 under Dr Brian O'Brien. For the first time, headway was made. Gerald Ford, later US President and then a congressman, ensured that the O'Brien recommendations for university research into UFOs were adopted. Ford also pressed for Blue Book's file to be made public, but this idea was rejected.

The air force invited a team from the University of Colorado to carry out a two-year study into the phenomenon. It was headed by Dr Edward Condon, a nuclear physicist of international reputation who had worked on the development of radar, the atomic bomb and the design of space capsules. Unfortunately for ufology, he was highly sceptical of the whole subject, openly ridiculing the more off-the-wall cases. It didn't help that Condon's number two was Robert Low, who, in August 1966, wrote a memo which rendered Condon's whole report, submitted two years later, meaningless:

> The trick would be, I think, to describe the project so that, to the public, it would appear a totally objective study but, to the scientific community, would present the image of a group of non-believers trying their best to be objective, but having an almost zero expectation of finding a saucer.

Some might view Low's private correspondence as an example of healthy scepticism; I find it an example of blinkered bigotry. By the end of the two years, two members of the team had been sacked and the administrative assistant had resigned.

The Condon report, or the 'Scientific Study of Unidentified Flying Objects', was produced at the end of 1968. Condon concluded that 'little if anything has come from the study of UFOs in the past twenty-one years which has added to scientific knowledge'.

This may have been music to the air force's ears, and Project Blue Book was duly officially closed down by the secretary of the air force, Robert Seamans Jr. His press release said: 'The continuation of Project Blue Book cannot be justified either on grounds of national security or in the interest of science.' It further concluded:

> No UFO reported, investigated and evaluated by the Air Force has ever given any indication of being a threat to our national security. There has been no evidence submitted or covered by the Air Force that sightings categorized as unidentified represent techno-logical developments or principles beyond the range of present-day scientific knowledge. There has been no evidence that sightings categorized as unidentified are of extraterrestrial vehicles.

The suspicion was that the Condon report had been a set-up, designed to give the air force a cop-out clause, a chance to extricate itself from what had become an increasingly embar-rassing problem with too many unanswered questions. Robert Low's memo makes it perfectly clear that the report's conclusions and recommendations were pre-planned. In fact, the Condon committee completely ignored many of the most fascinating cases from Project Blue Book. Of the ninety recent cases that the committee had examined, even after Condon's researches, nearly 30 per cent still remained unexplained.

Undoubtedly the most positive aspect to come out of all this paper-shuffling was the part played by J. Allen Hynek. As an astronomer, he began his work with Sign as something of a sceptic, but, as a scientist who probably had more access than any other to UFO reports and witnesses, he became convinced that there was a hard core of good-quality sightings that were neither cases of misidentification nor hoaxes. Becoming increasingly frustrated with the biased prejudice of those charged with looking open-mindedly into the UFO phenomenon, he distanced himself from Condon and Low and made several public criticisms of Project Blue Book. When it was closed in 1969, he determined to carry on.

The result was the Center for UFO Studies (CUFOS), set up in 1973. Based in Illinois, it continues to operate, scientifically and objectively, today. Since Hynek's death in 1986, it has been renamed the J. Allen Hynek Center for UFO Studies.

Another series of projects dedicated to honest research is known collectively as the Search for Extraterrestrial Intelligence (SETI) programmes. SETI's standpoint is a curious anomaly as far as UFOs are concerned, because while it holds that intelligent life may exist on other planets, it does not accept that that life has the technology to reach Earth. Much of SETI's work involves beaming messages into space via radio frequencies and listening for signals that might be artificial in origin. These programmes, co-ordinated by NASA, have been very well funded. The latest, which began in 1992, had a budget of $100 million although they are now privately-funded. SETI is currently conducting two parallel searches – a general sky search, which probes for signals, and a targeted search of each of the 100 nearest stars to our own sun. The results so far have been inconclusive, with no real evidence of artificially created signals being picked up, despite the odd anomalous return.

We are still, as we have done for centuries, asking the age-old question, 'Is there anybody out there?'

THE COVER-UP

G room Lake, Nevada is described by *UFO Magazine* as 'one of the most inhospitable places on Earth'. It lies in the desert 120 miles north-west of Las Vegas, in Emigrant Valley. Groom Lake is not shown on any modern American map. The older maps call it 'Area 51' and there can be no more secret place in the world.

In Chapter 1, we looked at the distinct possibility that the rash of sightings in the 1890s and before the First World War were in reality airships and aircraft being built in what was arguably the world's first arms race. We know that Germany and Britain were racing each other in a bid to build the biggest, fastest and most deadly warships, so why not planes as well? This notion is likely to be the explanation of some UFO sightings today, and Area 51 is the most likely home of some decidedly unconventional aircraft.

We know that prototypes of aircraft like the Stealth fighters and bombers will have been built and tested years before they are commissioned for service. These tests, for obvious reasons of secrecy, will probably have been made at night. Even a pilot in the 1970s, seeing the black triangle of a Stealth fighter hurtling past at high speeds, might well have filed a UFO report. For such a revolutionary aircraft would be unknown to most of the military – its existence would be strictly on a need-to-know basis. If the witness's account appears in a UFO magazine, rather than in serious journals like *Flight International* or *Jane's Defence Weekly*, it is all the more fortunate as far as confidentiality is concerned. And if the mainstream media bother with it at all, it will be in the usual tongue-in-cheek silly-season way and the protoype secret will remain secure.

Take this argument a stage further. Knowing that prototype aircraft are likely to be reported as UFOs and consequently ignored by most people, mightn't a shrewd designer hit upon the idea of making an aircraft look like a flying saucer? Look at some of the designs in *Jane's All the World's Aircraft*. Let one example suffice: the Chance–Vought 'Flying Flapjack', also known as the Navy Flounder. This aircraft, built in the pre-jet age, was of an irregular saucer shape and could take off nearly vertically, fly as slowly as 35mph an hour, yet reach speeds of more than 400mph. In other words, in flight behaviour and appearance, it had all the attributes of a classic UFO.

Carry this idea to its logical conclusion and someone may well have come up with a circular craft with a bank of rotating coloured lights, just like something out of Spielberg's *Close Encounters*. Imagine that this craft can drop bombs using a laser designator to mark its target, which is the technique employed to such devastating effect in the Gulf War, enabling bombs to be put through skylights in the roofs of specific buildings. A saucer-shaped craft, with rotating coloured lights, firing a beam of light at the ground? A craft that is stealthy – that is, almost undetectable by radar? Consider the use of such a machine in a war: an unrecognisable warplane, which, if seen, is dismissed by the military and scientists as just another UFO. Take out a few key military bases with it; hit command and control centres, radar sites, communications centres. This would be a decisive first blow in a war without the need for nuclear weapons. An idea worth developing? Very probably. Has it been done? I don't know. It depends on what you believe about Aurora.

On the question of Aurora, ufologists are joined by aviation journalists and 'groupies'. The story started in 1985, when the American Department of Defense issued a budgetary document which outlined funding for a variety of projects. Most of these were well known, and to journalists used to keeping their ears and eyes open around government circles, carried no surprises. Except one. Under the section entitled 'Strategic Reconnaissance' was a reference to a project called Aurora. Not only had nobody ever heard of it, but nobody in government was prepared to answer questions on it, either. Was its inclusion an error, a glitch left in by a careless computer operator when the document was being declassified for press release? Whatever it was, it appeared to be a secret or 'black' project, and an expensive one at that. The sum quoted was $2 billion over the subsequent two years alone.

The Lockheed SR-71 spy plane, itself the successor to the CIA's A-12, was officially retired in 1990, although a few have now been recalled to active duty. Aviation experts agree that this aircraft, capable of flying at nearly 100,000ft, could not be taken out of service unless there was something better to take its place. Hopeless optimists might argue that now the Cold War is over, the era of the spy plane is no more; that it has been consigned to the history books along with the U-2 and the Cuban Missile Crisis of 1962–3. Technologists might argue that in the age of the satellite, aircraft themselves are unnecessary. But satellite orbits are known, and consequently it is possible to schedule sensitive activities around them. Even cloud cover causes problems, despite the infra-red cameras that most satellites now routinely carry.

In the late 1980s, speculation grew about a replacement for the SR-71 which was hypersonic, that is, capable of travelling at many times the speed of sound. Such an aircraft could only be 'black', and it would be expensive.

The role of Groom Lake as a secret airbase began in 1954. The CIA gave the giant Lockheed Aircraft Corporation the contract – and this land in the middle of nowhere – to develop a spy plane capable of greater altitudes than anything then available. In 1984 another 89,000 acres was grabbed by the government, and there was a further attempt to expand in 1993. Access to the base is strictly forbidden. There are warning signs everywhere, some featuring the threat 'Use of deadly force authorised'. It is still possible to see into the base from three local vantage points – White Sides Mountain, Freedom Ridge and Tikaboo Peak. Local computer programmer Glenn Campbell, from Rachel, a nearby hamlet, has compiled a visitors' guide, complete with information on how to evade security patrols – the 'Cammo Dudes' – and even what to do if you're caught.

Sightseers regularly witness mysterious lights over Area 51 at night and are regularly watched by military personnel in unmarked black helicopters. It was in 1989 that the lights and rumblings often associated with UFO sightings were noticed for the first time. Witnesses reported hearing a pulsing noise and seeing ringed contrails, which gave rise to speculation that a radical new type of engine called Pulsed Detonation was in use. It is in the S-4 section of Area 51, 10–15 miles south of Groom Lake, beside Papoose Dry Lake, that engineer Bob Lazar claims he worked in the late 1980s on reverse-engineering and testing alien craft. It is impossible to prove that Lazar is telling the truth, but on the other hand, it is impossible to prove he isn't.

There is some evidence that Aurora, if it exists, has been operating over Britain. A report sent to the Ministry of Defence tells of two men out walking at Calvine, a remote area twenty miles north of Pitlochry near Blair Atholl in Tayside. It was 4 August 1990. The two men became aware of a low humming sound and turned to see a large diamond-shaped object which hovered for about ten minutes before flying off vertically at great speed. What was really intriguing was that a Harrier jet also made a number of low-level passes, as if the pilot had seen the object as well and was homing in for a closer look. One of the men on the ground had a camera and sent the photographs he took to both the ministry and the *Scottish Daily Record*. The Harrier remains untraced; the object unidentified. I kept a blow-up of one of his photographs on my office wall until one day my Head of Division noticed it and took it away.

Expert analysis had revealed that the photographs were not fakes, but neither the experts nor I accepted the Aurora theory. And even if it exists, it is most unlikely that Aurora could function in the way described in the encounter. It seemed to me to be the perfect way for UFO sceptics to explain away a difficult sighting. The Calvine report remains one of the most intriguing cases in the Ministry of Defence's files. The conclusions, however are depressingly familiar: object unexplained, case closed, no further action.

Calvine was not the only possible Aurora sighting. On 5 November 1990, a patrol of RAF Tornados was flying over the North Sea when they were overtaken at high speed by what the pilots could only describe as a large aircraft of some sort.

In 1991 came the most peculiar reports. The United States Geological Survey recorded on their earthquake-monitoring equipment a series of strange sonic booms. They were able to calculate from their data that an airborne object had been travelling at a speed of at least Mach 3. In other words, it was moving at three times the speed of sound, some 2,100mph. And it was heading for the Nellis Air Force Base in the middle of Area 51. At around the same time, an RAF air-traffic controller reported having tracked a target in the vicinity of RAF Machrihanish on the remote Kintyre Peninsula on Scotland's west coast at a similar astonishing speed. Other witnesses claimed to have seen odd aircraft shaped like paper darts in the area. The rumour grew that not only did Aurora exist, but that it was undergoing test flights between the United States and the UK, stopping overnight at RAF Machrihanish. The remote base would certainly be suitable for such a purpose: it is as forbidding in its own way as Area 51, with watchtowers and miles of barbed wire fences. It looks like a prison camp.

The American authorities have always vigorously denied the existence of Aurora. The then secretary of the air force, Donald Rice, stated categorically that the United States had no aircraft remotely resembling the descriptions being circulated about Aurora. If there really is no Aurora, what is it that are we dealing with?

Questions were asked in the House. Did the government know about Aurora or any other craft operating clandestinely in our airspace? The MP's question, together with the response from the minister for the armed forces was as follows:

> **Mr Llew Smith**: To ask the secretary of state for defence how many Aurora prototype aircraft of the United States Air Force are based at the Machrihanish Air Force Base in Argyll, and for what period permission has been given for basing these aircraft in the United Kingdom.
>
> **Mr Soames**: There are no United States Air Force prototype aircraft based at RAF Machrihanish and no authorisation has been given by Her Majesty's government to the United States Air Force, or any other US body, to operate such aircraft within or from the United Kingdom.

It was a cheeky question, because it made the assumption that Aurora exists.

Another MP tried an oblique approach, not mentioning Aurora at all. Mr Soames' response was as follows: 'No new types of high-altitude, long-range reconnaissance aircraft have been based or are being considered for basing in the UK.'

Formal inquiries were made through the American embassy in London and all relevant American military branches. They were all pressurised to tell us whether such an aircraft exists, and they all assured us it didn't.

If this is a lie, the consequences for Anglo-American relations would be dire, and it would seem foolish in the extreme to jeoparadise such a strong alliance for the sake of an aircraft, however technologically dazzling. In fact, when inquiries were made with the Americans, they intimated that they themselves were wondering whether some of their own UFO sightings might not be British experimental aircraft. This was either the most brilliant of double-bluffs or the Americans – those I spoke to, at least – do not have an Aurora at all.

There is a lighthearted side to the Aurora controversy. An American toy manufacturer has produced a model which they claim is a faithful representation of the phantom craft. It is shaped like an arrowhead and has a smaller, piloted craft mounted on top, rather as the space shuttle was mounted on top of a Jumbo jet as part of its initial testing programme. When speculation was rife about the Stealth fighter, similar excited rumours spread. Toys were produced, aviation experts wrote critiques and drew sketches. When the Stealth fighter was finally unveiled to the world, some were right, some were not. We shall have to wait and see whether the Aurora toy lives up to expectations – assuming that Aurora, exists, of course!

The serious question is, if there is an Aurora and it isn't American, who does own it? And are they flying, unimpeded, over our airspace? If Aurora does not exist, and never has done, what is it that has been seen in our skies? My Head of Division would have had to do some serious rethinking about the photograph that he took off my wall. If military planners are using the UFO phenomenon to mask the development of increasingly advanced aircraft, are these machines, as Bob Lazar and others contend, in fact the product of research into genuine alien vehicles? Or, just as sinister, could alien intelligence be using 'black' projects as a cover, relying on scientists and military and government personnel to write off an unexplained triangle in the sky as just another secret prototype they don't know about? Who exactly is fooling whom?

Occasionally, at parties, people would come up to me, drink in hand, and say, 'What do you do for a living?' The reply 'I investigate UFOs for the government,' was guaranteed to be something of a showstopper. Invariably, though, being surrounded by a circle of intrigued people gave me an opportunity to gauge public opinion. A few scoffed, of course, but most were fascinated and their enquiries were quite intense. One question, above all, would be asked over and over again. 'Is there an official cover-up?' My answer was always 'Not in Britain'.

All I can say is that I am telling the truth. I hope that the ufologists I have worked with and who know me accept that I have never told a lie on this subject and never will. Quite apart from any personal code of honour, to tell one lie would completely undermine my position. It would be like removing one card from a house of cards – tell one lie and the whole fabric collapses. This entire book is pointless if for one moment one reader regards it as fiction.

There are those who will not accept this. Some con-spiracy theorists will assume that I am guilty because I am the spokesperson, as they see it, of a guilty government; others may be able to divorce the two. They may be quite prepared to accept my honesty, but will maintain that I have been the innocent dupe of unscrupulous masters. This group believes that secret studies and projects are going on all the time, for whatever sinister reason, and they would contend that I was simply not briefed about them. It is of course possible that there is a caucus in the civil service, a sort of Praetorian Guard, who know the truth and call the shots, and that the rest of us are merely pawns in their all-powerful game. But such arguments merely result in the sort of stand-off I did my best to avoid in my three years in the job.

From a practical point of view, if I was deliberately kept in the dark about the UFO phenomenon, the situation would have been unworkable. I was the only member of the civil service with the responsibility to check UFO reports. Anyone wishing to manipulate this information would have had to have gone through me to obtain the relevant data and to find out who knew what in the world of ufology. No such approaches were ever made.

In short, I have worked for ten years in the civil service and I am convinced that the UK government is in no way involved in a UFO cover-up.

So why is the conspiracy theory so persistent? The major reason, I'm afraid, is that the Americans have muddied the waters. Ground Saucer Watch (GSW), an American UFO group based in Arizona, were so convinced of the existence of a government conspiracy that they brought a lawsuit against the CIA for failing to obey the Freedom of Information Act. The amount of evidence they have compiled is impressive, cataloguing as it does witness manipulation by agents (who may or may not be the original Men in Black), 'loss' of photographic evidence, and the physical ploughing up of indentations in the soil.

When Blue Book was wound up in 1969, Brigadier General C.H. Bolender might have made an important slip in a memo when he said: 'Reports of unidentified flying objects which could affect national security are made in accordance with JANAP 146 or Air Force Manual 55–11 and are not part of the Blue Book system.' In other words, Blue Book could have been a front for a covert operation that was researching into UFOs elsewhere. Todd Zechel of GSW has written: 'To give Blue Book full support would have been a waste, since it would have been duplicating research already being conducted by the CIA. Therefore, and for the most part unwittingly, Blue Book's facade enabled the CIA to pull off the greatest propaganda fraud in history.'

If this alleged cover-up did happen what was the motive? Perhaps the answer lies in a memo from Edward Tauss, acting chief of the weapons and equipment division of the OSI (Office of Scientific Intelligence), dated August 1952. 'It is strongly urged, however, that no indication of CIA interest or concern reach the press or public, in view of their probably alarmist tendencies to accept such interest as "confirmatory" of the soundness of unpublished facts in the hands of the US government.'

In other words, panic in the streets, though such a reaction is not, as far as I am aware, supported by any modern psychological research. It is certainly the stuff of American movies, whether the extras are fleeing hysterically from King Kong or aliens, as in *Earth versus the Flying Saucers*. Some people cite the famous radio broadcast by Orson Welles in 1938 of H.G. Wells's *The War of the Worlds* as proof of the gullibility of American audiences. Welles did not make it clear at the outset that the account was fictitious (in fact he transplanted the story to America to add 'authenticity') and it sounded for all the world as if hostile aliens were actually here. 'Ladies and gentlemen, I have a grave announcement to make. Incredible as it may seem, strange beings who landed in New Jersey tonight are the vanguard of an invading army from Mars.' The extent of the panic has been grossly exaggerated and has become a modern urban myth, rather like the vast numbers who were supposed to have thrown themselves off skyscrapers all over New York when Wall Street crashed in 1929.

The radio show was live, and no fewer than four announcements were made during the broadcast to reassure the listeners that this was science fiction. Its main effect was to establish Welles's notoriety at an early age: what panic there was was very localised and the national media blew the story out of all proportion.

Much more recently, and as with Welles's *The War of the Worlds*, broadcast on Hallowe'en, the BBC presented *Ghostwatch*, which purported to be a live investigation of a haunted house. There were certainly complaints from the public, but only a tiny minority were taken in by it, impressive and 'realistic' though the spirits were.

It may be that in the 1950s the panic-in-the-streets theory held water. It was the early phase of the Cold War, there were 'reds under the bed' and the cinemas were filled with tacky scare movies. Nowadays I doubt whether anyone could seriously suggest that society would behave like that. We are inured to the idea of the existence of other life forms and would tend to be fascinated and curious rather than terrified.

The recently released movie *Roswell* tells the story of the New Mexico alien crash in flashback and cites as a reason for the 'top brass' wanting to keep the whole issue quiet that world religions would be undermined if the news leaked out. The same kind of fear surrounded the work of evolutionists like Charles Darwin and Thomas Huxley in the nineteenth century. Because they, and geologists like Sir Charles Lyell, were able to show that the Garden of Eden/Creation story was not literally true in the way Genesis told it, the great concern of the Church was that if one section of the Bible could be disproved, the whole basis of Christianity might be challenged. A moment's reflection, of course, would have allowed die-hard Bible-bashers to incorporate the evolutionists' idea into the Creation story. Isn't evolution and natural selection an infinitely more sophisticated and omnipotent means of creation than, say, making Eve out of a spare rib of Adam's? And today, of course, the acceptance by many people of the Genesis version as a parable is no bar to religious belief.

The Big Bang theory of creation, which addresses problems Darwin and Huxley never contemplated, was once thought to destroy the notion that God made the world, yet now this too has been absorbed into a religious concept of a God who operates beyond the confines of time and space. The same should apply to the possible existence of alien life forms elsewhere in the universe. Recent discoveries in the fields of cosmology and quantum mechanics have, if anything, only proved the inherent strangeness of the universe. It can be argued that the stranger the universe, the more that new evidence flies in the face of orthodox science, the more, not less likely the existence of a creative God becomes. And if there is a God, why should S/he not be a God of the universe (or multiverse), rather than merely a God of the Earth?

There are in fact recorded close encounters which have a strong religious theme. In 1965, Sid Padrick claimed to have come across a landed UFO and its crew in California. They were able to communicate with him, by actual speech, and they made him a unique offer. 'Would you like,' they asked, 'to pay your respects to the Supreme Deity?' We have already discussed some Biblical visitations and the parallel between visitations by angels and alien encounters is obvious. Some faiths are now giving serious thought to the idea of extraterrestrial life. They no longer maintain that the existence of other beings contradicts religious doctrine. The Vatican has recently funded an observatory and the cleric in charge of the project, Father Coyne, has said that he sees no reason why extraterrestrials, if they exist, should not be baptised and welcomed into the Catholic Church. After all, for centuries missionary groups like the Jesuits have braved all sorts of dangers to convert people of different races and cultures who must have seemed as alien to them as Greys are to us.

Another strong reason for the belief in a cover-up is that there have been so many in the past. There is a widespread view that politicians habitually lie, that it goes with the territory. Benjamin Disraeli, no slouch himself when it came to deviousness, was rightly suspicious of government figures – 'There are,' he said, 'lies, damned lies and statistics.' In Napoleonic France in the early nineteenth century the regular statements of policy (the rough equivalent of our white papers today) were so notorious for being untrue that the phrase 'to lie like a bulletin' was in common use for years. In fact, however, in Western democracies lying is unusual, even if politicians are past masters at evading the question, changing the subject or refusing to answer at all. Where there is proof that a politician lied, then the result is usually resignation and sometimes the fall of a government. In 1963 the war minister, John Profumo, knowingly misled the House of Commons and the country when he said that there was 'no impropriety whatever' in his relationship with call-girl Christine Keeler. Ten weeks later, he admitted the lie and resigned. Harold Macmillan's government did not survive the next election.

Politicians in Britain and America, on the rare occasions when they are forced to deliberate on UFOs, have consistently stated that they are not aware of any evidence which would support the existence of extraterrestrial life. This does not preclude the possible existence of the 'inner circle' discussed earlier, who are fully 'in the know' and prepared to hide the truth from their colleagues, but even the most potent military secret of all time, the atom bomb, could be kept secret for only a relatively limited period. The counter-argument is that the secret has *not* been kept, and that Roswell, Rendlesham Forest and perhaps Area 51 are all evidence of that.

If it could be proved that governments in the past have lied on the UFO question, then present administrations would be in severe trouble. Most of the accusations have pointed the finger at the United States, but what is the position in Britain?

In an extract from 'The Age of the UFO' in *The Unexplained File* series, the editor has produced an interesting view of my department in the 1980s, to which I have applied my own lie-detector test.

> The British Ministry of Defence (MOD) has been collecting UFO reports since the 1960s [false: records actually go back to at least 1959] and continues to do so [true]. Its Whitehall offices ... house files that would, if ever released [some of the earlier ones have been – others are outlined for the first time in this book], prove extremely interesting to ufologists [true]. The number of UFO reports for 1981 alone – as quoted in the House of Lords ... in March 1982 – show that the MOD collected over five times as many cases during that year as Britain's leading civilian UFO society, BUFORA [a healthy sign that we were 'open for business'].
>
> The MOD says that UFO reports are the province of a department that has responsibility for low-flying aircraft. [Sort of. This is Sec(AS)2b, across the corridor from me in Sec(AS)2a.]

The rest of the article deals with UFO researcher Jenny Randles' attempts in 1983 to obtain access to ministry files and to force a policy statement out of the MOD. Their response was the one we have already seen many times: 'The sole interest of the Ministry of Defence in UFO reports is to establish whether they reveal anything of defence interest.' The statement went on: 'There is no unit within the ministry appointed solely for the study of UFOs [this is still true] and no staff are employed upon the subject on a full-time basis [true – I had other duties, too].'

In an article for the January–February 1994 issue of the *International UFO Reporter*, Jenny Randles had revised her view of the Ministry of Defence. After cataloguing her woeful experiences over twenty years of dealing with the ministry, she referred to a change in 1992. 'We now had,' she wrote, 'our own Edward Ruppelt . . . a man named Nick Pope.' I very much hope she was thinking of the early Ruppelt, before whatever pressure it was that caused him to change his attitude on UFOs was brought to bear.

Conspiracy theorists see conspiracies everywhere, 'the smiler with the knife'. The Ministry of Defence routinely destroys files, and we saw why in Chapter 9; radar operators routinely wipe tapes for economic reasons. The extremists won't accept either of these practical situations. To them, the destruction of files and tapes is just more proof of a cover-up. Sec (AS) routinely asks other sections to help with various investigations – I did so myself on a regular basis. We do not name these departments or give unnecessary details, and the cover-up merchants smell a rat once again. We *must* be hiding something. A constant criticism of the ministry is that we are keeping secret the most emotive files of all: those which deal with close encounters. It is unfortunate that one of my predecessors went on record as saying that these do not exist, but I believe this stems from a lack of familiarity with the files rather than from anything underhand.

I was often asked by ufologists whether there were any plans to introduce a Freedom of Information Act here, based on the American model. This is a political decision which cannot be made by the Ministry of Defence. At the time of writing, the Conservative administration has no such plans, although John Major's Citizen's Charter is an open government initiative. The Labour party has said that, if elected, they would instigate a Freedom of Information Act. Such a move would be welcomed in many quarters.

The American Freedom of Information Act has already released an incredible 30,000 UFO documents, all previously classified. These have come from the DIA and the NSA, the United States Air Force and the FBI, and some even from the CIA, who, like the FBI, previously denied having any documents on the subject at all! However, there are many UFO papers that the American government still refuses to release. The only possible reason for this is that national security is involved. And here we have a classic paradox: how can national security be involved if, as the American government says publicly, UFOs are not extraterrestrial and they do not pose any threat? I received no joy on this question from the United States embassy in London. I received no joy from the British embassy in Washington. I did meet a highly co-operative colonel of marines but his attempts to help came to nothing.

The prospect of a government cover-up is certainly frightening. Just consider the scene from the film version of Budd Hopkins' *Intruders* in which a character criticises a general for not telling the public that extraterrestrials are real. The general asks whether, in all seriousness, the President of the United States could stand up and tell the world that alien spacecraft regularly evade our air defences, land and carry out genetic experiments on our people without the government or the military being able to stop them.

My conclusion to the cover-up question in Britain is akin to Jenny Randles' and Lord Hill-Norton's. We do not possess vast amounts of secret information about aliens; we are not hiding crashed saucers and dissecting the technology they use; we do not have little graves of Greys; we have not signed treaties with them in some sort of uneasy truce. In Britain, the problem is the other way around. We all know too little about a phenomenon which is as real as toast. As long as we are all afraid of ridicule, the UFOs are going to be ignored.

Perhaps we ignore them at our peril.

DANGER IN THE SKY

Whether or not UFOs are extraterrestrial, whether or not humans are being abducted by aliens, one thing is certain: people *have* been endangered, hurt and even killed by UFOs. This is not speculation; it is fact.

The date was 7 January 1948; the location Godman Air Force Base, Kentucky. It was only months after Kenneth Arnold's seminal 'saucer' sighting and rumours were rife. A spate of similar sightings occurred all over America and someone rang the air base to report a strange bright light hovering nearby. Four P-51 Mustang aircraft owned by the National Guard were ordered to break off their routine flight and investigate. Three pilots – Hammond, Clements and Mantell – climbed in pursuit of the object, but at 20 to 22,000ft, where the air was thin, Hammond and Clements had to give up because of a lack of oxygen. Instead they continued on their routine flight to Standiford Field. A fourth pilot, Hendricks, was unable to follow the order at all, presumably because of a fuel shortage, and he flew direct to Standiford, arriving forty minutes ahead of the others.

So Captain Thomas Mantell was now alone in the sky, at the

highest altitude his plane could manage, chasing an inexplicable object. He radioed the control tower at Godman. 'It appears to be a metallic object, tremendous in size, directly ahead and slightly above. I am trying to close for a better look.'

Minutes later, Mantell's P-51 was littered over a wide area near Franklyn, Kentucky, and the pilot was dead. The official board of inquiry came to the conclusion that the crash had been caused by anoxia (oxygen deprivation). Mantell had blacked out and lost control of his aircraft. In the hysteria over Arnold's sighting and the first, heady days of Project Sign, all sorts of rumours started to circulate. Mantell was buried in a closed casket, it was said, because his body was not actually there. It had been 'lifted' out of the P-51 by the alien crew of whatever he was chasing. Other stories held that Mantell's body had inexplicable wounds. Much of this was nonsense. It doesn't take much imagination to understand why a plane-crash victim should be buried in a closed coffin, however contrary this may run to usual American practice.

But what was Mantell chasing? Even some of the more 'enlightened' UFO books of today claim it was a weather balloon. As in the Roswell incident of the previous year, we can assume that Thomas Mantell, like Jesse Marcel, knew what a weather balloon looked like. Other accounts claim it was probably Venus, the nearest planet to ours, with its brilliant blue-white light. But Mantell's last radio message – 'a metallic object, tremendous in size' – rules out both these possibilities, though the sceptics, of course, won't have it. The tremendous size, they say, was simply an hallucinatory distortion created by the lack of oxygen. Mantell, however, was an experienced pilot – he knew what anoxia could do and it was unlikely that he would have risked his life to chase something he could explain perfectly well. Whatever the truth, Captain Thomas Mantell became ufology's first known 'martyr'.

*   *   *

The Bass Strait, the narrow channel that lies between Australia and Tasmania, has been likened more to the infamous Devil's Triangle off Bermuda. In this particular ufocal, no fewer than seventeen aircraft were lost during the Second World War. What is odd about this is that there was no enemy action over the Bass Strait in that war.

In October 1978, Frederick Valentich, a civilian pilot, took off from Moorabbin airport in Melbourne. He had been in the air for about forty-five minutes when he radioed the Melbourne Flight Service Unit to report that he was being 'buzzed' by an aircraft he couldn't identify. Melbourne had no knowledge of another aircraft in the Bass Strait area and asked Valentich to describe it. He said it was large, bright and metallic and carried a green light. It passed about 1,000ft above him, then circled and vanished, only to reappear overhead, hovering dangerously close to his plane. Whatever the craft was, it was clearly playing some sort of game with him. His last radio message, to controller Steve Robey, said: 'My intentions are ah to go to King Island ah Melbourne that strange aircraft is hovering on top of me again . . . it is hovering and it's not an aircraft . . .'

Robey was alarmed by the rising panic in Valentich's voice, but all attempts to raise him again failed. The radio channel was clear: Valentich simply didn't or couldn't respond.

An air, sea and land search was instigated by Search and Rescue as soon as it was apparent that Valentich had not reached King Island. For five days the search teams combed the area, but no trace of plane or pilot has ever been found. Frederick Valentich had become another victim of a UFO.

That year, 1978, was something of a peak one for Australian UFO sightings. Green lights had been seen over the strait and just twenty minutes before Valentich's disappearance another witness, Roy Manifold, had taken a photograph of something odd. When the film was processed a huge, black denseness seemed to hang over the sea, swirling up the water. Australian ufologist Bill Chalker destroyed the Australian Air Force's claim this was clouds. For clouds to have appeared quickly enough to match the timing of the shots, they would have to have been cruising at 200mph.

I was drawn into a debate over a similar case which had allegedly taken place in the autumn of 1970. Radar at RAF Binbrook, near Market Rasen in Lincolnshire, had picked up an unexplained blip in British airspace on 8 September. A number of aircraft from different bases were scrambled. Captain William Schaffner, an American exchange officer based at Binbrook, took his Lightning plane out over the North Sea beyond Grimsby, chasing something that, according to the radar screen at least, was varying its speed between 600 and an incredible 17,000mph. Schaffner described a dazzlingly blue light and reported that as he closed in, he could make out that the object was cone-shaped and had a spherical section which appeared to be made of glass. At one point the craft (or one of them – there may have been two) hurtled towards him and he had to bank sharply to avoid a collision. On the radar screen something extraordinary happened. The blips representing the Lightning and the UFO actually merged, then stopped altogether. A second later, the UFO blip was careering away at a speed estimated to be in excess of 20,000mph.

Radio contact was re-established with Schaffner, but he sounded dazed and disorientated and his compass wasn't working. He was ordered to ditch in the sea. The Lightning sank in minutes. For some reason, Schaffner had been unable to eject from the cockpit and get into his survival dinghy. But the cockpit was empty and his body was never recovered. It was an amazing story, but was it true, and why had the story only surfaced now?

The local angle on this was handled by Pat Otter from the

Grimsby Evening Telegraph. Tony Dodd, an ex-police sergeant and top UFO researcher, took up the case for Quest International. Because I was beginning to field questions from journalists and ufologists I had the file on the loss of the aircraft sent to me from the archives and took a closer look at what had happened.

The Lightning had been involved in a routine exercise designed to practise the intercepting and shepherding of low-speed targets, an operation often undertaken in the Cold War years, when Soviet bombers would fly quite regularly into British airspace just to test our defences. On this dummy run, the target was an RAF Shackleton. The file implied that Schaffner had simply flown into the sea while attempting to intercept it and was missing, presumed drowned. Any lights he had reported were simply those of the Shackleton.

I found no evidence of any unusual circumstances surrounding the crash, but I felt uneasy nonetheless. Why on earth would anyone make up something like this some twenty years after the event? Nobody had anything to gain, and a number of witnesses appeared to be able to vouch for at least part of the story. The file told me no more. All I could do was watch and keep a close eye on the loss of military aircraft (every year there are, tragically, several) and, of course, an open mind.

The Bermuda Triangle, written about in thousands of books and articles, remains the most mysterious swallower of aircraft, ships and people. Disappearances at sea (or in the sky over the sea) are by no means unusual. The vast areas involved mean that it is notoriously difficult to find the wreckage of a tiny craft: it is literally like looking for a needle in a haystack. Not surprisingly, there is a theory (among many others, natural and supernatural) that the disappearances off Bermuda are uforic in origin, that aliens for years have been lifting whole planes out of the sky and ships out of the sea, for what purposes we can only guess.

What makes the Mantell and Valentich sightings remarkable is the radio reports they were able to transmit. How many others might have died without the opportunity to communicate that one, last, telltale message?

Near-misses in the skies also happen very frequently, and if there is a lull in world events, or if excited, garrulous or furious airliner passengers talk about such a close shave, the shock-horror merchants in the media will run a story on it and there will be demands for a full inquiry and so on. Undoubtedly, some of the near-misses are with UFOs. The Civil Aviation Authority requires its pilots to log all near-misses, no matter what the other craft may be, but here the ridicule factor comes into play again. Some pilots will not report a near-miss with a UFO to avoid the sniggers in the airport lounge. But if passengers see something and a radar blip confirms it, then they will have to. In these circumstances, however, it is likely to be a standard near-miss report rather than a UFO report.

I was able to investigate two such incidents during my time at the UFO desk, although the first had occurred a few months before my posting. The first was on 21 April 1991 over Lydd, near Romney in Kent. The pilot of an Italian MD80 reported that a grey, missile-like object flashed past his aircraft at 22,000ft. A radar blip confirmed the sighting. Before doing anything else I checked the army range at Lydd, but I was not surprised to draw a blank – missiles are not fired off indiscriminately, especially into the air close to a well-established civilian flightpath. And in any case, Lydd had no missile capable of reaching that sort of height. A passenger aircraft had come within a few feet of being blasted out of the sky, but the incident was never explained. No defence significance?

On 15 July of the same year, there was a similar near-miss, again over Kent. At a height of 15,000ft, the pilot of a Boeing 737 saw a black 'lozenge-shaped' object pass very close to his wing tip. He reported the matter and there was a full investigation. The unsatisfactory conclusion was that there had been the risk of collision between the Boeing and an 'unidentified object'. No defence significance?

Beyond the requirements of the near-miss rules, pilots are not keen to discuss UFOs. I have spoken to one very experienced civil aviation pilot who told me he has seen several UFOs from his cockpit. His employers were not happy about him talking about these to anyone. He holds the lives of hundreds of people in his hands every day, and one whiff of instability – 'The pilot is seeing things off the port bow!' – and the damage to his career would be terminal.

There are also a number of cases in which harm has resulted from close encounters on the ground. However, there is no concrete evidence that the UFOs concerned were alien in origin, still less that the suffering caused was intentional.

Falcon Lake, Ontario, seventy-five miles east of Winnipeg, is the site of Canada's most famous encounter. On 20 May 1967, at about midday, amateur geologist Stephen Michalak, wearing protective clothing including gloves and goggles, was chipping away at rock strata. He saw two red, cigar-shaped UFOs coming in to land near him. One just hovered and then sped away, vanishing in the cloud cover. The second actually landed and appeared to cool down, its colour changing from a glowing red to gold. Michalak estimated the craft's dimensions as 12ft high and 35ft in diameter. With astonishing presence of mind, he drew a sketch of what he saw and made notes on its appearance. There were narrow slits at the base of a dome-shaped projection on top and grilles he took to be ventilation panels, or possibly an exhaust, on each side of the fuselage. Purple light was shining out of these and he was aware of the noise of an engine and the strong smell of sulphur.

Suddenly a door opened on the craft's left side. What he had taken to be an exhaust was clearly a hatch. He heard voices inside and walked towards it. He called out in English, French Russian and the smatterings of other languages he'd picked up over the years. There was no response and the hatch closed again. Michalak could feel the heat on the craft's surface. He reached out to touch it and his glove melted. Without warning there was a blast of hot air from the exhaust vent on the right side. He fell back, his coat and shirt burning, and the craft took off.

The instinctive reaction of most of us would be to dismiss this account as a hoax. But Michalak's health suddenly deteriorated and he was admitted to hospital. On his stomach was a mark exactly matching the grid pattern of the exhaust vent, a series of thirty circular burns. He suffered from skin infections, weakness, weight loss, dizziness, diarrhoea, blackouts and vomiting, long after the burns had healed. Nearly two dozen specialists who tested him came to the conclusion that he was suffering from radiation burns, and that a longer exposure would have killed him.

An even more disturbing experience was that of Betty Cash of Dayton, Texas. On 29 December 1980, fifty-one-year-old Betty, who ran a grocery store and restaurant, was out for the day with a friend, fifty-seven-year-old Vickie Landrum and Vickie's grandson, Colby, then aged seven. They had driven in Betty's Oldsmobile Cutlass to find a bingo game, but the halls were closed in preparation for New Year parties. Instead they had a meal in New Carey and began their journey home to Dayton. It was around nine o'clock and Betty was driving along Highway FM1485 through this swampy area, where Lake Houston and its various tributaries run south to Galveston Bay. It was chilly and the car windows were closed and the heater on. The night sky was clear after a day of intermittent rain. There was a three-quarter moon and the area was bright from the streetlights of Houston, thirty miles away.

Colby saw it first – a bright, glowing object racing them above the tops of the oaks and pines that edged the road. It seemed to be about three miles ahead of them, but rather than diminishing in size, as a passing aircraft would, it grew larger and seemed to be making for the road ahead of them. Betty's instinct was to outrun it, but the Oldsmobile wasn't fast enough. She was forced to brake hard as the object came in and hovered in front of them, about 25ft off the ground, straddling the highway. In descriptions the three witnesses gave – and have continued to give with unerring consistency – it was, in Vickie's phrase, 'like a diamond of fire'. It seemed to be made of aluminium, and the four points of the diamond were rounded. It had a row of blue lights across the centre and emitted bleeps from time to time.

Vickie, a committed Christian, genuinely believed that this was the Day of Judgement and cradled a terrified Colby in her arms as the object rose and fell slightly on downblasts of flame ahead of them. She told Colby not to worry. 'When that big man comes out of the burning cloud, it will be Jesus.' They'd be safe.

Betty got out of the car. She stood in front of the bonnet, as though mesmerised by the light, apparently unaware of the intense heat the object was giving off. Vickie and Colby screamed at her to get back inside, but when she tried, the door handle was too hot to hold and she had to use the leather sleeve of her jacket to open it. No sooner had Betty got back into the car than a swarm of helicopters – they counted twenty-three in the next few minutes – arrived from nowhere and moved off again, along with the glowing craft.

Betty drove on and all three of them were still able to see the diamond, glowing in the sky about five miles away, its light illuminating the helicopter escort. They were not they the only witnesses, either. An oil worker in Dayton saw the UFO – 'It was kind of diamond-shaped and had two twin torches that were shooting brilliant blue flames out the back.' A bakery clerk in

Eastgate, eight miles west of Dayton, reported a bright light in the sky over New Carey. An off-duty Dayton policeman and his wife saw the helicopters, as did an inhabitant of Crosby. They flew right over his house.

For Betty, Vickie and Colby the physical symptoms began almost at once. When Betty dropped the Landrums at their home that night, Vickie complained of a headache and sickness. Over the next few days, grandmother and grandson showed signs of acute sunburn. They vomited and suffered from diarrhoea which lasted for days. Vickie lost 30 per cent of her hair; Colby too lost hair, but much less. Both had pain in their eyes and their sight deteriorated. Vickie still fears she will eventually go completely blind and worries for Colby, who, doctors told her, could develop leukaemia if the problem is radiation sickness, as suspected.

Betty fared worse. She had blinding headaches and felt she was going to die. Huge blisters appeared on her skin, so disfiguring that friends who called to see her in hospital could not recognise her. She developed an aversion to anything hot – the sun, even warm water. A month later she had lost over 50 per cent of her hair and suffered from a continuous eruption of skin conditions. More recently, she also developed breast cancer and had to have a mastectomy.

The encounter left its mark emotionally, too. Both women, previously bright and vivacious, are now withdrawn and nervous. Both have been in and out of hospital and neither has been able to work again.

What happened on that Texas highway in the dying days of 1980? The presence of the helicopters (and this is not the only instance of terrestrial craft being seen with UFOs) gave rise to the belief that the 'diamond of fire' might have been an unshielded nuclear reactor which the helicopters were taking somewhere for disposal after some sort of accident – an American Chernobyl.

Neither Betty Cash nor the Landrums could be shaken on their testimony. Of the helicopters they saw; some were large, double-rotor CH-47 Chinooks, which have an unmistakable 'telephone' shape in the air; others were smaller, single-rotor types of the Bell Huey variety. Other witnesses agreed that what they had seen with the UFO were Chinooks. Betty and Vickie sued the United States government for physical and emotional damage and loss of earnings, but the case failed after representatives of the US Army, Navy and Air Force, and from NASA, testified that they neither owned nor operated any such craft. But of course, ufologists have pointed out that there are other agencies who weren't in court that day, and who gave no such assurances. The army base at Fort Hood near Killeen didn't know of anybody who could put that number of helicopters in the air. The Houston Intercontinental Airport Federation Aviation Administration said that nearly 400 helicopters operated commercially in the Houston area, but not one of them was a Chinook.

This encounter is an extraordinary example. There are too many witnesses to shout 'hallucination'; the physical symptoms are visible for all to see. And the Landrums and Betty Cash have suffered too much for the motive of publicity or financial gain to be laid at their door. US Army press officer Major Tony Geishauser spoke to the local paper. 'I don't know what it could be . . . unless there's a super-secret thing going on, and I wouldn't necessarily know about that.'

Here we are back once again in conspiracy country. Either the American government is lying and has lied consistently about the UFO phenomenon, and its helicopters did escort a real UFO out of American airspace, or it covered up a nuclear near-miss and it was a miracle that only three people were physically hurt. It is certainly the view of some elements of the UFO lobby that the craft was an alien one being test-flown out of Area 51 by military pilots.

I can't pretend to provide the answers. What I can do is to note the date: 29 December 1980. That same night, something was stirring in the Suffolk woods, thousands of miles away at a place called Rendlesham Forest.

IS THERE ANYBODY
OUT THERE?

The extraterrestrial hypothesis (ETH) is probably the most popular in ufology. This theory holds that UFOs are alien spacecraft and their crews 'not of this world'. Is this possible? Could such life exist, and if so, is it capable of crossing the vast distances between its world and ours? Bearing in mind that the nearest galaxy to our own is 170,000 light years away; bearing in mind that the nearest star to us, Proxima Centauri, is 40 billion km away (in a Jumbo jet, the journey would take 5 million years).

The Earth is one of nine planets orbiting the sun. Mercury, a shrunken, shrivelled world, unchanged for millennia, is nearest to it; next come Venus, with its intense heat, suffocating atmosphere and acid rain; third, Earth; fourth, Mars, the most popular of the science-fiction planets. It looks red through a telescope and in 1976 the Viking space probe found no signs of life on it. Fifth, and a long way away from the sun's orbit, is Jupiter, a stormy, violent planet bigger than all the others put together. It has sixteen moons and a pale ring. Sixth is Saturn, with its 1,000 ringlets made of sparkling ice. It has eighteen known moons, probably more. Seventh comes Uranus, another gas planet with eleven rings and five moons. Neptune is eighth, jockeying for position furthest from the sun with Pluto. It has eight moons, four rings and wild, tempestuous storms. Pluto is the smallest planet. Its moon, Charon, is half its size.

The solar system also contains an asteroid belt, clusters of tiny planets (actually bits of rock), some as small as a few metres across, and comets, like Halley's, only one of millions that circle the sun. The sun itself is, in effect, a giant hydrogen bomb.

It is generally assumed that there is no life elsewhere in the solar system, but this is orthodox science's arrogant view, based on the fact that life on Earth is dependent on carbon, hydrogen, nitrogen and oxygen. Since other planets do not possess these elements in the same proportions, QED, there is no life on other planets. I doubt whether many established scientists watch *Star Trek*. This is a pity, because the oft-quoted comment from Mr Spock when he reads an alien presence on his console aboard the *Enterprise* – 'It's life, Jim, but not as we know it' – is rather more humble. Perhaps you need to be a half-alien to accept the possibility. But why shouldn't there be life forms that don't need carbon, hydrogen, nitrogen and oxygen to survive? We wouldn't last more than a few seconds in Pluto's 2,000mph winds, but does that mean nothing can? Our minds don't have the scope to encompass what might really be out there.

True, space probes like Viking have flown past planets and some have landed, notably on Venus and Mars, without finding signs of life. But then, in a recent and highly embarrassing incident, NASA equipment aboard an orbiting space probe only 1,000 miles above us failed to detect any signs of life on Earth, either! If life has developed anywhere in the solar system other than on Earth, the most likely place is Mars (although some of the moons around Jupiter – especially Europa – also have possibilities). Its similarities to Earth are striking. Its 'day' is almost the same length as ours (forty-one minutes longer), it has seasons and its crusty surface has mountains, canyons, deserts, even polar ice-caps. Although the 'canals' visible through telescopes in the last century, which were thought to suggest the possible existence of extraterrestrial life, are optical illusions, it is nevertheless likely that Mars did have running water at some time in its history. Only this could explain the rift valleys and similar geological formations. When Viking I's landing craft touched down on Martian soil in 1976, it carried out three types of experiments designed to check for signs of life, at least at microscopic level. The first experiment with soil samples indicated that living cells were present, although NASA later announced that the readings had a un-organic cause. As some might say, 'they would, wouldn't they.' In any case, the experiments were all based on assumptions about life which may have been incorrect.

The Viking Orbiters have sent back a fascinating array of photographs over a period of several years now. Two of these, both taken in 1976, are worthy of note if you happen to believe in intelligent life on Mars, if only as an historical fact. The pictures seem to show artificial structures on the planet's surface. The first is a pyramid, not unlike those found in ancient Egypt and the Mayan, Aztec and Inca civilisations in Central and South America. The second, and more astonishing, is the mile-long geological feature which so closely resembles a human face. The photograph was taken from Viking I as it searched for a possible landing site for Viking II, from 1,162 miles above the planet's surface. It has of course been dismissed by many as a freak accident of lights and shadows working on a susceptible human imagination, but the resemblance to a face is still uncanny.

Uncanny, too, is the fact that a number of probes have malfunctioned or simply gone missing near the surface of Mars. In 1993, NASA lost contact with its Mars Observer probe which had cost $980 million. There are those who believe that life does exist on Mars – underground. If that life is there, invisible to our nosy probings, perhaps it doesn't welcome our intrusion.

The sun is life to us – without it, we would die. But the sun is only one star in a galaxy, one in an estimated 200 billion stars we call the Milky Way. And the Milky Way itself is just one of millions of galaxies. The figures quickly become mindboggling. We don't know how many stars there are in the universe, but the smart money settles on something around 10,000 billion billion. If these stars have developed their own clusters of planets, orbiting them as we orbit the sun, then it is not unreasonable to suppose that some of those planets would have similar chemical building blocks of life to those that we possess. And the complex chain of reactions which gave rise to life on Earth could occur – or have occurred – elsewhere. Given the sheer number of stars involved, the odds against life not developing somewhere else would seem to be astronomically high. In short, why us?

Such speculation is all we have until someone with the clout of governments or with a scientific reputation does some serious work on the subject. Life on Earth has evolved through adaptation to changing environment. The 'survival of the fittest' is not likely to be an exclusively earthly phenomenon. It could apply to any life form on any planet, successful examples passing on their genes to successive generations. Random genetic mutation would do the rest.

If we can stretch our minds to encompass the possibility that life is not unique to Earth, what about intelligence? By the same token, there is no logical reason why humans should be alone in the universe. Intelligence of a sort, of course, exists in all animals of a certain order. Chimpanzees are known to use tools, as our primitive ancestors, *homo erectus* and *homo habilis*, did. Several chimps have been taught American sign language and have a large vocabulary, expressing emotions and teaching their young. Sea otters float on their backs on the surface of their habitats, holding rocks on their chests with which to crack open sea urchins and clams. Dolphins in particular show a sophisticated level of intelligence and appear to have developed a complex language. This clearly involves thought processes and goes some way beyond mere instinct. Intelligence itself is probably one link in the chain of evolution, intended to secure the survival of certain species. Humans are slow and weak; we can't outrun a gazelle and haven't the teeth or claws to bring it down. What we do have is the opposable thumb needed to pick up objects, the close-set eyes of the hunter to watch our prey and a mind to reason. That mind enables us to catch a gazelle by a bringing it down with an arrow, to hack off its meat for food, strip off its skin to keep ourselves warm. No other animal in our world is as resourceful as the human, or as deadly.

If these processes can happen here they can happen anywhere, given the right conditions. Through the random laws of chance, you could expect life to develop just as often as it didn't – the cosmic joker idly turning the pack of cards. There are those who argue that life cannot develop at all around a binary star system (that is, a solar system which has two 'suns'), nor around a star that is too hot, too cold, too old, too young, too large or too small. Perhaps our life form could not have developed in those adverse conditions, but that does not preclude the creation and evolution of other types. And even if we insist, as orthodox science does, that these essential forms can only grow on an Earth-like place, who is to say there aren't a billion earths in other galaxies? More and more scientists are beginning to take the view that the universe is likely to be teeming with life.

Let us assume for the moment that it is, and that some of this life is intelligent. Could it reach us? The main obstacle to interstellar travel is the vast distances involved in relation to the speed that we can move. The Earth is about 93 million miles from the Sun, but this is a tiny distance in interstellar terms.

Greater distances need to be measured by a different gauge, the light year. Light travels at around 186,000 miles a second. The light from the moon takes a little over one second to reach Earth. Light from the sun takes eight minutes. If light travels 93 million miles in eight minutes, how far will it travel in a year? The nearest star to our sun is over four light years away, and this is only a tiny fraction of the diameter of our galaxy (about 60,000 light years); the distance between ours and Andromeda, a nearby galaxy, is 2 million light years. Could a spacecraft make such a journey?

Albert Einstein postulated in his theory of general relativity that it was not possible to travel faster than the speed of light. When an object accelerates, its mass increases. When an object accelerates to very high speed, close to that of the speed of light, time for the object begins to slow down. This sounds bizarre, but it is a proven scientific fact. In a famous experiment, two clocks were synchronised. One was left on Earth, the other orbited Earth in a rocket at great speed. When the rocket returned to Earth, the clock on board was fractionally slower than the one on Earth. In theory, if an object accelerates fast enough, its mass becomes infinite and time stops. It follows, then, that it would be impossible to build a conventional spaceship and accelerate it to the speed of light.

In practice, however, space travel is already here. Unmanned probes have left our solar system already; what they have not yet done is to go fast enough. The probes travel at only a fraction of light speed and would not reach even the nearest star for thousands of years. But there are ways around this. We have the technology to build an interstellar ship in space, perhaps on the orbiting space station Mir or the planned American station, Freedom. Such a craft, if it could attain a speed of even half that of light, could reach any one of a small number of stars in, say, fifty years. Materials could be ferried up on space shuttles. The advantage of this is that most of a rocket's fuel is used in getting it off the ground. Build it above the Earth's atmosphere, and the fuel problem becomes less critical. Space is a vacuum, with no air resistance, so an object accelerated to a given speed will continue at that speed until some force stops it. Fuel is therefore only required for the initial acceleration and any subsequent manoeuvrings, not for the journey itself. The slingshot effect could also come in to play. A number of our existing probes have been handled this way, flying towards a planet, orbiting around it at ever greater speeds, then hurtling out of orbit at a far greater speed than that at which it entered it.

The problem with building an interstellar craft is not impossible technology, but impossible amounts of money. The costs would be astronomic themselves and the world's economy would suffer. And our priorities change according to the state of our own world. The mood of the 1960s, for example, was one of expansion, exploration. The American government in particular became obsessed with the space programme, seeing the race to beat the Russians to the stars as an extension of the Cold War. The 'giant leap for mankind' in 1969 was the logical culmination of this, but, brilliant achievement though putting men on the moon was, it did not begin to unlock the secrets of the universe beyond. The mood since has been more cautious. The collapse of the USSR has reined in the Russian space programme. In the careful 1990s, the West tends to use its money for other things.

The long-term effects of life in space on humans are not known. There were those who objected to the railways in the 1830s because they believed that at speeds of more than 15mph the human body would disintegrate. We proved those fears to be groundless, but space travel is more complex. In orbit round the Earth, astronauts experience weightlessness which leads to 'space sickness' – dizziness and nausea – because our bodies are not designed for or used to the situation. In the longer term, the flow of bodily fluids changes. This makes astronauts look younger, albeit temporarily, but no one knows the ultimate effects on the liver and heart. In the cramped conditions of today's space capsules, muscles can waste and it is necessary for astronauts to work out to combat this. The loss of calcium will certainly weaken bones. The psychological effects, too, of years in space have yet to be measured. In science fiction, this problem is conveniently avoided by the use of cryogenics, whereby the ship's crew can 'sleep' in suspended animation until the time of arrival at their destination planet. In reality, however, we have no technology for that as yet. A journey to another galaxy, then, would essentially be one-way, with the original crew dying of old age before arriving. We would need to use the 'ark in space' concept, with distant descendants of the original team completing the journey.

True interstellar travel of a practical, as opposed to a theoretical, kind, is currently beyond our technological capability. But this might be surmountable. The theory is there, and it all depends on the one force we know least about: gravity. There are four fundamental forces in the universe: electromagnetic, strong nuclear, weak nuclear and gravitational. Gravity is a product of mass, which explains why the sun's gravitational forces are powerful enough to hold the planets in orbit. Einstein saw time and space as one entity, which he called simply space-time. Any object distorts spacetime to a limited extent, but this distortion is more pronounced around massive objects such as red giant stars, where space-time is warped in the same way as a water bed would be, if a bowling ball had been placed on it. In 1919, during a solar eclipse, light rays from a distant star were seen to bend around the sun. It was not the light itself that was bending, but, because of the sun's gravitational pull, space-time itself.

If you took a sheet of paper, and drew two points, A and B, at opposite ends, what would be the shortest distance between them? The inevitable straight line? No. If you folded the paper so that point A was on top of point B, there would be no distance between them at all. Cheating? Perhaps, but if we could find a way to 'fold' spacetime in on itself, perhaps by amplifying gravity, then we would have cracked the basic problem of covering the vast distances of space. We cannot do this, but it is possible that nature can do it for us, bending spacetime around a huge object like a black hole (the compressed corpse of a decayed star).

All this is theoretical physics, but scientists are beginning to carry out serious research into gravitational and anti-gravitational propulsion. And Bob Lazar, contentious though his claims are, alleges that his reverse-engineering work in the S-4 section, south of Area 51 on the Nellis Range involved craft using systems not dissimilar from the one I have just described.

In short, then, there are no theoretical reasons why intelligent life shouldn't exist elsewhere in the universe and no theoretical reasons why interstellar travel is not possible. The fact that scientists and governments are prepared to spend money and time on the SETI programmes described in Chapter 9 is an acknowledgement that such possibilities, at least, exist. One example of an intentional message to any receptive extraterrestrial neighbours, the Arecibo message, was beamed in 1974 from the 305m wide dish of the world's biggest radio telescope at Arecibo in Puerto Rico. It consisted of 1,679 on-off or binary commands, which could be mathematically converted into pictures. The message was aimed at M13, a globular cluster at the edge of our own galaxy, the Milky Way. If there is intelligent life out there, we can expect an answer in 50,000 years' time.

Put together the two assumptions we have discussed, the existence of intelligent life and spacetime bending, and you have the possibility of the extraterrestrial hypothesis in a nutshell. Human beings, the highest form of intelligence on Earth, are endowed – some might say cursed – with an unquenchable curiosity. Just as a small child will ask its irritated parents, 'Why is grass green?', so adults throughout the centuries have been pondering the imponderable. If we could fly to other galaxies, wouldn't we do it? And isn't it reasonable to presume that intelligent aliens would do the same? If such a race were a few thousand, or even a few hundred, years more advanced than us, isn't it at least likely that they would be reaching out to explore the universe across the great void of space?

Staying with the ETH, and accepting that alien curiosity exists, what exactly is the mission of UFOs, and what are the implications of their presence for us? Estimating the likely extent of UFO sightings, and taking into account a 95 per cent rational explanation factor, we are still left with hundreds of thousands of unexplained sightings worldwide. We have looked at some of these in this book: the Roswell incident with its indestructible metal; the wave of sightings over Belgium, backed by radar lock-ons; the Rendlesham Forest encounter and the telltale radiation in the woods; the loss of aircraft after encounters with UFOs; the countless testimonies of witnesses, contactees and abductees who independently recalled the same experiences long before they became public knowledge; the unexplained photographs and videos. And all this evidence only scratches the surface.

Time, whatever may be done to bend it, does not stand still. Since the time I began writing this book, more cases from the 1960s will have been released under the thirty-year rule and the Freedom of Information Act, and thousands more sightings will have taken place, some of which will have been reported. Taken individually, some of these cases provide strong evidence that some UFOs are extraterrestrial. Taken collectively, they leave no doubt in my mind that this is indeed the truth.

More complex theories abound. The Greys are beings from another dimension; they are time travellers (in other words, they are the beings humans will evolve into, travelling back to their past – our present). But William of Occam knew a thing or two, with or without his razor. The simplest theory is the best and the most likely: UFOs are the craft of alien visitors to Earth. This will not be proved until some direct and clear contact is made. Only then will the doubts go away, and Patrick Moore and Carl Sagan and the millions of doubters in the world will shake their heads and say, 'Well, I'll be damned!' If this is so, the doubters ask, why don't aliens simply touch down on the front lawn of the White House? After all, if their intelligence is that advanced, they'd hardly need to issue the order so beloved of 1950s sci-fi moviegoers – 'Take me to your leader.' They would know who the world's leaders are and where to find them.

There are many possible answers. Aliens may well be aware that the White House is surrounded by controlled airspace. Any intruding object would be assumed to be hostile and would be engaged. Even in the event of an appalling breach in security, like the one in September 1994 when a light aircraft crashed on the famous lawn, the barrage of secret service agents and their firepower would be awesome. In any case, the pilot of that plane was killed. I doubt whether aliens would be so careless.

Then there is the issue of biological hazard. Earthly germs may well be lethal to alien species, just as their micro-organisms might be the kiss of death to us. Human history is full of such examples. The terrifying bubonic plague which swept out of China in the mid-fourteenth century wiped out between a third and a half of Europe's population. In the Americas, hundreds of thousands of Native Americans died as they fled from the European settlers. But it was not the repeating rifle that brought most of them down – it was influenza, typhoid and smallpox. They had no natural immunity to disease – and this despite the fact that all humans of whatever race share the same basic genetic make-up. It may well be that the uncontrolled exchange of vastly different micro-organisms would lead to the swift and terrible collapse of one or both species when worlds collide.

Perhaps aliens do not even wish to make contact. Perhaps they have probed us for longer than we know and have come to the conclusion that humans do not care for each other, or for their planet. In galactic terms, perhaps we are the slob-like neighbours nobody wants to know. We know nothing of alien culture, so how can we know what, if any, moral stand they take? We let thousands of people die every year of starvation while we build butter mountains and splash about idly in lakes of wine. Are they sickened by this, or frightened by it? Is fear, in fact, the key to the whole mystery? Why was there a sudden upsurge in UFO sightings just after the Second World War, the very time when we had developed and used weapons of terrifying capabilities? Was it that with our atomic weapons and with our new rocket technology, we now threatened worlds beyond our own and that this new situation needed watching?

And what of the genetic theory used to provide a possible explanation for animal mutilation and human abduction? The first is a proven fact, although the cause remains unknown; the second is so universally described that there has to be an element of truth in it. Are aliens, as some claim, a dying race desperately trying to inject fresh life into themselves? Are those pale children shown to abductees really the hybrid salvation of civilisations on the brink of extinction? Are we simply laboratory rats to the aliens, at the mercy of their curiosity? And if the UFO phenomenon is an evolving one, as some ufologists claim, what little experiments may they be developing for us next?

Or perhaps, as most early science fiction supposed, the aliens are simply coming to invade, to steal our natural resources and enslave our people. In this case, perhaps the whole UFO phenomenon is a prolonged exercise in reconnaissance. Fly overhead, following ley-lines or modern highways or railway tracks, test their air defences, probe their fields at night, kill their cattle, abduct them on lonely roads. Are the aliens simply sizing up our people and technology, as a boxer sizes up his opponent before going on to the attack?

The whole process might be more benign than that. If fear is the key and the aliens dislike our genocidal tendencies, perhaps it is their mission to change us, to genetically remove or breed out the most negative of our traits. Perhaps it is no coincidence that abductees feel they have 'grown' as a result of their experiences. Many of them have got involved in environmental issues and become more spiritually aware. Is this because they now know that we are not alone in the universe, or has something been deliberately cultivated in them, along with the physical implants which some claim have been found in the bodies of abductees?

And what of claims by Larry Warren at Rendlesham, that he saw superior officers apparently communicating with aliens? Of Betty Cash and the Landrums, who saw a UFO escorted by helicopters? Of Bob Lazar, who worked on the reverse-engineering of UFO craft? Of the Roswell nurse who saw autopsies being performed on shrunken little creatures later buried in coffins small enough for children? If this liaison is real, is it simply a matter of trade? Are we bartering with the creatures from the sky? Do we do business with Greys?

Yet in suggesting these reasons we make what is probably the very basic mistake of trying to apply human logic to the question. The dictionary definition of alien as an adjective reads: 'Foreign, strange, odd, weird, bizarre, peculiar, abnormal, outlandish, unfamiliar.' If aliens are visiting us, their motives may be completely beyond our understanding, and what we see as logical may make no sense to them at all. We can but tentatively suggest that the covert, furtive appearances of UFOs implies that have no wish to make direct, open contact. If they ever did, ufologists would have to add another category to their classification table – a close encounter in which alien life forms come out of the closet and tell us what they are doing here.

Our own history does not bode well for us. There are no cases in it where a less advanced civilisation has survived contact with a more sophisticated one. The latter always exploits, enslaves, ultimately destroys. We can but hope that alien visitors are a better and nobler race than we are.

So what is to be done? The UFO lobby have argued that a full study into the UFO phenomenon is needed, and it should go much further than Blue Book. All previous studies, they argue, most of which were American, involved varying degrees of whitewash. They were glorified public-relations exercises in which a few, well-intentioned individuals like J. Allen Hynek and, in his early phase, Edward Ruppelt, struggled against the collective apathy and scepticism of their colleagues. They believe that we need an international body, perhaps under the auspices of the United Nations, with the money, the muscle and above all the will to do the job properly. Their remit would be to centralise and evaluate all the data held to date and to act as a worldwide co-ordinating collection point for all UFO and UFO-related phenomena. They would liaise with military, scientific and government authorities, with rapid response teams of trained investigators, able to travel at a moment's notice to the scene of a sighting. They would analyse radar blips, photographs and soil samples, interview witnesses and break down the barriers of secrecy and bigotry which have for far too long dogged the whole subject. Above all, they would be a completely open organisation, publishing accounts of all their findings and making the evidence available to you and me.

This would cost money, but relative to a space project or the huge cost of defence budgets, the sums involved would be small. The lobbyists for such a body maintain that the stakes are too high for us not to take this sort of action. Even if UFOs, however they have been described – as angels, fairies or mowing devils – have been with us for millennia, there can be no doubt that in recent years the pace has been hotting up. Sightings are increasing, contact is more interactive, and there is no reason to suppose it will suddenly stop.

One thing is certain. If there is anybody out there and if they do make full contact with us, it would be the most significant event ever in the history of the human race.

EARTH VERSUS THE FLYING SAUCERS

There is a commonly held belief among many ufologists that the phenomenon they study points to the existence of a benevolent 'space brothers' entity – the 'feelgood factor' evinced in the final reel of *Close Encounters of the Third Kind*. I make my judgements on actual evidence, on the situation which actually exists. And the evidence, which I have tried to draw together in this book, whether it is from the Ministry of Defence files or elsewhere, is, I believe, far from reassuring.

We have seen examples of aircraft being brought down or disappearing in mysterious circumstances, of people being taken against their will under some form of hypnosis and subjected to terrifying pseudo-medical examinations for unknown purposes. We have seen cattle butchered and mutilated in our fields and people becoming seriously ill with all the symptoms of radiation poisoning. If any of these occurrences could be proven to be the result of human action, their perpetrators were caught and convicted, they would face long prison sentences. In some parts of the world, they would face death. Yet, in most cases, only a very limited investigation was ever carried out. Mention the words

'UFO' or 'alien' and the sniggers start at once, the shutters of bigotry and unreason come down. Only the UFO lobby persists in researching what they can in their own time and with their own limited funds, and the UFO lobby are still regarded as eccentric, to say the least.

I believe that there is a war going on, a one-sided war so secret we aren't even aware that it is happening. If any of these incidents can be attributed to an alien presence, then that presence is carrying out what can only be described as crimes against humanity. If we could set up the kind of international investigative force I would like to see and if that force established that the alien presence was real, then we would be able to open up a dialogue with it. We would ask the aliens to stop their harmful activities, following the conventional lines of diplomacy used on Earth. A polite official request, if ignored, becomes a demand; a demand, if ignored, becomes an ultimatum. An ultimatum, if ignored, becomes a war. 'War,' said the nineteenth-century military theorist von Clausewitz, 'is the continuation of politics by other means.' Could we win a war against an extraterrestrial force?

If aliens are here, their main defence at the moment is that very few people realise it and nobody seems in a position to prove it. Strip away that cloak of secrecy and, who knows, we might be more evenly matched than most would suppose. In this unimaginable Armageddon, we'd be fighting on home ground with what strategists call interior lines of communication. Moreover, we'd be defending our own patch against a force more alien than any we've known before, and people fight well for those things. The motto of many British yeomanry regiments in the 1790s as they raised themselves to repel a possible invasion from the French was *Pro Aris et Focis* – for hearths and homes. And against this common enemy, wouldn't we band together? Wouldn't national frontiers come down, old animosities fade, old quarrels be forgotten?

Yet in any war, the winner of battles is not the brave cause, or the morale of the fighter, important though these things are. The winner of battles is technology. In 1870, when Prussia rumbled to war by train against a swaggering and overconfident France, it did so on twenty-six railway lines. The French had one. The result was annihilation at Sedan and the rise of Germany and the unbalanced, tempestuous world of the twentieth century. Although alien technology is an unknown quantity, according to the concept known as cultural tracking it might not be quite as far in advance of our own as may be supposed. When the airships of the 1890s were reported as UFOs, their speeds were not very much greater than the aircraft we knew all about. As our earthly craft have improved in speed and manoeuvrability, so have UFOs. The abductee accounts of the 1960s featured talk of control panels, switches and reel-to-reel tape-recorders. There was no mention of liquid quartz read-outs until we'd invented them ourselves. This might simply be a question of humans relating to things they recognise and ignoring what they don't, or it could mean that in some respects alien technology is only one step ahead of ours, and they may have to develop quickly to stay that one step ahead.

Consider our radar systems – ground-based, airborne, multi-frequency, highly sensitive. Some UFOs are picked up on these systems, others are not. But our own Stealth aircraft are virtually undetectable by radar too, so there is nothing remarkable in this. If radar operators re-evaluated their current procedures of disregarding slow-moving or stationary 'clutter', if they tied in their blips with visual reports as they did in Belgium in 1990, then we might learn a little more of the intruders' capabilities. If we used our alert systems, scrambled our aircraft, chased and intercepted what we saw, then we might find ourselves on surprisingly equal terms.

We have a range of formidable weapons now: air-to-air and

surface-to-air missiles capable of travelling at several times the speed of sound; missiles that can home in on heat sources or objects emitting radar waves. We have lasers and other projected-energy weapons. These things are being planned, designed and tested now, whether in Area 51 or your backyard doesn't, in the end, matter. Every day science fiction is becoming fact.

What else can aliens do that seems beyond our own capabilities? The abduction stories are probably the most frightening, but we use hypnosis ourselves for medical purposes and our lasers and stun weapons produce a similar effect to the paralysing beams of light that have been reported. The medical probe through the navel has its human counterpart in keyhole surgery, now a well-established medical practice. And what of the return of the abductees with little or no memory of the event? Drugs might cause this, or hypnosis itself, but we know from conventional psychiatry that some experiences are too horrible for us to want to remember, too bizarre to believe. The mind is its own river of forgetfulness. Human abduction by aliens, if it happens, is frightening, but it is not inexplicable.

Of course, it would be madness to go to war with the extraterrestrials unless it was absolutely unavoidable. For all our capabilities and the sheer, dogged guts of the human species, our iron will to survive, it would be a war we could not win. If aliens have harmed us, perhaps we have brought this on ourselves. In the paranoia of the Cold War, American pilots certainly, and probably Russian pilots, had orders to intercept and, if necessary, shoot down unidentified flying objects, since these were likely to be enemy aircraft. What if some of them were actually alien craft?

If aliens are here, we must at least show them we know what is going on. It is for this reason that governments should take the issue seriously, investigate sightings and announce their conclusions, however bizarre or unsettling they might be. As

I said, the covert nature of aliens' activities seems to be their main defence. Blow that wide open and perhaps we can force a dialogue which might be mutually advantageous. At the very least, governments should draw up contingency plans, rules of engagement, as they do for every conceivable facet of terrestrial warfare. As far as I am aware, nothing of the kind has ever been done. I did float the idea with various members of the ministry and it was clear that the suggestion was unwelcome. The silence said it all. So, if a UFO were to land on the White House lawn tomorrow, there is no specific system which would be kicked into operation to deal with it.

Either we are alone in the universe or we are not. Perhaps either alternative is equally profound and terrifying. I have tried to be dispassionate and even-handed in my approach, but time and again I come back to the extraterrestrial hypothesis, the alien visitor. I believe that the evidence tells us that intelligent life exists out there and that an alien hand is reaching out to us across the void of space. Whether that hand is reaching out to us in friendship or for some sinister reason, we cannot yet tell.

When Winston Churchill was speaking to the people of Fulton, Missouri, in March 1946, he was talking about a different threat, a different enemy, but his words ring hauntingly down the years to us. 'The dark ages may return on the gleaming wings of science. Beware, I say. Time may be short.'

THE ROSWELL FILM FOOTAGE

The arguments over the existence of extraterrestrial visitors rage on. Ufologists work themselves into a frenzy over the authenticity of the latest sighting reports, documents and photographs; they tear their hair out in frustration. Why won't people accept what's going on? Just how much proof do people want? Scientists shake their heads sadly, hoping that the whole subject will go away. Their slavish adherence to the convention of empirical repeatability means that they ignore most paranormal phenomena and mysteries, which tend to be transitory and spontaneous. If you can't repeat it in a laboratory, forget it. They frown at the UFO researchers particularly, perhaps because they have had the presumption to invent the word 'ufology', which gives the whole subject a pseudo-scientific respectability.

The scientists want proof; the ufologists think they have proof. The scientists demand something absolutely watertight. Enter stage left a man called Ray Santilli, touting film footage purporting to show an autopsy being performed on alien beings. Cue the biggest row ever to hit the world of ufology, and a debate that was finally to involve not just scientists and ufologists, but the world media and the general public, who were belatedly introduced to a subject that had been exercising some minds for nearly fifty years.

Ray Santilli is managing director of a London-based firm called Merlin Communications Ltd, part of the Merlin Group. A few years ago, while Santilli was researching a documentary on Elvis Presley, he heard about an American cameraman who claimed to be the first person ever to film Elvis on stage. He flew over to meet the man, who was in his eighties by this time. Santilli purchased some film footage from the cameraman, who then offered him some canisters containing 16mm film of what he maintained were various autopsies carried out on alien beings who had been killed in the supposed UFO crash at Roswell. Santilli bought all the footage, allegedly paying some $100,000. The cameraman's identity has not been made public, although he has been given the pseudonym of Jack Barnett. It is claimed that he was serving in the US Army in 1947, and was called upon to record the aftermath of the Roswell crash, including the site and the autopsies. He somehow managed to spirit some of this footage away, and kept it for nearly fifty years before deciding to sell it.

Rumours about the existence of this film had been circulating among a few ufologists since 1993, but it was not until spring 1995 that the story broke. During April I had received a call from Philip Mantle, director of investigations at BUFORA, who briefed me about the film, and gave me advance warning that there was to be a secret screening of some of the footage in a few weeks' time at an unspecified location.

By this time I had moved on from the UFO desk, but I was still very much in the thick of things, and was continuing some of my research privately. I was in a very strange position, really, midway between the camps of officialdom and ufologists. Some ufologists will never regard me as anything other than the man from the ministry, while the department itself would occasionally pick my brains on a particular sighting or query. Among other ufologists, however, I had made many friends in my three-year tour of duty and Philip was one of a number of key figures with whom I had kept in touch.

A few weeks later Philip rang again to tell me that the film would be screened on Friday 5 May in the lecture theatre beneath the Museum of London. I arrived shortly after 12.30am, and, having been subjected to a rigorous search to ensure that no cameras were brought into the room, I was ushered into the auditorium. There were about 200 people present, a mixture of ufologists and journalists from all around the world.

Shortly after 1pm the lights went down and an edited section of film, lasting for about eighteen minutes, was shown. It dealt with one of the autopsies. (Philip Mantle had seen two other segments of the footage, one allegedly showing an on-site examination of an alien, which takes place in a temporary structure like a tent, and the other a second autopsy.) The journalists had been in a lighthearted mood, doubtless quite pleased at being able to spend their Friday afternoon on a UFO story, which they were probably planning to write up in their usual jocular style. There had been some laughter and general tomfoolery, but once the screening began, this soon gave way to gasps of amazement and horror.

There was something lying on the autopsy table, and it wasn't human. It is difficult to estimate the height, but it was probably around 5ft, perhaps a little less. It was essentially humanoid, with a bulbous, hairless head. The eyes seemed slightly larger than ours, although this might have been an illusion created by the fact that they were completely black. The nose and mouth were basically humanoid, although the nose appeared slightly smaller and the mouth was frozen in an expression of horror, and the ears were decidedly strange. The torso looked muscular, especially the upper arms and thighs. The creature seemed to have a pot belly, leading some to believe that it might be a pregnant female. It had six fingers on its hands and six toes on its feet. The upper left leg appeared to be seriously injured, and the left hand almost severed at the wrist. These, presumably, were injuries sustained in the crash.

Two individuals wearing hooded one-piece protection garments of some sort examined the body, and there was a third masked figure visible behind a screen. The footage we saw was edited, clearly short extracts from a fairly lengthy operation. The actual procedure (judging by a clock on the wall) took several hours.

After the examination had taken place, the black membranes covering the eyes were removed. It was at this point that the scalpels were brought out, and the autopsy became a dissection. The body was slit open at the front and various organs were removed. I do not have any specialist medical knowledge, so am unable to speculate on the nature of these organs. As each cut was made, a small amount of dark, viscous liquid seeped from the wound. The scene ended with a medical hacksaw being used to cut off the top of the head and remove the brain.

By this time there was much uneasy coughing and a faint smell of sweat in the auditorium. People were shifting uncomfortably in their seats, and many averted their eyes from the screen, watching only occasionally, or out of the corner of their eyes. I had not seen an autopsy before, and although I am not squeamish, I must confess that I found the whole thing extremely unpleasant.

When the lights went up at the end of the screening, the perplexed media turned on the unfortunate Santilli, angry that there had been no introduction, and no opportunity for questions to be asked. He soon found himself surrounded by predatory hordes of reporters and had to be escorted from the room by a minder.

We filed our way out of the auditorium and tucked into the

free wine and sandwiches with gusto (although not before a number of ashen-faced individuals headed for the toilet) and the debate began. Some ufologists present began to offer their views, although most, sensibly, decided to stay on the fence, saying simply that the footage was extremely interesting, but that it raised a lot of unanswered questions.

In the course of the next few months there was a steady build-up of interest, and – predictably – a split developed in the ranks of ufologists. Part of this stemmed from the invitation list at the 5 May screening. Santilli had been working very closely with Philip Mantle, who was suspected of having deliberately snubbed some of his ufological rivals. Jenny Randles, the previous director of investigations at BUFORA, had not been invited, nor, it seemed, had anyone like Tony Dodd or Graham Birdsall from the other main British group, Quest International. Independent researchers such as Timothy Good were not invited either. Also notable for their absence were the world's most renowned researchers on Roswell, people like Stanton Friedman, Kevin Randle and Don Schmitt.

Graham Birdsall wrote a powerful attack on the whole affair in Quest's *UFO Magazine*, while Kent Jeffrey from the American Operation Right to Know organisation (who had been at the screening) contributed a detailed critique to the Mutual UFO Network *UFO Journal*. There were certainly some important questions: why was the original cameraman not prepared to speak out and be questioned, so that details of his military background could be authenticated? Why had he held on to the film for nearly fifty years before coming forward? Perhaps most importantly, why did the aliens shown not match the descriptions given by some of those who claimed to have seen the original entities from the Roswell crash?

Many people who have seen the film have expressed doubts as to whether it could have been faked. I suppose that in these days of Hollywood special effects anything is possible, but the corpse certainly looked real, and special effects on such a scale would almost certainly have had to involve a lot of professionals, any one of whom, surely, could have let something slip. At this point, an extremely unpleasant rumour began to circulate, which held that the corpse was a human one. Could it be the body of someone suffering from some sort of genetic or radiation-induced deformity, people wondered, or might an ordinary corpse have been doctored somehow? If this was the case, it was suggested, criminal charges might be brought against those responsible. This was not the only legal problem facing Santilli. If the films had, as was claimed, been taken from the US Army, surely that was theft, and the films belonged to the US Army? Of course, if they were genuine, it would be rather difficult for some American general to come forward and claim them.

The debate soon spread into the media, and for once it was picked up in a big way by the quality broadsheets as well as the tabloids. The *Guardian* ran a big feature on the footage, which was also discussed in *The Sunday Times* and the *Independent*.

In the summer of 1995 Santilli began to market the footage in a serious way. He combined all the available clips on one video, which he offered for sale at £33 per copy. Interestingly, and again dealing with a legal point, the order form contained the following statements:

'Whilst the film stock has been verified as manufactured in 1947, we cannot currently warrant that the contents were filmed in 1947.

'Although our medical reports suggested that the creature is not human, this cannot be verified.

'Although we have been informed that the footage emanates from the Roswell incident, this has not yet been verified.'

On Monday 28 August 1995, extracts from the film were shown in a Channel 4 documentary made by John Purdie of

Union Pictures. The extracts were also broadcast in America and Japan. In the aftermath of these screenings the debate on UFOs reached a new intensity. Many claimed this was the final proof that extraterrestrial life exists, and has visited us on Earth. Scientists still disagree, maintaining that it is possible to hoax virtually anything these days. I suppose they are right, although I suspect that some scientists have such a closed mind on the subject that they wouldn't even accept the existence of aliens even if the proverbial UFO landing on the White House lawn happened before their very eyes.

I am still asked by ufologists and journalists alike what I think of the film. I have said simply that it is interesting, although there are still questions to be answered. As for its authenticity, I keep an open mind, but have to say I am inclined to think it is a very clever hoax. Even if it is a hoax, it does not necessarily follow that something bizarre and very probably extraterrestrial did not crash at Roswell in 1947. The shame of the whole business is that if the film is proved to be a forgery, the public will simply assume that the whole Roswell incident never happened. Perhaps, say the conspiracy theorists, that is exactly the aim – to use a cynical piece of disinformation to discredit the whole Roswell saga. If so, it is fooling very few people, and certainly not local congressman Steven Schiff, who continues to maintain that something bizarre happened at Roswell, and that somewhere within the ranks of officialdom in America there are people who know exactly what it was.

Perhaps it is fitting to end this chapter with a quote from Richard D'Amato, national security aide to Senator Robert Byrd. 'If it happened, if there is even one credible piece of evidence that Earth has been visited by aliens, it changes everything. It only had to happen once.'

CONCLUSION

It is with mixed feelings that I look back on my time as the government's expert on UFOs. In one sense, I enjoyed my three years in Secretariat (Air Staff), and relished my unique position as the only person in the ministry with an opportunity to investigate UFOs, abductions and the alien threat – not to mention cattle mutilation, crop circles, rogue comets, ghosts, and anything else weird and wonderful that happened to come my way. I enjoyed being the 'real Fox Mulder', and I found it fascinating to plough through the 'real X-Files', and to open a few of my own. My joy at being promoted and posted to pastures new was tinged with sadness at having to leave. Yet this was not merely the sadness associated with missing out on interesting cases, to come, but a deeper sadness stemming from a feeling that, much as I had achieved, I was leaving a job unfinished.

Certainly my attitudes, both as a civil servant and personally, changed. The more knowledge I accumulated, the more patently obvious it became that the UFO phenomenon could not be wholly explained away by conventional science. I hadn't solved the UFO mystery, but I believed I had taken an important step down that road by realising that the mystery needed proper official study. And now I had to walk away from the situation, not knowing how my successor would see the subject, and unsure of whether she would follow up the research I had began.

As I have pointed out, the subject is one that lends itself to personal prejudice. It is difficult for career civil servants to shake off their preconceived notions about UFOs, to open their eyes to the situation and their minds to the possibilities. I freely admit that I myself failed to grasp the enormity of what was going on straight away. My conversion was a slow one, but no less extraordinary for that. It is certainly unusual for the Ministry of Defence's UFO desk officer to come out and say that some UFO sightings are probably extraterrestrial in origin. It is not that I've gone mad, not that I've made a blind leap of faith, but that the conclusion I have drawn is the only one borne out by the evidence.

I consider myself to be intelligent and rational. A career civil servant with ten years of experience at the ministry who has reached the ranks of middle management is not supposed to believe in an alien presence. Indeed, I started my tour of duty believing in aircraft lights, but I ended it believing in aliens. Not surprisingly, the change in my attitude has been jumped upon by the newspapers, and I've found my views being quoted widely. On occasion this has made things difficult for me at the ministry, and I sometimes suspect that my next promotion might be a long way off. And yet, as we've already seen, I'm not a lone voice in the wilderness any more.

If you happen to watch a television documentary about UFOs these days, the people interviewed won't all be wide-eyed believers who have just spent the night camped out on top of some hill waiting for flying saucers. Nowadays you're likely to run across Harvard professors, Ministry of Defence under-secretaries, or maybe even a former chief of the defence staff. And when people of that calibre line up on the side of the believers, perhaps it's time to recognise that, despite some of the more pessimistic comments I've made here about attitudes, things might just be changing for the better. The great and the good, whatever they may say publicly, cannot fail to pay attention when such distinguished scientists, public servants and soldiers insist that we have an ongoing situation that causes them concern.

It is that concern which has led me to write this book. I believe that by the time I vacated the UFO desk I had changed the minds of many people within the ministry, simply by showing them the evidence, and this book gives me the opportunity to take my message to a wider audience. And the message is this: know that there are people who watch our skies to protect the sleeping masses. Know that we keep a round-the-clock watch on our airspace, using sophisticated radar technology. But also know that not all potential intruders into our airspace have two wings, a fuselage and a tail, and not all show up on our radar. These unusual intruders are not necessarily here for any reason that a Royal Air Force air defence expert might anticipate.

The idea of a technological threat of non-human origin may seem like science fiction, but it is not. It is science fact. There *is* a threat, despite what some people may say. Perhaps those who disagree would care to speak to the Belgian F-16 pilots who were ordered to intercept a UFO which could, and did, run rings around their aircraft. Perhaps they would like to speak to Stephen Michalak, blasted in the chest by the heat from a landed UFO, or Betty Cash, who developed radiation sickness after her terrifying close encounter. Or perhaps these sceptics should talk to the families of those who did not survive their encounters with UFOs, like Thomas Mantell and Frederick Valentich. Perhaps they would care to meet farmers who have had cattle mutilated, as if by a laser. Or perhaps they ought to spend time, as I have, with some of the thousands of people who claim to have been experimented on by non-human intelligences;

people who generally shy away from publicity, and only want some answers; people whose encounters are increasingly being recognised as genuine by mental-health professionals. We all like to think that we are in control. But what happens when we're not? What happens when we refuse to accept that a threat even exists, let alone do anything to counter it? This is the ultimate dilemma about UFOs which we must face. We can't begin to find any solutions until we first acknowledge that there is a problem.

Appendices

Appendix 1

Numbers of UFO Reports Made to Ministry of Defence

1959: 22	**1977**: 435
1960: 31	**1978**: 750
1961: 71	**1979**: 550
1962: 46	**1980**: 350
1963: 51	**1981**: 600
1964: 74	**1982**: 250
1965: 56	**1983**: 390
1966: 95	**1984**: 214
1967: 362	**1985**: 177
1968: 280	**1986**: 120
1969: 228	**1987**: 150
1970: 181	**1988**: 397
1971: 379	**1989**: 258
1972: 201	**1990**: 209
1973: 233	**1991**: 117
1974: 177	**1992**: 147
1975: 208	**1993**: 258
1976: 200	**1994**: 250
	1995: 373

Appendix 2

The Form Used for Reporting UFO Sightings

REPORT OF AN UNIDENTIFIED FLYING OBJECT

1. Date, time & duration of sighting	
2. Description of object (No. of objects, size, shape, colour, brightness, noise)	
3. Exact position of observer (Indoors/outdoors, stationary/moving)	
4. How observed (Naked eye, binoculars, other optical device, camera or camcorder)	
5. Direction in which object first seen (A landmark may be more useful than a roughly estimated bearing)	
6. Angle of sight (Estimated heights are unreliable)	
7. Distance (By reference to a known landmark)	

8. Movements (Changes in 5, 6 & 7 may be of more use than estimates of course and speed)	
9. Met: conditions during observations (Moving clouds, haze, mist etc.)	
10. Nearby objects (Telephone lines, high voltage lines, reservoir, lake or dam, swamp or marsh, river, high buildings, tall chimneys, steeples, spires, TV or radio masts, airfields, generating plant, factories, pits or other sites with floodlights or night lighting)	
11. To whom reported (Police, military, press etc.)	
12. Name & address of informant	
13. Background of informant that may be volunteered	
14. Other witnesses	
15. Date and time of receipt	
16. Any unusual meteorological conditions	
17. Remarks	

Appendix 3

Ministry of Defence Response
to UFO Witnesses

 MINISTRY OF DEFENCE
From: Mr N G Pope, Secretariat(Air Staff)2a, Room 8245,
Main Building, Whitehall, London SW1A 2HB

	Telephone (Direct Dialling) 0171 218 2140
	(Switchboard) 0171 218 9000
	(Fax) 0171 218 2680

Mr A Smith	Your reference
1 Nonsuch Road	
Anytown	Our reference
County	D/Sec(AS)12/3
AT1 0SP	Date
	26 July 1994

Dear Mr Smith,

Thank you for your letter dated 20 July in which you described the
strange object that you saw in the sky recently.

I should begin by explaining that our only interest in the subject of
UFOs relates to the issue of defence. Unless there is evidence to
suggest that any sighting poses a threat to the defence of the UK, we
do not investigate further.

Although there are clearly many strange things to be seen in the
skies, we believe that most of them can be explained in terms of known
objects or phenomena. Examples that spring to mind include aircraft
lights, airships, satellites and meteors. Having said this, we do
accept that a small proportion of UFOs appear to defy explanation, and
we keep an open mind on these.

If you wish to take the matter further, might I suggest that you
contact one of the civilian groups involved in UFO research, who will
doubtless be very interested to hear from you, and may well have some
ideas about what you saw. I would suggest the British UFO Research
Association on 01924 444049 or Quest International on 01756 752216.

I hope this is helpful.

Yours sincerely,

Nick Pope

Appendix 4

UFO Organisations

The following organisations will be able to give you general information about UFOs, and can investigate specific sightings. Where the organisations are national they will generally refer you to a researcher in your local area. These groups also organise lectures and conferences.

British UFO Research Association
BM BUFORA
London
WC1N 3XX
Telephone Number: 01924 444049

London UFO Studies
10a Tudor Road
Barking
Essex
IG11 9RX
Telephone Number: 0181 270 9919

Quest International
18 Hardy Meadows
Grassington
Skipton
North Yorks
BD23 5LR
Telephone Number: 01756 752216

Strange Phenomena Investigations
41 The Braes
Tullibody
Alloa
Clackmannanshire
Scotland
FK10 2TT
Telephone Number: 01259 724033

UFO Magazine
1st Floor
66 Boroughgate
Nr Otley
Leeds
LS21 1AE
Telephone Number: 01943 850860

Operation Right to Know (Britain)
20 Newton Gardens
Ripon
North Yorks
HG4 1QF
Telephone Number: 01765 602898

Appendix 5

Lt-Col Charles Halt's Report on the Rendlesham Forest Incident

DEPARTMENT OF THE AIR FORCE
HEADQUARTERS 81st COMBAT SUPPORT GROUP (USAFE)
APO NEW YORK 09755

REPLY TO
ATTN OF: CD

13 Jan 81

SUBJECT: Unexplained Lights

TO: RAF/CC

1. Early in the morning of 27 Dec 80 (approximately 0300L), two USAF security police patrolmen saw unusual lights outside the back gate at RAF Woodbridge. Thinking an aircraft might have crashed or been forced down, they called for permission to go outside the gate to investigate. The on-duty flight chief responded and allowed three patrolmen to proceed on foot. The individuals reported seeing a strange glowing object in the forest. The object was described as being metalic in appearance and triangular in shape, approximately two to three meters across the base and approximately two meters high. It illuminated the entire forest with a white light. The object itself had a pulsing red light on top and a bank(s) of blue lights underneath. The object was hovering or on legs. As the patrolmen approached the object, it maneuvered through the trees and disappeared. At this time the animals on a nearby farm went into a frenzy. The object was briefly sighted approximately an hour later near the back gate.

2. The next day, three depressions 1 1/2" deep and 7" in diameter were found where the object had been sighted on the ground. The following night (29 Dec 80) the area was checked for radiation. Beta/gamma readings of 0.1 milliroentgens were recorded with peak readings in the three depressions and near the center of the triangle formed by the depressions. A nearby tree had moderate (.05-.07) readings on the side of the tree toward the depressions.

3. Later in the night a red sun-like light was seen through the trees. It moved about and pulsed. At one point it appeared to throw off glowing particles and then broke into five separate white objects and then disappeared. Immediately thereafter, three star-like objects were noticed in the sky, two objects to the north and one to the south, all of which were about 10° off the horizon. The objects moved rapidly in sharp angular movements and displayed red, green and blue lights. The objects to the north appeared to be elliptical through an 8-12 power lens. They then turned to full circles. The objects to the north remained in the sky for an hour or more. The object to the south was visible for two or three hours and beamed down a stream of light from time to time. Numerous individuals, including the undersigned, witnessed the activities in paragraphs 2 and 3.

CHARLES I. HALT, Lt Col, USAF
Deputy Base Commander

Appendix 6

Details of UFO Files Held in the Public Record Office

AIR 16/1199
AIR 20/7390
AIR 20/9320
AIR 20/9321
AIR 20/9322
AIR 20/9994
AIR 2/16918
AIR 2/17318
AIR 2/17526
PREM 11/855

Appendix 7

File PREM 11/855

PRIME MiNISTER'S
PERSONAL MINUTE

5

SERIAL No. M. 412/52

SECRETARY OF STATE FOR AIR

LORD CHERWELL

What does all this stuff about flying saucers amount to? What can it mean? What is the truth Let me have a report at your convenience.

W.S.C.

28 July 1952

AIR MINISTRY, 4
WHITEHALL,
S.W.1.

PRIME MINISTER

The various reports about unidentified flying objects, described by the Press as "flying saucers", were the subject of a full Intelligence study in 1951. The conclusions reached (based upon William of Occam's Razor) were that all the incidents reported could be explained by one or other of the following causes:-

(a) Known astronomical or meteorological phenomena

(b) Mistaken identification of conventional aircraft, balloons, birds, etc.

(c) Optical illusions and psychological delusions

(d) Deliberate hoaxes.

2. The Americans, who carried out a similar investigation in 1948/9, reached a similar conclusion.

3. Nothing has happened since 1951 to make the Air Staff change their opinion, and, to judge from recent Press statements, the same is true in America.

4. I am sending a copy of this to Lord Cherwell.

S.L.B.

9ᵗʰ August, 1952.

Put by

Appendix 8

Number of UFO Reports made to Projects Sign/Grudge/Blue Book

Year	Total sightings	Unidentified
1947	122	12
1948	156	7
1949	186	22
1950	210	27
1951	169	22
1952	1,501	303
1953	509	42
1954	487	46
1955	545	24
1956	670	14
1957	1,006	14
1958	627	10
1959	390	12
1960	557	14
1961	591	13
1962	474	15
1963	399	14
1964	562	19
1965	886	16
Totals	10,047	646

Bibliography

Berlitz, Charles and Moore, William: *The Roswell Incident* (Granada Publishing, 1980).

Bord, Janet and Colin: *Alien Animals* (Granada Publishing, 1980).

Bryan, C.D.B.: *Close Encounters of the Fourth Kind: Alien Abduction and UFOs – Witnesses and Scientists Report* (Weidenfeld & Nicolson, 1995).

Butler, Brenda, Street, Dot and Randles, Jenny: *Sky Crash: A Cosmic Conspiracy* (Neville Spearman, 1984).

Delgado, Pat and Andrews, Colin: *Circular Evidence: A Detailed Investigation of the Swirled Crops Phenomenon* (Bloomsbury, 1989).

Evans, Hilary (ed.): *Frontiers of Reality* (Guild Publishing, 1989).

Goldman, Jane: *The X-Files Book of the Unexplained, Volume I* (Simon & Schuster, 1995).

Good, Timothy: *Alien Liaison: The Ultimate Secret* (Arrow, 1992); *Beyond Top Secret: The Worldwide UFO Security Threat* (Sidgwick & Jackson, 1996).

Hopkins, Budd: *Missing Time* (Richard Merrick, 1981); *Intruders: The Incredible Visitations at Copley Woods* (Random House, 1987).

Howe, Linda Moulton: *An Alien Harvest* (Linda Moulton Howe Productions, 1989).

Hynek, Dr J. Allen: *The UFO Experience: A Scientific Inquiry*, (Ballantine Books, 1974).

Jacobs, David: *Secret Life* (Simon & Schuster, 1987).

Lindemann, Michael (ed.): *UFOs and the Alien Presence: Six Viewpoints* (The 2020 Group, 1991).

Mack, John E.: *Abduction: Human Encounters with Aliens* (Simon & Schuster, 1994).

Nagaitis, Carl and Mantle, Philip: *Without Consent: A Comprehensive Survey of Missing-Time and Abduction Phenomena in the UK* (Ringpull, 1994).

Noyes, Ralph (ed.): *The Crop Circle Enigma* (Gateway, 1990).

Randle, Kevin and Schmitt, Don: *UFO Crash at Roswell: The Truth About the UFO Crash at Roswell* (M. Evans Publishing, 1994).

Randles, Jenny: *UFO Study: A Handbook for Enthusiasts.* (Robert Hale, 1989).

Ruppelt, Edward J.: *The Report on Unidentified Flying Objects* (Doubleday & Co. Inc, 1956).

Schnabel, Jim: *Round in Circles: Physicists, Poltergeists, Pranksters and the Secret History of the Cropwatchers.* (Hamish Hamilton, 1993);
Dark White: Aliens, Abductions, and the UFO Obsession (Hamish Hamilton, 1994).

Shuker, Karl: *Mystery Cats of the World* (Robert Hale, 1989).

Spencer, John: *Perspectives: A Radical Examination of the Alien Abduction Phenomenon* (Macdonald & Co., 1989);
The UFO Encyclopedia (Headline, 1991).

Strieber, Whitley: *Communion: A True Story* (Century Hutchinson, 1987);
Transformation: The Breakthrough (Century Hutchinson, 1988).

Vallée, Jacques: *Dimensions: A Casebook of Alien Contact* (Souvenir Press, 1988);
Confrontations: A Scientist's Search for Alien Contact (Souvenir Press, 1990);
Revelations: Alien Contact and Human Deception (Souvenir Press, 1992).

von Däniken, Erich: *Chariots of the Gods?* (Souvenir Press,

Walters, Ed and Frances: *The Gulf Breeze Sightings* (Bantam Press, 1990).

'The Age of the UFO' *in Unexplained File* (Orbis, 1984).

Fortean Times (Various Issues)

UFO Magazine (Various Issues)

UFO Times (Various Issues)

The Halt Package (Tape and Documents)

PICTURE CREDITS AND PERMISSIONS

Index